Study Guide

Social Studies
for CSEC®

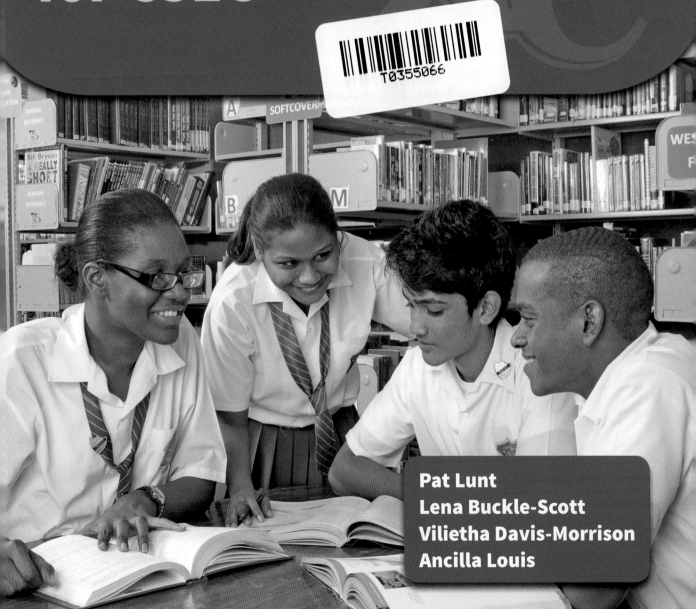

Pat Lunt
Lena Buckle-Scott
Vilietha Davis-Morrison
Ancilla Louis

OXFORD
UNIVERSITY PRESS

Great Clarendon Street, Oxford, OX2 6DP, United Kingdom

Oxford University Press is a department of the University of Oxford.
It furthers the University's objective of excellence in research, scholarship,
and education by publishing worldwide. Oxford is a registered trade mark of
Oxford University Press in the UK and in certain other countries

First published by Nelson Thornes Ltd in 2012
This edition published by Oxford University Press in 2015

British Library Cataloguing in Publication Data
Data available

978-1-4085-1662-1

17

Printed in Great Britain by Bell and Bain Ltd, Glasgow

Acknowledgements

Cover photograph: Mark Lyndersay, Lyndersay Digital, Trinidad
www.lyndersaydigital.com
Illustrations: Jo Taylor and Richard Jones (Beehive Illustrations), and Katie Mac
(NB Illustration)
Page make-up: Pantek Media, Maidstone

Although we have made every effort to trace and contact all
copyright holders before publication this has not been possible in all
cases. If notified, the publisher will rectify any errors or omissions at
the earliest opportunity.

Links to third party websites are provided by Oxford in good faith
and for information only. Oxford disclaims any responsibility for
the materials contained in any third party website referenced in
this work.

The manufacturer's authorised representative in the EU for product safety is
Oxford University Press España S.A. of El Parque Empresarial San Fernando de
Henares, Avenida de Castilla, 2 – 28830 Madrid (www.oup.es/en or product.
safety@oup.com). OUP España S.A. also acts as importer into Spain of
products made by the manufacturer.

Contents

Contents

Introduction

This Study Guide has been developed exclusively with the Caribbean Examinations Council (CXC®) to be used as an additional resource by candidates, both in and out of school, following the Caribbean Secondary Education Certificate (CSEC®) programme.

It has been prepared by a team with expertise in the CSEC® syllabus, teaching and examination. The contents are designed to support learning by providing tools to help you achieve your best in Social Studies and the features included make it easier for you to master the key concepts and requirements of the syllabus. Do remember to refer to your syllabus for full guidance on the course requirements and examination format!

Key terms are emboldened in the text, and defined in the glossary that begins on page 184.

At the end of the units are practice examination-style questions to test your knowledge. Note, however, that as the examination for the options in Section C does not include multiple-choice questions, the usual end-of-unit questions in this section are replaced with two pages of structured questions covering all the material in Section C.

Inside this Study Guide is an interactive CD that includes electronic activities to assist you in developing good examination techniques:

• **On Your Marks** activities provide sample examination-style short answer and essay-type questions, with example candidate answers and feedback from an examiner to show where answers could be improved. These activities will build your understanding, skill level and confidence in answering examination questions.

• **Test Yourself** activities are specifically designed to provide experience of multiple-choice examination questions and helpful feedback will refer you to sections inside the study guide so that you can revise problem areas.

This unique combination of focused syllabus content and interactive examination practice will provide you with invaluable support to help you reach your full potential in CSEC® Social Studies.

What is a family?

Concept of the family

The family is a basic unit within most human societies. At its simplest level, a family is a group of people who share certain connections and attachments. In the past, these connections have traditionally been understood to mean that the people are related 'by blood', which suggests a biological linkage, or through a particular form of relationship, such as marriage. Such blood relationships are known as **kinship**. Typically, members of a family unit will usually share the same residence.

Understanding the so-called 'traditional family' allows for comparison with some of the different family types and unions found across the Caribbean.

The basic functions of the family

The family functions as:

- a unit of procreation
- a unit for the socialisation of individuals
- an economic unit for satisfying basic needs
- a social unit for satisfying emotional and psychological needs.

The family as a unit of procreation

When humans produce offspring, this is called procreation. Human procreation allows for a society to continue since this process produces new members to replace those who die or migrate. Procreation does not take place only in a family situation, but many people argue that a family provides the best environment in which to raise children.

The family as a unit of socialisation

The family provides for the **socialisation** of its members. Socialisation is to do with developing an attitude in children and young people that encourages them to make a useful contribution in society.

Children, in particular, are taught about:

- accepted behaviours in society, **values**, attitudes and aspects of culture
- how inappropriate behaviour receives sanctions
- their roles and responsibilities
- basic skills.

In a family, children learn how to behave in the society into which they have been born. They learn about the kinds of behaviour that are accepted and expected, including, for example, the basic sets of manners used in greetings and in making requests. As they learn

Many people believe the family provides the best environment for raising children

these skills, children are taught about the values that underpin them, such as respect and consideration.

Children also learn about the **roles** and responsibilities they currently have and those they will have when they become adults.

Children learn basic skills to help them to become independent.

The family as an economic unit

Different family members take on different roles and responsibilities, share out the workload and pool resources. By working together, the family is more likely to be able to meet its basic needs for food, clothing and shelter.

A family that meets its own basic needs will not require financial assistance from the government. The working members of a family will be making a contribution to society through the payment of taxes.

The family as a social unit

Our wellbeing as humans relies on more than simply having our physical needs met (for food, clothing and shelter). We also have emotional and **psychological** needs. We need to know that we are loved, wanted and protected. Our family should provide the environment in which these needs are met. Our family also gives us a sense of identity and a feeling of belonging.

EXAM TIP

In studying the family, you will need to know and understand the concept of the family and the family functions. Be ready to explain how families can help themselves to function and the supportive strategies governments can employ.

ACTIVITY

Take each of the functions of the family as described above.

1 Explain how a society benefits from each function and what the consequences for a society might be if that function was not fulfilled.

2 Suggest some ways a family can ensure that these functions are fulfilled.

How governments and other organisations assist the family

The family unit needs to function well if a society is to survive and to be healthy. When families struggle to function properly or effectively, the government and other agencies can support them with financial or other assistance. For example, a government might provide:

- welfare payments to help meet basic needs
- facilities, such as day nurseries to help working mothers
- feeding programmes
- counselling programmes
- foster homes or foster care for children who cannot live at home or who have lost their parents
- care services for people who are old or incapacitated and for those who have mental health issues or physical disabilities.

Other organisations, such as schools, also have a part to play in preparing children for their roles as members of society.

KEY POINTS

1 A family produces new members for a society.

2 A family trains children to fit into society.

3 A family nurtures individuals to help them become fulfilled and well adjusted.

4 A family helps meet the basic needs of its members.

Different family types and unions

Family types

The idea of a family is found in almost every human society, but the form and structure of a family is not fixed. Variations in family types result from such things as changing views and attitudes within a society or alterations in a country's economy. A family, whatever its actual type, is still a grouping of people who form a unit and seek to fulfil some or all of the functions described in topic 1.1.

Nuclear family

The term 'nuclear family' is most commonly used to describe a father and mother who, together with their children, share a dwelling. The children can be the biological offspring of one or both parents or they may be adopted.

Extended family

An extended family is one that extends beyond the limits of a nuclear family. Extended families include individuals from more than two generations and a wider range of kinship relations, including aunts, uncles, cousins, nieces, nephews and grandparents. Extended families in Caribbean society have important functions such as providing childcare when parents are at work or away from home.

Sibling families

In **sibling** families, both parents are absent because of **migration**, imprisonment or death, and an older brother or sister takes care of younger siblings and manages the upkeep and maintenance of the dwelling.

Single-parent family

In a single-parent family only one parent is present and in most cases this is the mother.

Life for the head of a sibling family can be very challenging

Emerging family patterns

Changes in society usually produce changes in family types and structures. Some women, for example, choose to live alone and yet give birth to, or adopt, children. In recent times, other family patterns have emerged in different countries across the region. Some of these families include children who are adopted, who belong to only one of the partners, or are born to a **surrogate mother**.

Family unions

All of the following unions can be the basis for a family, meaning that children may be part of the relationship. The children may be the offspring of the present union, they may belong to one of the partners from a previous relationship or they may be adopted.

Legal marriage

A legal **marriage** is a lawfully recognised union between a man and a woman. The married couple will usually share the same residence. Traditionally, marriage has been seen as the ideal environment in which sexual relations can occur.

Monogamy and polygamy

Monogamy is a form of marriage in which a person has only one wife or husband at one time. In **polygamy**, a person may have more than one wife or husband at the same time. **Polygyny** is where a man has more than one wife, and **polyandry** is where a woman has more than one husband. If the law states that a person may only marry one person at a time and someone marries another person while a previous marriage still exists, this is known as **bigamy**.

Visiting relationships

In a visiting relationship, the man and woman are not married and do not share the same residence although they do have sexual relations.

Consensual/common law union

In these relationships, a man and woman are not legally married but they do share a common residence and also have sexual relations.

Family trees

A family tree is a chart that shows the names and relationships of different generations of the same family.

In the family tree in Figure 1.2.1, male family members are in blue and female family members are in red. The 'm.' between two names indicates that these two people are married.

ACTIVITY

Using the family tree in Figure 1.2.1, answer the following questions.

1 Who did Jean Roberts marry?

2 Name two of Bryan and Michelle Roberts' grandchildren.

3 What is David Ramsey's relationship to Sarah Booth?

4 Who are Sarah Booth's cousins?

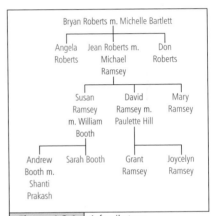

Figure 1.2.1 | A family tree

CASE STUDY

'I will not see the New Year,' whispered Clara's mother on a late December day. 'Promise me you will look after your brother and sister.' Two days later she passed away, another victim to AIDs. Clara was an orphan and, at 16 years of age, she had the responsibility of bringing up her 10-year-old brother and 7-year-old sister. She saw her dreams of becoming a doctor turn to dust.

Questions

1 What kind of family is Clara now heading?

2 What are some of the problems faced in such a family?

3 What else might cause such a family to exist apart from the death of parents?

EXAM TIP

Make sure you are familiar with the different types of families and unions. You must be able to identify and describe these, as well as indicating some of the advantages and disadvantages that might be associated with each one.

KEY POINTS

1 There are a number of familiar family types in the Caribbean region: the nuclear family, the extended family, the single-parent family and the sibling family.

2 There are a number of unions around which a family can be based: legal marriage, consensual or common law, and visiting relationships.

Roles, relationships and responsibilities in the family 1

At the end of this topic you will be able to:

- examine the roles, responsibilities and relationships of adults and sibling members of a Caribbean family.

Traditional adult roles and responsibilities

Families exist within the context of a wider society. A society where men have a dominant role in social organisation and are seen as the head of the house is known as **patriarchal**. Where such roles and responsibilities fall to women the society is **matriarchal**. Family patterns where the father has responsibility for the family are known as **patrifocal**, while those where the mother has this responsibility are **matrifocal**.

The role a person has indicates the functions they should fulfil in that position. The responsibilities that go with that role are the actions that need to be carried out in order to fulfil the role. Each person in a family occupies a certain **status** (or position) which will determine the roles and responsibilities of that individual. A person might be a father, mother, son, daughter, sister or brother and could have more than one status at the same time. For example, a person might be a father, son and brother and have different responsibilities for each of these roles. Sometimes there is 'role conflict', where one role interferes with the performance of another.

Some responsibilities have traditionally been associated with particular male family roles, while others are seen to be more in line with female roles. For example, women have traditionally been associated with responsibilities in and around the home and with childrearing. Some male roles have traditionally involved activities that take them away from the home, such as earning an income.

Males

An adult male member of a household may have the role of husband or father or both. As a husband he would have a responsibility to love, cherish and care for his wife. As a father he would have a responsibility to love, care for and socialise his children and to earn an income to satisfy the economic needs of the family.

Traditionally, the main roles for men have been seen as those below.

- Disciplinarian. A disciplinarian is responsible for discipline. Discipline is about giving instruction and moral training, establishing rules for acceptable behaviour and maintaining order through ensuring that these rules are obeyed. Applying punishments or sanctions for unacceptable behaviour may be a part of this.
- Breadwinner. The breadwinner in a household earns the money to satisfy the family's basic needs.
- Decision-maker. In this role, the male would be seen to make all the important decisions that affect the family.

- **Matrilocal** refers to when a couple lives with the wife's parents.
- **Neolocal** refers to when a couple establishes their own residence.
- **Patrilocal** refers to when a couple lives with the husband's parents.
- **Matrilineal** refers to when rights, duties and responsibilities follow the mother's lineage.
- **Patrilineal** refers to when rights, duties and responsibilities follow the father's lineage.

Females

An adult female member of a household may have the role of wife or mother or both. As a wife she would have a responsibility to love, cherish and care for her husband. As a mother she would have a responsibility to love, care for and socialise her children and be largely responsible for childrearing. She may also earn an income to help satisfy the economic needs of the family.

Traditionally, the main roles of women have been seen as those below.

- Caregiver. In giving care, a person shows concern for another and seeks to ensure the other person's safety and wellbeing, perhaps offering protection from those things that might harm. In a family situation, meeting physical needs, largely through preparing and cooking meals, and offering emotional and psychological support would be part of this.

- Socialising agent. Socialisation is about helping people to become members of society. Part of this is teaching children about accepted behaviours in society and about values, attitudes and aspects of culture.

- Economic provider. Although not a main breadwinner, a woman would have been expected to produce food from a backyard garden or to make items of art and craft, either for use in the house or for sale.

- Homemaker. In homemaking, a person is responsible for creating a pleasant home environment. A large part of this involves keeping a dwelling clean and tidy.

- Counsellor. As counsellor, a woman would be responsible for meeting emotional and psychological needs as well as considering religious aspects of life.

One of the traditional roles for women in the Caribbean has been that of counsellor

ACTIVITY

Carry out a survey among members of your class to establish how far the traditional male and female roles are reflected in different households. What do your findings show about the extent to which these traditional roles apply in families in your community?

KEY POINTS

1 The status and role a person has comes with certain responsibilities.

2 There are traditionally accepted roles for men and women in Caribbean families.

3 Role conflict occurs where one role interferes with the performance of another.

EXAM TIP

You should be able to explain how the traditional roles of men and women in Caribbean families would have contributed to a successful household.

Roles, relationships and responsibilities in the family 2

Traditional roles for children

Children in a family have different roles and responsibilities, which often change as they grow older. Many traditional responsibilities involve helping parents with different chores around the house, running errands or fetching supplies and, for older children, sharing in caring for their younger siblings. If the family has a plot of land on which to grow food, the children can help here too and so make a contribution to the economic function of the family. Traditionally, different roles would have been given to boys and girls.

All these activities allow children to play their part in helping the family to function as a unit. If a child helps with chores, or with looking after a younger sibling, this means that parents are able to spend more time on other activities. In some cases, this may enable the parents to go out to earn money, which would not otherwise be possible.

ACTIVITY

Decide which member of a household would traditionally be expected to carry out each of the following activities. Explain how carrying out each activity contributes to the functioning of the family.

• Disciplining the children
• Running errands
• Washing clothes
• Bathing a baby
• Holding a full-time job

Performing a role well

There are a number of reasons why a person may not fulfil their role adequately. This might be because:

• one role interferes with the performance of another
• the person lacks the necessary knowledge or skills
• there are insufficient financial or other resources
• the person is indifferent about performing their role
• another family member frustrates their attempts to fulfil the role.

ACTIVITY

Think of an example of how each of the situations described in 'Performing a role well' could arise. For example, a mother's role as homemaker would be frustrated by other family members not being tidy.

Relationships and responsibilities

Maintaining good relationships within a family is vital if that family is going to function properly. However, there are many reasons why conflict might arise and why there may be a breakdown in relationships.

Conflict between parents

A wife may be in conflict with her husband if he is not:

- assisting with the housework
- assisting with raising the children
- contributing enough to the family's expenses
- being open and honest
- spending enough 'quality time' with her.

A husband may be in conflict with his wife if she is not:

- keeping the household tidy
- preparing sufficient wholesome food for the family
- effectively socialising children
- being open and honest
- spending enough 'quality time' with him.

Conflict between parents and children

Children can be in conflict with their parents if they are not:

- doing their share of household chores
- obeying rules
- conforming to household values and attitudes.

A common cause of conflict between parents and children is the **generation gap**. This term is used to describe the fact that the generations may have different ideas about the way things should be done. The following reasons for conflict can be said to arise because of the generation gap:

- Parents and children have different ideas and values.
- Parents want their children to follow their way but children do not always agree.
- Children often think their parents' ideas are old-fashioned.

Children often think their parents' ideas are old-fashioned

ACTIVITY

1 Carry out some research among your peer group to identify common areas of conflict between children and their parents. Ask parents if they can remember being in conflict with their own parents. Find out what the reasons were for family conflict in their experience. What do your findings show you about children's attitudes today compared with a generation ago?

2 Suggest some ways in which the generation gap might be bridged.

KEY POINTS

1 Children have traditionally had roles and responsibilities within the household.

2 The performance of a role involves interaction and relationships with others.

3 Family members have different personalities, opinions, aspirations, ideas and values. These differences can create conflict and relationships can suffer.

1.5 Changing roles in the contemporary Caribbean family

Being aware of the traditional roles within the family (see topics 1.3 and 1.4) will help you to appreciate the changes that have taken place in these roles in contemporary Caribbean society. You also need to understand the circumstances that have brought about these changes and what the results of the changes have been.

Status of women in society

An individual's status in society is the social role they have. For example, a person might be a doctor, a parent or a community leader. In the past, generally speaking, women were expected to have a particular status or only certain roles, such as mothers, and were not expected to pursue certain types of education or employment. A change in the status of women is a result of changes in attitudes within society regarding aspects of **equality**, women's rights and the way in which women are viewed. As a result, women today:

- are no longer seen as being less important or subordinate to men
- have challenged their traditional gender roles in a household and demand a greater involvement in decision-making
- have rights to equal educational and employment opportunities and to equal pay for equal work.

Choice of employment

There are more opportunities for women in employment and they are more able to take advantage of those opportunities.

- Women are no longer seen as being solely responsible for the home and there is greater sharing with men of household chores and childrearing activities. This allows them more possibilities to seek employment.
- It is more acceptable for a woman to share the role of breadwinner in a household. The high cost of living sometimes means it is necessary for a woman to have paid work. A single mother is often the sole breadwinner in a family.
- Employment that has been traditionally male, for example construction, is increasingly open to women.

Available technology

Technology has affected women's availability for employment and the types of employment they can undertake. It has also stimulated the need and desire for self-improvement and advancement among women.

- Labour-saving devices in the home have reduced the time taken for some household chores. This has allowed women greater access to education, training and employment.

LEARNING OUTCOMES

At the end of this topic you will be able to:

- explain the causes and effects of the changes in the roles of family members in Caribbean society.

ACTIVITY

1 Carry out some research to establish the current rates of employment among women in your country. Find out how these rates compare with rates in the rest of the region and the world.

2 Carry out some research into your own family situation. Describe the similarities and differences between the roles your parents have and those of your grandparents when they were the age your parents are now. See if you can establish how the opportunities available for women and the attitudes to traditional roles have changed between those generations.

10

- Changes in workplace technology mean that some traditionally male work can be carried out by women. Factories that were once workplaces for many people can now be controlled by computers, and managed and operated by just a few workers.
- Television has brought many programmes made in developed countries, particularly the US, into Caribbean homes. These programmes reflect a society in which women are successful and powerful. They have also altered people's aspirations and expectations regarding lifestyle. In some cases, achieving such a lifestyle has meant that both partners in a relationship need to work. The information available through the internet has had similar effects.

Educational opportunities

Women increasingly have the same access to education and training as men. This means they can acquire the same knowledge and skills needed for any job.

Leisure activities

The changing status of women in the household and as individuals with their own money to spend has combined with a greater amount of time available for leisure. Women are increasingly able to spend time away from the home in the same kind of leisure activities as men.

Family planning

Many of the changes in women's roles have come about because of 'family life education' programmes. Family planning allows a woman to choose to have fewer children, which in turn results in more time being available for her to develop her own knowledge and skills, take up employment and consider her own quality of life.

Non-traditional employment opportunities for women have increased rapidly

The results of changing roles in the Caribbean family

LEARNING OUTCOMES

At the end of this topic you will be able to:

- explain the causes and effects of the changes in the roles of family members in Caribbean society.

The roles of men and women in the household and in the workplace have been changing in recent times within the Caribbean. More women are pursuing education and taking paid work outside the home and more men are sharing household duties and responsibilities. There is a greater sharing of decision-making within the home. The changes have generally had positive effects for women's views of themselves but there are indications that, for some men, the effects have been negative.

Identity crisis

Our sense of identity is largely gained from the roles we have within different situations, but especially perhaps within the family. We have seen, in topic 1.3, that a person can have a particular status, such as a mother. This status forms part of her identity. She is a mother and she understands where this puts her in relationship to other people.

The changes in traditional roles have meant, among other things, that more women are seeking full-time employment. This might conflict with her identity as a mother, especially if she has to place her children in someone else's care while she is at work. Similarly, sharing household decision-making may cause her conflict if she feels uncomfortable challenging traditional roles.

A man might be a father and also think of himself as the breadwinner and as head of the house. These are elements of his identity and he might feel able to prove himself by setting and achieving goals and by providing for his family. Such ideas will possibly be stronger if he comes from a patriarchal or patrifocal household.

If a man's understanding of his male identity is as the 'provider' and 'head of the house', then this identity might be threatened when his wife is also earning an income and sharing household decision-making. This is known as **identity crisis**.

Marginalisation of males

If a thing is marginalised, it has moved from a more central position out to the edges. When we talk of the marginalisation of males, we are referring to situations where males are much less dominant or central than they once were.

Women today are frequently joint breadwinners and so the family is less dependent on the male for meeting its needs. Females have been taking up and succeeding in education at ever-increasing rates and are found in many types of work that were once the place for males only. For many men, there is a sense that their place in family and society has become much less certain or secure.

Prepare a presentation for youth group leaders in your local community that outlines a strategy for helping male youths to adopt a positive male identity. Your presentation should briefly describe the changing roles in Caribbean families and the effects of these.

Role conflict

Role conflict is usually applied to the situation where the ability to perform one role is hindered by the need to perform another role at the same time. For example, a father will find his caring for his family role in conflict with his role as breadwinner if he has had to move away in order to find work.

Conflict can also arise due to roles within the home. Although there is an increased sharing of duties in the home, some of the traditional distinctions between male and female roles still apply. For example, a working mother might find it difficult if her husband still regards housework and raising children as a mainly female role.

Development of self-esteem and confidence in women

Women are increasingly able to develop **self-esteem** and confidence because they are:

- earning their own income, which makes them less dependent on a male partner
- making a greater contribution to society through developing and using knowledge and skills
- balancing working at home and developing a career
- enjoying equal pay for equal work
- freed from the sole burden of household chores and childrearing
- having smaller families, which frees up time
- sharing in decision-making in the family with their male partners.

EXAM TIP

Be aware of the notion that women have generally benefited from the changes in traditional roles while some men struggle to make the necessary adjustments.

Women are frequently joint breadwinners today

KEY POINTS

1 Traditional male and female roles are disappearing.

2 Some males struggle to understand what makes a positive 'male identity' in these circumstances.

3 Males are less central in the household, in the family, in education and in employment.

4 There can be conflict with people trying to fulfil different roles.

5 Women have developed greater self-esteem and confidence through increased rights and opportunities.

Preparing for parenthood and effective parenting

Preparing for parenthood

Becoming a parent is not something to do without careful thought about all the implications.

Aspects of readiness

Physical maturity and health

Your body changes as you reach puberty and many changes are to do with sexual reproduction. Even though a girl might be able to become pregnant, her body may not be sufficiently developed in other ways to allow her to have a safe pregnancy and to be able to give birth without endangering her health or even her life. A difficult birth can also have long-lasting or permanent implications for the baby's health and wellbeing.

As well as being physically mature, parents need to be healthy. This is perhaps especially true for the mother-to-be during pregnancy. She should monitor her weight and ensure that she is eating a balanced diet to provide all necessary vitamins and nutrients for her and the unborn child.

Financial resources

Becoming a parent has major financial implications. A child is an additional family member with basic physical needs that must be met. If both parents are earning an income, then adjustments will need to be made if one is to leave work, however long that may be for. If the parents are economically unprepared, this can mean that the child may be brought up in poverty. Poverty can mean that children are disadvantaged in a number of ways.

Acquiring skills for employment through education or training is important to ensure adequate family income.

Emotional and psychological readiness

Becoming a parent changes a person's life because the needs of the baby must be taken into account. A couple will have less time to spend on personal leisure activities and with each other. Parenthood is an enormous responsibility which can be exciting and challenging and can bring great joy as well as times of anxiety.

Obtaining knowledge and skills

Experiencing good parenting while growing up may help an individual to become a good parent in their turn. In recent years, there has been a growth in 'family life education' which provides a comprehensive approach to family issues such as:

- human sexuality
- reproductive health
- self-esteem

A number of governments have parent support programmes to help prospective parents gain the necessary knowledge and skills for parenting

- values
- relationships
- parenting
- family planning and contraception
- sexually transmitted infections.

Characteristics of good parenting

Knowledge

Parents must have knowledge of:

- the values, **mores** and **norms** of society if they are to pass them on to their children (see topic 2.3)
- nutrition and healthy lifestyles
- family planning methods to limit family size and so be better able to provide for their family
- education systems and expectations.

Skills

Parents need to have a range of skills, dealing with different aspects of running a household and bringing up children. They should be able to:

- communicate effectively, speaking clearly, honestly and openly, and listening to the questions, feelings and concerns of their children
- set guidelines for behaviour, fix boundaries that should not be crossed and be ready to impose suitable discipline in a calm but firm manner
- manage the household's money to ensure that income is allocated to pay fixed costs and that sufficient money is available to meet the family's basic needs.

Attitude

Parents need to demonstrate an attitude of caring, nurturing and encouragement which will help children develop into healthy and fulfilled individuals.

ACTIVITY

Choose one of the following topics:

- Self-esteem
- Relationships
- Values
- Family planning and contraception

Write a short explanation of how a talk on this subject could help to prepare a young person for responsible parenthood. You will need to think about the aspects of parenthood that are relevant to your chosen subject.

EXAM TIP

You should be ready to identify the characteristics that make a good parent and to explain the part each characteristic plays in effective parenting.

CASE STUDY

Although he was quite strict when it came to behaviour, Dewain's father was good fun to be with. He would even be able to get Dewain doing his chores in the yard with good humour. Once, however, when Dewain had complained about having to do so much, his father's face became serious. He explained that Dewain's mother worked hard to keep the household clean and to put good food on the table. He said that it was only right that Dewain play his part in the family.

Question

What kind of parent is Dewain's father? Give reasons for your answer and describe the attitudes and behaviour you think Dewain might develop as he grows older.

KEY POINTS

1 Preparation for parenthood includes physical, emotional, psychological and practical aspects.

2 Good parenting requires certain knowledge, skills and attitudes.

Contemporary social issues influencing Caribbean family life 1

Parents may not want a delinquent child living in the home because of negative influences on other siblings

Social issues are defined as widespread behaviour that:

• a large section of the population thinks is undesirable or unacceptable
• directly or indirectly affects large numbers of people
• conflicts with what society generally agrees to be right or good
• is generally viewed as a problem
• is not easily solved.

Some current social issues

Juvenile delinquency

Juvenile delinquency is the term used to describe antisocial and sometimes criminal behaviour carried out by young people. Many factors can contribute to delinquency, such as an abusive home, poor parent-to-child communication and negative peer pressure.

Delinquency may be avoided if struggling parents receive counselling or training, if a child experiences a loving and nurturing environment, if after-school facilities are provided and young people can be engaged in positive activities.

Strategies to alter the behaviour of juvenile delinquents can include:

• holding after-school life-skills classes
• arranging parenting skills sessions with a psychologist.

Street children

Street children are deprived of homes, affection, protection, food and education. They suffer poor health and constantly face the threat of violence. They may beg for money and some join gangs.

Children may avoid ending up on the streets if their parents receive training to prevent problems that can lead to children leaving home, and if more help is available for families struggling with poverty.

Strategies to prevent the problems experienced by street children include provision of:

• greater numbers of foster parents
• day centres to provide food and health care
• counselling to assist with trauma
• facilities to teach vocational skills which could lead to employment
• specialist educational facilities
• childcare for the children of street children.

Sexually transmitted infections

Sexually transmitted infections (STIs) are passed from one person to another through sexual contact. Many common STIs can be cured. Left untreated, some can lead to serious long-term health problems, infertility and even death. The most serious sexually transmitted infection is the HIV virus which can lead to a person developing AIDS, for which there is no cure.

Good sex education and access to items that prevent the transmission of infections, such as condoms, can reduce infection rates. Those already infected need care through counselling and support, and also medical treatment.

Substance abuse

Substances that are legal, such as alcohol and tobacco, and illegal, such as marijuana and cocaine, can be abused. These substances can be physically addictive, because of chemical reactions in the body, or psychologically addictive, because the person desires to experience the associated pleasurable effects again. Prolonged use and over-indulgence or abuse can lead to:

- long-term health problems and even death
- under-achievement at school
- loss of work
- negative outcomes in families.

Strategies to deal with substance abuse include:

- education concerning the effects of substance abuse
- assistance for parents in helping their children avoid substance abuse
- counselling for individuals and families.

Trafficking in persons

Human trafficking is about moving persons against their will, by force, coercion or fraud, away from their usual place of residence to another location. It is most commonly associated with the transport of children and women for forced labour or sexual exploitation purposes. The Caribbean is a region of supply, transit and destination for trafficked persons.

Strategies to combat trafficking include:

- prevention, by educating potential victims about the dangers and by tackling the demand for people to work in the sex industry or as bonded labourers
- protection, by supporting victims if they act as witnesses, helping them to regain documentation and ensuring they are given fair treatment by immigration authorities
- prosecution of those who traffic and those who are the clients
- reintegration, by counselling victims of trafficking and providing support services such as shelters, educational and vocational training, financial assistance and job placement.

Alternative lifestyles

There are several alternative lifestyles that are felt by many to be unacceptable. For example, people can choose to live a promiscuous lifestyle with many sexual partners. Some people see such lifestyles as challenging the accepted and established patterns of family and society.

Worldwide, it is estimated that anywhere between two and four million men, women and children are trafficked across borders or within their own country every year. This woman's child was stolen by a child-trafficking gang.

KEY POINTS

1 Social issues concern behaviours that large numbers of people see as being undesirable.

2 Social issues are complex and difficult to solve.

3 Social issues have consequences for society as a whole but also affect individuals and families.

Contemporary social issues influencing Caribbean family life 2

Current social issues

Teenage pregnancy

Teenage pregnancy is a troubling social issue because a young mother can face risks to her physical health, especially when giving birth, and also to her emotional and psychological well-being. There may be a strain on family relationships and finances, her education will be disrupted or perhaps ended, and she and her child face poor outcomes.

Child abuse

Child abuse can take a number of forms including: neglect, where basic needs are not met; a lack of care and protection; physical, sexual or emotional abuse, or the requirement to do inappropriate work.

Incest

Incest is sexual intercourse between biologically related siblings or children and biological parents.

Some professionals and others include intercourse: between a child and a non-biological parent such as an adoptive or step-parent.

Research indicates that incest exists across all social classes although there are some social factors that might make it more likely to occur. For example, in some households children and adults have to share the same bedroom or even the same bed.

Domestic violence

Domestic violence involves an attack on one family member by another. It undermines the home which should be a place where people feel safe and secure. It is also psychologically damaging because it involves violence and terror at the hands of those who should be the most trusted.

Desertion

Desertion occurs when one partner in a relationship leaves without intending to return. It is most commonly associated with a man leaving his wife and family. Desertion is no longer grounds for seeking a **divorce**, but a woman can seek maintenance from her partner if this is for the welfare of any children involved. A deserted family may face financial hardship and there will be emotional and psychological effects.

Care for older people and those with special needs

In the past, older people may have expected their grown-up children to care for them in their old age. This is not so common today because families are fragmented, with people migrating for work and so on. Traditional, informal support networks no longer exist and AIDS is having an impact on the generation who would be providing much of the care.

Providing care for older people and those with special needs is time-consuming. A person who becomes a caregiver will experience a reduction in, or a complete loss of, his or her ability to earn an income.

Living in poverty can affect people's health and deprive young people of opportunities

Poverty

Poverty is usually considered in relation to the general level of wealth of others in society. Poverty can affect health and nutrition and deprive young people of some possibilities and opportunities. Poverty affects individuals differently. Some become resigned to it, while others are motivated to escape by succeeding in a career or business venture. Some become so desperate that they are drawn into criminal activities to obtain money.

Strategies for dealing with social issues

A general strategy for dealing with social issues is the prevention of the circumstances that give rise to the issue in the first place. This might involve improving education or providing individuals with the attitudes and skills to help them avoid poor choices. Individuals and organisations working on the issues also need support.

The impact of social issues on family life

The impacts on family life are varied and include extra financial burdens, conflict in or break-up of the family, alienation of family members, negative effects on health and children being deprived of proper parenting.

ACTIVITY

'Violence against women is a manifestation of historically unequal power relations between men and women which have led to domination over and discrimination against women by men and to the prevention of the full advancement of women ...'

Source: United Nations Declaration on the Elimination of Violence against Women, General Assembly Resolution, December 1993

1 Carry out some research to find out how common domestic violence is in your country.

2 Prepare a presentation that a community leader might give to young people in the area to explain why domestic violence is not acceptable.

KEY POINTS

1 Teenage pregnancy usually limits the life chances of the mother and results in poor outcomes for the child.

2 Child abuse takes many forms.

3 Incest is found in all social groups and classes.

4 Domestic violence and desertion are particularly damaging because they undermine home and family.

5 Caring for older people or those with special needs is more difficult today because of changes to family structure and increasing economic pressures.

Governments introduce certain laws to protect the interests of individual family members.

Laws related to inheritance

Inheritance is the money or property that passes from a deceased person to his or her successors. A person receiving an inheritance is called a **beneficiary** and what each should receive is described in a person's **will**.

Inheritance laws prevent relatives from taking money or property that rightfully belongs to the intended beneficiary of a deceased person.

In a number of countries, earlier distinctions made between the rights of children born 'in wedlock' and those born 'out of wedlock' have been removed. Amendments to the law are important in the Caribbean because there are increasing numbers of children born to parents not in a legal marriage.

Many countries now regard partners in a range of unions as having the same rights as married couples.

Laws related to childcare

Family law legislation (such as the Child Care and Protection Act in Jamaica) seek to establish in law the responsibilities of parents to provide maintenance for any unmarried children they have up to the age of 18. In some circumstances, the court can extend this requirement beyond 18 if, for example, it is proven that the child needs support in order to complete their education or they have a physical or mental disability.

Other laws attempt to ensure that:

• a single parent receives money for the maintenance of a child from the other parent
• parents do not leave their child or children unattended for long periods without making provision for their safekeeping.

Laws related to legal separation

A **legal separation** is the separation of a married couple by an order of the court. It is often a step taken before a couple divorce. A legal separation does not end the marriage but it gives married partners certain rights while they live separately and will usually involve some legally binding agreements being made concerning monies due to both parties.

Leaving a child alone at home for extended periods of time is recognised as neglect. Laws have been introduced to try to prevent this happening.

Laws related to divorce

A divorce is the legal termination of a marriage and is the only way in which a marriage can be legally ended. Such an ending is known as an **annulment**. Long-standing grounds for divorce have been matrimonial offences such as adultery, cruelty or desertion. Other reasons for seeking a divorce have also been introduced and accepted in law.

A partner seeking a divorce is a **petitioner**. He or she must prove to the courts that the marriage has broken down and that the relationship is unlikely to improve. This is known as an 'irretrievable breakdown of the marriage'. To satisfy the courts that this is the situation, it must be proved that the couple have separated and lived apart for at least 12 months.

Couples who have been married for less than two years will not be granted a divorce unless the courts are satisfied that all efforts have been made to retrieve the marriage, including receiving assistance from marriage counsellors.

Divorce law also provides that one party to the marriage is liable to maintain the other party if that other party is unable to support themselves for any of the following reasons:

• the partner has to take care of a child of the marriage who is under 18
• the partner's age or physical or mental condition prevents them from working to earn a living
• any other reasonable reason.

The money a court orders a partner to pay to another is called **alimony**.

Laws related to domestic violence

The governments of many Caribbean countries are introducing laws to prevent violence, particularly against women and children. Member governments of the Organisation of Eastern Caribbean States (OECS) have ratified the UN Convention on the Elimination of all forms of Discrimination Against Women (CEDAW). In some territories family law is being drawn up or reformed to ensure that:

• a wider range of unacceptable behaviours beyond violence are addressed by the legislation
• individuals in different domestic relationships are equally protected.

ACTIVITY

Find out about the laws in your country that deal with inheritance where the deceased person has not left a will.

KEY POINTS

Laws exist to ensure that:

• a deceased person's successors receive their proper inheritance
• children receive proper care and support
• when a long-term relationship ends, neither party is left in difficult circumstances
• domestic violence is prevented.

EXAM TIP

You should be able to explain how the laws protect individuals in relation to inheritance, divorce, lack of care and maintenance, and domestic violence.

SECTION 1: Multiple-choice questions

1 In a patrifocal family:

   a the woman does all the housework

   b the male children are given chores

   c the man is head of the house and has responsibility for the family

   d their residence is the home of the man's father

2 Which of the following best defines a nuclear family?

   a A mother and father sharing a residence together with their children

   b A family with only one child

   c A family where parents and children share a residence with uncles, aunts and cousins

3 Marriage is increasingly seen as a partnership in which a husband and wife share the responsibility for household decision-making. This statement suggests that in marriages today:

   a a husband has the final say in everything

   b the roles of husbands and wives are complementary

   c wives have a submissive role

   d husbands and wives each have specific roles

4 One way in which children can avoid conflict with their parents is to:

   a leave their belongings around the house

   b refuse to run errands

   c help with household chores

   d show a lack of respect

5 Many women now share the role of breadwinner in a household. This means that women:

   a spend more time with childrearing duties

   b have paid work and contribute to the family's income

   c spend a lot of time baking

   d do voluntary work in the community

6 One result of the changing roles in Caribbean society is that some men feel marginalised. This leads to:

   a boys working harder in education

   b men sharing in household duties

   c males having a dominant role in the household

   d men losing self-esteem and their sense of identity

7 One aspect of effective parenting is passing on the accepted behaviours within a society. These are called:

   a norms

   b functions

   c rules

   d values

8 Sexually transmitted infections are passed from one person to another by:

   a shaking hands on meeting

   b eating a meal together

   c unprotected sexual contact

   d sharing toilet facilities

9 When a person abandons their family and has no intention of returning, this is called:

   a adultery

   b cohabiting

   c migration

   d desertion

10 A beneficiary of a deceased person's will is a person who:

   a helps to draw up a will

   b inherits property or money from the deceased person

   c looks after the will until it is read out

   d reads out the will

Further practice questions and examples can be found on the accompanying CD.

SECTION 2: Structured questions

1 a Write a brief explanation of the functions of the family and describe at least three family types that are found in the Caribbean region.

   b Using the three types of family you chose in a, discuss the advantages and disadvantages each family might have when attempting to fulfil each of the functions of the family that you have identified.

   c Describe the role you think the government of a country has in helping each type of family to:
   • meet its basic needs
   • socialise the children
   • encourage health and wellbeing.

2 The roles and responsibilities traditionally assigned to males and females are changing across the Caribbean. Explain the following:

   a The traditional roles of men and women

   b The way in which these roles are changing

   c What has brought about the changes

   d The effect the changes are having on men and women and on society.

3 The rate of occurrence of sexually transmitted infections (STIs) is rising rapidly in the Caribbean and is a social issue of major concern.

   a Briefly define STIs, explain how they are passed from one person to another, and why they are a major social issue.

   b Describe at least two factors that you feel contribute to the rise in instances of STIs.

   c Explain the role you think the following groups or individuals have in dealing with the issue of STIs:
   • Parents
   • The education system
   • The health services
   • Adolescent teenagers

   d Explain why the issue of STIs is a difficult social issue to solve.

4 There are a number of laws in Caribbean countries that are designed to protect the rights of children. These laws cover issues such as work, inheritance, education, and emotional and physical wellbeing.

   a Explain why it is important to have laws concerning children and work.

   b Describe what can happen if a child's parents die without leaving a will.

   c Describe how a child's life might be affected if they are denied access to education.

   d Say why you think laws are in place to prevent children being abused.

Further practice questions and examples can be found on the accompanying CD.

2 Social groups and institutions

2.1 Caribbean culture

LEARNING OUTCOMES

At the end of this topic you will be able to:

• account for the cultural diversity of the Caribbean region.

The culture of a country or region is shown by many things, including the customs, ceremonies, religions, festivals, music, food, dress and language that can be found in that place.

Cultural diversity

People who come from the same part of the world and share the same culture are known as an **ethnic group**. If ethnic groups from different parts of the world come to live together in one area and aspects of their different cultures are evident, we say that area has cultural diversity. The longer these different ethnic groups live together, the more the cultures mix. As this happens, a new culture develops. So a Caribbean culture is forming that is made up from elements of the different ethnic cultures of its people.

Historical, geographical and social factors

A number of factors have led to the Caribbean having one of the most culturally diverse societies in the world. We are a people whose forefathers came from parts of South America, Africa, Asia and Europe.

The people who we call Amerindians came from South and Central America and arrived in the Caribbean region in about 4000 BC. In about 500 BC, the Taino people came from the area of South America's Orinoco River. As Amerindian societies developed, so did agriculture, houses, permanent settlements, and ways of ruling and keeping order.

The Amerindians lived in the Caribbean until the arrival of the Europeans in 1492. The Europeans destroyed the Amerindian settlements and wanted to enslave the people. The diseases that the Europeans brought with them also killed many Amerindians because they had no resistance to them.

The coming of the Europeans also saw the arrival of another ethnic group into the region: the people brought as slaves from Africa. This began as early as 1518 but, as the colonies developed and the importance of certain crops increased, so did the demand for slaves. Hundreds of thousands of slaves were transported over a period of about 300 years until the abolition of the slave trade in the nineteenth century.

Following the end of slavery, people from India and China came to work as cheap or 'indentured' labourers. This happened from the 1830s onwards and, although these people were free to return home after their period of indenture, many chose to stay and became the nucleus of the Indian and Chinese communities in the Caribbean today.

The immigration process continues and some countries have seen significant arrivals of other groups from, for example, Syria, Lebanon and other Middle Eastern states.

ACTIVITY

Identify the different ethnic groups in your country. Prepare a list of cultural features that are evident as a result of this group's presence.

Promotion of ancestral customs and crafts

The descendants of the Amerindian populations have settled in parts of St Vincent, in the Carib Territory on the east coast of Dominica and at Arima in Trinidad. The younger Kalinago are keen to promote their culture by:

- recreating dances, music and song
- using art to tell the stories of their way of life and their myths
- discovering the uses of their traditional herbal medicines
- designing and selling traditional basket work.

There are also initiatives to celebrate and remember African culture and heritage which have influenced Caribbean music, food, literature and art.

The Amerindians were the first people to settle in the Caribbean. Their traditional crafts are still being practised today.

Tolerance of different cultural patterns

Given the varied histories of the people who make up the Caribbean, it is not surprising that there are many different cultural patterns within the region. This diversity of cultures is one of the region's most exciting features, but it also presents one of its greatest challenges. It can sometimes be difficult for people from different cultural backgrounds to live alongside one another. We all want to be free to enjoy and celebrate our own culture. In a healthy society, citizens can appreciate different cultures and allow all people to follow their own cultural traditions.

Commercialisation of culture

Some aspects of Caribbean culture are becoming **commercialised**, particularly through the tourist industry. For example, people are drawn to the region because of the many festivals that celebrate aspects of our culture such as music, dancing or food. Once in the region, tourists are often interested in traditional artefacts. Producing and selling these artefacts provides an income for traditional craftspeople.

EXAM TIP

You need to be familiar with the sequence of settlement of different ethnic groups and the cultural practices and influences that each has brought to the region.

4000 BC	First humans artefacts
500 BC	Arawaks
1450 AD	Caribs
1492 onwards	European settlement and colonisation
1500s onwards	Africans arriving as slaves
1845	First Indian indentured labourers
1849	First Chinese indentured labourers
1850–1950	European, Middle Eastern immigration

Figure 2.1.1 Timeline of settlement of different ethnic groups

KEY POINTS

1 Caribbean culture consists of elements from many different ethnic groups.

2 The ancient culture of the people who first settled on the islands is being rediscovered and celebrated.

3 Many aspects of Caribbean culture attract visitors from outside the region.

Social groups

DID YOU KNOW?

There are groups that are both primary and formal, or primary and informal. For example, your class at school is a primary group because there is frequent face-to-face contact between members. It is also a formal group because there are, among other things, rules governing behaviour, and a uniform.

ACTIVITY

1 Make a list of all the formal and informal groups you belong to. Decide whether they are primary or secondary groups.

2 Choose one formal and one informal group and decide what the benefits are for you of belonging to each.

Which type of group do these members of a sports club belong to?

What is a social group?

A social group consists of two or more people who:

- interact frequently
- share common interests
- share a feeling of unity
- work towards a common goal or objective
- have common expectations of behaviour that conform to established guidelines.

Other groups that do not have these characteristics are not classed as social groups. For example, a group gathering at a sports fixture is not a *social* group since it does not meet all or any of the above criteria. Such a group would be a transitory (temporary) group.

Primary and secondary groups

Social groups can be categorised by size, and by the frequency and quality of interaction between members (see Table 2.2.1). Families and friendship groups are examples of primary groups. Schools, political parties or trade unions are examples of secondary groups.

Feature	Primary groups	Secondary groups
Size	Small size	Larger size than a primary group
Degree of interaction	• Members interact frequently with one another and do so face to face • Each member interacts with all others	• Interaction is less frequent than in primary groups • A member may only interact with some, not all, of the other members • All members are rarely in direct contact
Relationships	• Relationships are personal and intimate • Members are accepted because of who they are not what they can bring to the group	• Relationships are less personal and can be based more on function and formality • Members may be expected to make a contribution in order to be accepted

Table 2.2.1 Primary and secondary groups

Informal and formal groups

Social groups can be classified as formal or informal, depending on how they are organised (see Table 2.2.2). Schools, Girl Guides and trade unions are examples of formal groups. Many such groups help in the socialisation of children and young people. A group of friends within a church, office or school would be an example of an informal group.

Characteristic	Formal	Informal
Structure	Clear structure and hierarchy, status, roles and lines of authority, including an elected or appointed leader	No clear structure, possibly with an unofficial leader. Operates on personal relationships of members
Common goals	Clearly defined and lasting goals or purposes	Goals or purposes change with time and type of activity
Rules	Written rules with sanctions	No written rules
Membership	Set requirements for joining and members need to formally leave	No set requirements for joining and members can simply leave
Marks of identity	There may be a uniform or dress code, set behaviour, a badge or symbol	May develop a mode of dress or speech
Common needs, interests, values	Exists to protect its members' interests or to meet external needs. Members' values reflected	Exists to share interests and needs and to offer support. Formed of individuals with common values
Interaction determined by rules and regulations	Contact and interaction between members may be formalised and limited	Interaction between all members is unstructured and open
Established patterns of behaviour	Often laid down in writing and outlining behaviour expected of members, both within the group and when dealing with others	Patterns may develop and become established but not recorded
Cooperation to achieve group goals	Cooperation required of members	Cooperation a product of personal relationships not a formal requirement
Sanctions	Formally laid down as part of rules and regulations	Informally developed within the group

Table 2.2.2 Informal and formal groups

Peer groups

A **peer group** is made up of people of a similar age who share a similar social status and have similar experiences, interests and values. People might be friends with their peers but a peer group does not always consist of friends. **Peer pressure** is the influence a peer group places on an individual to conform to the values and behaviour of the group. Children and adolescents are often said to be very vulnerable to peer pressure.

Interest groups

An interest group is a group of individuals who share an interest. The group may exist to protect the interests of its members and, when this is the case, it might be involved in activities that are intended to influence public opinion or policy. National associations of hotel owners, farmers or manufacturers are examples of such groups.

Pressure groups

Pressure groups seek to influence public opinion or policy and are usually involved with issues that affect people outside their membership. For example, a group may form to protest about a major road development that will destroy an area of unspoilt natural beauty.

EXAM TIP

You will need to be able to define a social group as a distinct entity. You should be able to identify and explain ways in which young people can benefit from belonging to formal social groups.

KEY POINTS

1 A social group is a number of people who personally interact frequently, according to an established set of norms, in order to meet shared needs.

2 Social groups can be primary or secondary, informal or formal.

3 Social groups can be classified according to the closeness of the members.

4 A formal group has a formally organised internal structure.

As well as providing formal education to students, schools also have a role in the socialisation of young people

The word 'institution' has two distinct meanings:

- In one sense, an institution means an established custom or pattern of behaviour in a society, sometimes called a **norm**.
- In another sense, an institution is a formal, specialised organisation, such as the church.

Social control

The norms of society are unwritten rules or standards that are generally accepted and that regulate behaviour in any given situation. Norms are passed on from one generation to the next as part of the process of socialisation. They can vary in importance and significance and some have sanctions that also vary in severity.

Some norms are known as **folkways**, which are behaviours that have developed among groups of people over time. Examples of folkways include behaviours such as shaking hands when greeting a person, or saying 'please' and 'thank you'. There might be mild sanctions for individuals who do not follow these practices. Other folkways include such events as birthday celebrations, funeral rites and wedding ceremonies.

Other norms are called **mores** – these are more serious and are closely associated with reinforcing moral values and behaviour. Important mores can become institutionalised, which results in them becoming subject to law. Violating such a more may result in a severe penalty.

Social norms reflect the agreed **values** of a group or society. Values are to do with the ideas and principles that a group or society has regarding what is good or bad, right or wrong, desirable or undesirable, important or unimportant. When a majority of people in a population share a value, this can shape the way a society looks and operates. For example, most people agree that using violence is undesirable behaviour and so there are mechanisms to prevent, discourage and punish violence.

If a society's values, attitudes and viewpoints remain constant, then the social norms that reflect them will endure over time. If a value, attitude or viewpoint changes, so the associated norm will be modified or even abandoned.

Institutional organisations

An organisation that is an institution is a secondary social group and a formal social group. Such an organisation has a number of characteristics:

- A hierarchical structure. There is clear line of authority within a clearly defined structure. Individuals have specific roles and a given status.
- A specific function. This will usually be to meet the particular interests of the members or to promote a particular issue within society.
- Written rules. These will cover all aspects of the organisation including membership requirements, codes of behaviour, operations and procedures.
- Sanctions. These are a form of punishment, used to ensure members obey rules and regulations. An institution can contribute to social control when its values are the same as those of society in general.
- Endurance over time. The functions of an institution go above and beyond meeting the needs of any individual or current member. Members should pass on the values of the institution to others. In some cases, the intention is to encourage ideas within a society over the long term, such as social order and cooperation.
- Symbols. Institutions sometimes have marks of identity. Such marks may be seen in the clothing of members or in the use of specific symbols. Such marks help to identify the institution within a wider society and also encourage a sense of belonging and identity for members.
- Ritual. Rituals are sets of actions, performed for a set purpose, which is often symbolic. Some ritual actions reinforce the ideas and values of an institution and might include the use of special gestures, words or even music. The requirement for people in a court to stand up when a judge enters is an example of a ritual. In this case, the ritual symbolically expresses the recognition of the judge's authority.

CASE STUDY

The CARICOM Commission on Youth Development (CCYD) was established in 2007 to analyse the challenges and opportunities for youth in the CARICOM **Single Market** and Economy (CSME) and to improve their wellbeing and empowerment. CCYD research published in 2009 showed that youth across the Caribbean region were concerned about a serious disintegration of **social institutions** and values.

Questions

1 To what extent do you agree with these research findings? What examples can you give to support your view?

2 What issues do you think the youth in the Caribbean are facing today?

3 What kind of institutional organisations would help to address these issues?

KEY POINTS

1 A social institution is a norm accepted by the majority of a society.

2 A norm develops in response to a specific need in society.

3 Norms and values can change over time but if the need remains so the norm will endure.

4 Norms, mores and values often serve to regulate behaviour and direct the workings of society.

5 Certain mores form the basis for some of a country's laws.

6 The word 'institution' can also mean an organisation such as a school or church.

7 These organisations often seek to maintain and develop the norms, mores and values of society.

Cohesion in groups and institutions

In topics 2.2 and 2.3, you learned that a social group is more than just a number of people who are in the same place at the same time or simply have some common characteristics. Members of a social group have a common goal, meet and interact frequently, and have established patterns of behaviour. This unit considers the factors that draw individuals to a particular group and those that help people stay together as a cohesive unit.

Requirements for cohesion

A common goal

Social groups are usually formed because of a desire to meet a particular need or achieve a particular goal. This goal will stimulate the interest of founding members and also attract new members. Commitment to the achievement of the group's goal will inspire commitment to the group itself, which will encourage members to remain and to work together.

Leadership

In most circumstances, a group needs one or more persons to be responsible for organising and coordinating actions, to give the group direction and to ensure that the members' needs are being met. Members who feel their needs are not being met will not be motivated to participate in the group's activities and may even leave the group.

Authority

The leadership in both formal and informal groups needs to have power and authority within the group. In an informal group, a leader can emerge from the membership and is given a power simply because other members look to that person to make decisions and take certain responsibilities. In more formal groups, a leader is elected or appointed and is given power in accordance with the group's written rules or constitution. The power of the leader means he or she has the authority to make decisions and to request actions or behaviour from members. A leader must be willing to use his or her power and authority in order to direct the activities of members, allocate resources and to apply sanctions.

Which of the requirements for cohesion do you think will be displayed in this particular group?

Control

Groups need to have a certain amount of stability if they are to remain organised and focused. To promote order and maintain this stability, the behaviour of the group members needs to be regulated. To achieve this, the group will formulate some written or unwritten rules, which will have varying degrees of formality. In addition to these, there will be sanctions that will apply to members who violate the rules.

Cooperation

Cooperation is about working together. People join a group because they have the achievement of a particular goal in mind. This goal might be the meeting of a need that they have or a desire to see something changed. People join a group because they recognise that this is the best way of achieving the goal, either because it would be impossible to achieve it alone (for example, playing a team sport) or it is more likely to be achieved if more than one person is involved (for example, the activities of an environmental group). In these circumstances, group members need to be willing to work together, to share ideas, offer skills and pool resources. If members split up into factions within the group, its chances of achieving its goal and even of staying together are limited.

Commitment and loyalty

Without the commitment and loyalty of its members, a group will not survive for long. Members may lose a sense of commitment if they:

- no longer feel interested in the success of the group
- are not allowed to participate in decision-making
- are dissatisfied with the way the group is being led
- are not getting the benefits from the group that they expected
- no longer share the same values as other members
- see that their inappropriate actions or those of others are not sanctioned
- think the group is insufficiently resourced to achieve its goals.

Benefits of belonging to a social group

Belonging to a social group can bring a number of benefits for the individual, who can learn to:

- accept authority
- cooperate with other members
- be tolerant of others' views and ideas
- deal with people with different personalities
- learn to resolve differences.

ACTIVITY

Analyse a social group to which you belong to identify aspects of the group that work towards maintaining cohesion, and aspects that might disrupt this cohesion.

Leadership, cohesion and interaction in groups and institutions

At the end of this topic you will be able to:

- describe the requirements for cohesion in groups and institutions
- explain the different types of interaction within and among social groups.

Types of leadership

Effective leadership is an important factor in stimulating cohesion within a group. There are different styles of leadership, which have a direct bearing on the way in which the group functions (see Table 2.5.1).

Type of leader	Characteristics
Democratic/ participative	• There is a two-way flow of information from the leader to the members and from members to the leader. The leader might inform the group about intentions and a planned direction. Group members can feed back their thoughts and even suggest ideas of their own • The members will participate in decision-making processes within the group • The leader will delegate some authority to group members
Authoritarian/ autocratic	• There is a one-way flow of information, from the leader to the members • The leader does not take feedback or suggestions from members • The leader does not delegate any authority to members
Laissez-faire	• The leader gives very limited direction to the group • Members are left to work out their own methods and processes for achieving their goals

Table 2.5.1 Types of leadership

Qualities of good leadership

The success of a group often depends on the quality of the leadership. In most cases, a democratic leader will be most successful, particularly in obtaining greater cooperation from members in the group. A good leader should have certain character traits, such as integrity and other skills in dealing with people. A leader's knowledge and experiences may also be relevant to a particular situation.

A good leader should be able to:

- communicate well with members
- command the respect of members
- initiate policies and set goals for the group
- delegate tasks and the authority for accomplishing them
- motivate members to achieve the group's goals
- display honesty and fairness
- allocate resources for achieving the group's goals
- take note of and apply good ideas from members.

EXAM TIP

Be ready to explain the consequences of the different aspects of interaction within and between groups.

Aspects of interaction within and between groups

Social interaction

Whenever people live or work in groups, there is interaction. This is the series of actions or communications that take place between them. The interaction is sometimes between individuals within a group and sometimes it is between groups. You need to be able to explain the different types of interaction.

Competition

There might be competition within a group if two or more members are seeking to take up the same position. There may be friendly competition when group members take part in a debate or sports activity. Organisations may compete if they are both trying to achieve the same goal. For example, non-government organisations (NGOs) may have to compete for funds, and political parties compete for votes during an election. Competition can lead to increased creativity and determination.

Cooperation is one form of interaction within a group. If group members interact in this way, it is more likely that the group's objectives will be achieved.

Conflict

Conflict can occur within a group for many reasons, simply because each person is an individual and it is unlikely that every one of those will always agree with everyone else. Conflict may also arise when members are:

- in competition
- unhappy with some of the behaviour within the group
- dissatisfied with the leadership.

The ability to prevent or resolve conflict is a useful skill for group leaders and members.

Cooperation

Cooperation involves working together. Individuals can cooperate within a group to see that the group's goals are achieved. Groups can cooperate together to see that wider objectives are fulfilled.

Compromise

This is about finding a way of resolution between two conflicting opinions or ideas. Each side makes concessions, which means they give up something in order to reach a settlement in which they get part of what they wanted.

KEY POINTS

1. For a group to survive it must have:
   - a goal that attracts and motivates members
   - effective leadership
   - rules
   - sanctions
   - committed members
   - cooperative members.

2. Members of social groups may compete with one another within the group and cooperate with one another to help achieve the group's goals.

3. Groups may compete with one another in terms of needs and interests, and cooperate when seeking to meet broader societal goals.

Functions of institutions

At the end of this topic you will be able to:

- evaluate the functions of institutions in society.

Religions often have values that reflect and enhance those of society. Many people benefit from the work of members of faith groups who are often volunteers.

At a very basic level a society must provide clothing, food and shelter for its members. As a society develops, increasingly complex systems of provision and administration are necessary, with organisations, or institutions, managing the whole process. In a modern developing society, such as in the Caribbean, the provision of even the basic requirements can involve a complicated series of interactions.

In the case of food, for example, the simplest form of transaction is where a producer sells direct to a **consumer**. In today's society, however, most people buy their food from a retailer. The retailer will have bought the food from a wholesaler, who may have purchased from a food processing company. All these stages require other systems and organisations, such as transport companies, financial institutions and regulatory bodies. Government will also be involved in establishing such things as food labelling and food safety standards, negotiating trade agreements for imported and exported foods, and occasionally having to fix prices.

The many needs of a society are usually allocated to one of the following categories: economic, educational, recreational, religious, or political.

Economic

The economy of a society consists of the various systems that produce and manage **resources** and the money that is used as the medium of exchange. Primary industries produce raw materials, such as ore and food. Secondary industries turn these raw materials into manufactured goods, such as furniture or packaged food. Tertiary industries are concerned with the movement of goods or with providing a **service** to people or to other industries. Examples of tertiary industries are tourism, transport, finance and insurance.

Since money is involved in almost all exchanges of wages and salaries for work, rents, investments and distribution of profits, the institutions involved in finance, including banks and **credit unions**, have a very important role.

Educational

The educational institutions of a society are the schools, colleges and universities. These institutions play a part in the **socialisation** of individuals. They also seek to increase people's knowledge and skills, to help them achieve their full potential, and to prepare them for the world of work. They do this by:

- teaching basic skills, such as literacy and numeracy
- teaching knowledge and skills for specific jobs
- transmitting the culture, beliefs, norms and values of society
- developing critical thinking skills
- addressing the spiritual, moral, educational and physical development of each individual.

Consider the different types of institution described and explain the contribution each one makes to society.

Recreational

Recreational institutions provide facilities for people to use in their leisure time for rest, pleasure and amusement, and in order to stay fit and healthy. These institutions help people maintain physical and mental wellbeing and in this way they contribute to the development of a country's human resources. Recreational institutions include sports clubs, theatres, music venues and tourist resorts.

Religious

The different faiths of the Caribbean have organisations or institutions to represent them to their followers. There are buildings such as churches, mosques, synagogues and temples, which are places of worship and teaching. There are also people within the organisations, such as ministers, imams, rabbis and priests, to whom believers may go for spiritual direction and support. A person's faith can be a fundamental part of his or her life. It can assist in social control when the values of the faith align with the values of society.

Political

The main organisation of the political institution of a country is the government. The government is responsible for ensuring that the society is able to grow and prosper and to be safe and secure. There are many competing and sometimes conflicting interests within a country and a government has to see that everyone's interests are taken into account and regulated. A government achieves this by:

- making laws and establishing sanctions for those who break them
- producing policies
- defending the nation state
- maintaining relations with other countries.

Government exists at national and local levels in most Commonwealth Caribbean countries. Local government can foster local democracy and ensure that local issues are addressed.

KEY POINTS

1 Society's needs are categorised as economic, recreational, religious and political.

2 Economic institutions are related to the production and management of goods and services.

3 Religious institutions help people in matters of faith.

4 Political institutions officially regulate the activities of society.

5 Recreational institutions provide for fulfilment in leisure time, for pleasure, amusement and health.

CASE STUDY

The Caribbean Wellness Day 2010 5km Run/Walk was formally launched by the Minister of Health of Trinidad and Tobago, Senator the Honourable Therese Baptiste-Cornelis in September 2010. The event was held on Saturday, 18 September 2010 at the Queen's Park Savannah. All members of the public were invited to participate and registration was free.

All citizens were encouraged to go to the Queen's Park Savannah from 1pm to take advantage of free screening checks for body mass index (BMI), blood glucose/sugar, cholesterol, blood pressure, HIV and pap smears. Information was also provided on leading a healthy lifestyle.

The 5km Run/Walk commenced at 4.30pm.

Questions

1 Why would a government spend time and money promoting a healthy lifestyle for its citizens?

2 Which social institutions do you think should have a role in helping individuals to be healthy?

SECTION 1: Multiple-choice questions

1 Cultural diversity means:
- **a** eating different foods
- **b** travelling to different countries
- **c** different ethnic groups living together
- **d** celebrating the lives of people from the past

2 To help towards achieving a safe and happy society, the best attitudes different ethnic groups can have towards each other are:
- **a** suspicion and mistrust
- **b** tolerance and acceptance
- **c** fear and hatred
- **d** dislike and rejection

3 What type of group is formed by a number of friends meeting after school?
- **a** Involuntary
- **b** Formal
- **c** Voluntary
- **d** Informal

4 People of a similar age who share some common values would be called a:
- **a** voluntary association
- **b** peer group
- **c** youth club
- **d** soccer team

5 A society usually has ideas about what people feel is right or wrong, desirable or undesirable, important or unimportant. These ideas are called:
- **a** values
- **b** rules
- **c** folkways
- **d** currency

6 Sanctions can be applied by an institution in order to:
- **a** reward people for good behaviour
- **b** prevent people enjoying themselves
- **c** punish people for disobeying rules and regulations
- **d** allow people to behave as they please

7 Which of the following is most likely to lead to cohesion within a group?
- **a** A lack of commitment
- **b** Weak leadership
- **c** Conflict
- **d** Sharing a common goal

8 Competition in a group can be useful when it leads to:
- **a** creativity and renewed determination
- **b** violent disagreements
- **c** members leaving
- **d** feelings of failure

9 Which of the following institutions have a role in the socialisation of individuals?
- **a** Factories
- **b** Educational establishments
- **c** Sports clubs
- **d** Banks

10 Theatres, sports clubs, music venues and cinemas are institutions whose function is mainly:
- **a** religious
- **b** economic
- **c** recreational
- **d** educational

Further practice questions and examples can be found on the accompanying CD.

1 The Orbit Youth Club has been running for three years and has attracted a good number of members. When asked what they like about the club, existing members say that they enjoy the activities offered and the opportunities they are given to suggest new activities that could be introduced. One recent suggestion was that club members might form an environmental team to help improve the local area. The club is facing a period of change because the leader is moving away and will need to be replaced. The club also needs to recruit some new members to make it more sustainable.

   a Describe some of the ways that young people benefit from membership of a club like the Orbit and how they could be used to attract new members.

   b Suggest at least three characteristics that should be considered by those responsible for selecting the new club leader.

   c Suggest how the club's leader might encourage members to work together to achieve their goal of improving their local environment.

2 One aspect of concern to the club leaders is that the members are almost all from one ethnic group.

   a Why might the leaders think it would be a good idea for club members to have more contact with people from other ethnic groups?

   b Make some suggestions that would make such contact between ethnic groups possible. How might group members be able to find out about and celebrate features of their own culture and those of other people?

   c Explain some of the problems the leaders might encounter as they try to encourage contact between ethnic groups and how these could be overcome.

3 The club offers a range of activities for its members. There is a basketball court in the club grounds and one room has recently been equipped with some computers where the club will be running short courses in IT. The club is acting as a social institution by providing these activities.

   a Explain what you understand by the term 'social institution' in this context.

   b What functions of an institution is the club performing by providing the two activities mentioned?

   c Suggest some other functions of social institutions that the club might be able to perform and provide examples of the types of activities that would be offered to achieve this.

4 The club has asked its members to help draw up a manifesto that states the aims and principles of the club. They have also asked for members' help in drawing up a list of expectations regarding behaviour and attitude, which will be expected of all members.

   a Write your suggestions for the contents of a manifesto for the Orbit Youth Club.

   b Write about the kinds of behaviour and attitudes you think members need to be encouraged to show, explaining why each one is important.

   c If the manifesto and the behaviour and attitudes list are made available for potential new members, do you think this will encourage them to join or not? Give your reasons.

> Further practice questions and examples can be found on the accompanying CD.

3.1

Different types of government

The concept of government

A society is made up of individuals who live and work in groups. All these individuals and groups have goals, needs and interests which at times may compete and sometimes conflict with others. There needs to be a means by which these conflicting goals and interests can be managed and regulated. This is usually achieved through the promotion of **norms** and **mores** and the use of legislation and the enforcement of laws. The body responsible for managing a country's goals and for regulating the activities of a society is the government.

The Caribbean situation

The majority of CARICOM member states are former British colonies. As colonies, these states were subject to Britain. This means that they were not independent and were under British rule. The situation has changed and the member states of CARICOM now have different types of government systems in place (Figure 3.1.1).

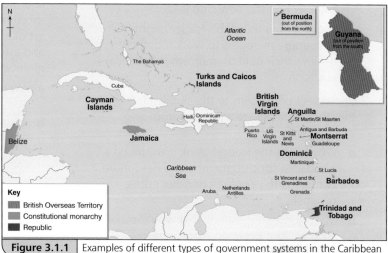

| Figure 3.1.1 | Examples of different types of government systems in the Caribbean |

Crown colony

A crown colony was a type of administration under the British Empire. The colony gave up its elected assembly and right to self-government. The government comprised a governor, an executive council and a legislative council. The councils were made up of officials who headed government departments in the colonies, together with members nominated by the governor. The governor had **executive**, **legislative** and **judicial** powers which gave authority to make and administer policies and laws. The councils were advisory, with no power themselves.

British Crown Colonies have been reclassified as British Overseas Territories. The form of government still reflects that of a crown colony. Montserrat, and Turks and Caicos are examples of British Overseas Territories.

Constitutional monarchy

A monarchy is a system in which one individual is **monarch** or sovereign, usually for his or her whole life. In a constitutional monarchy, a colony acquires political independence from the colonial power. The crown-appointed governor is replaced by a governor-general, who is head of state. This person is a symbolic representative of the monarch (or crown) and has only limited constitutional powers. So there is still a connection to the monarch of the previous colonial power, even if this has no direct bearing on the governing of a country.

The governor-general acts on the advice of the prime minister. The prime minister is in charge of the government of the colony, which is responsible for the internal and external affairs of the country.

Jamaica and Barbados are examples of constitutional monarchies.

A distinction between a monarchy and a constitutional monarchy exists in the relationship of the monarch to the law. In a monarchy, the monarch may be above the law or subject to the law. In a constitutional monarchy, the monarch is always subject to the law.

Republicanism

Countries where the monarch has been replaced by a president as head of state are republics. There are two types of republic in the Caribbean.

- In a presidential republic, run on the presidential system, the head of state or executive president is also head of government. The executive president has full constitutional powers. The government of Guyana is based on this system.
- In a parliamentary republic, with a parliamentary system, the head of state holds a ceremonial function and the prime minister is the head of government and, therefore, has the executive authority. Trinidad and Tobago, and the Commonwealth of Dominica have such a system, and the presidents there have limited constitutional powers.

Proposals for policies and laws are debated in parliament

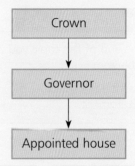

The structure of government 1: the legislature

The different branches of government are the legislature (parliament), the executive and the judiciary. Each branch of government should function independently of the others, and each should also act as a check on the others.

To achieve this check and to avoid abuse, the constitutions of Commonwealth Caribbean countries operate the principle of **separation of powers** which divides the powers of government between the three branches.

Regional heads of state and government gather to discuss issues such as economic integration, trade agreements and tourism

The legislature

Structure of parliament

The legislature (or parliament) can have one body, in which case it is called a **unicameral** legislature, or two bodies, which is known as a **bicameral** legislature. Guyana and Dominica have unicameral legislatures. A bicameral legislature comprises an upper house, sometimes called the senate, and the lower house, which is known as either the house of representatives or the house of assembly.

Legislatures have a limited term of office, usually five years, after which elections are held.

Composition of parliament

In a bicameral legislature, members of the senate (or upper house) are senators who are nominated, not elected. The senate might include:

• independent senators – nominated by the head of state
• government senators – nominated by the prime minister
• opposition senators – nominated by the leaders of the opposition parties with sitting members in the house of representatives assembly.

Independent senators are so-called because they do not represent a **political party**. They usually represent particular interests, such as business or education.

Where there is a prime minister, he or she is able to nominate a majority of senators. This means that the government will have the majority of votes in the senate. The government will also have a majority in the house of representatives since it will have most members there also.

The house of representatives (or lower house) is made up of members of parliament (MPs) elected from the governing party and members of the opposition party or parties. Some governing party MPs are appointed as ministers by the prime minister and together they form a **cabinet** (see topic 3.3).

The role of the opposition

The opposition parties criticise and oppose government policies with which they disagree. A strong opposition:

- ensures that the legislature keeps the power of the executive in check
- ensures that the government is accountable for its actions, revealing weakness, mismanagement or corruption
- introduces its own **bills** to improve the governance of the country.

The effectiveness of the opposition can be limited if:

- ministers use delaying tactics
- it is frequently out-voted because it is a minority.

The role of the prime minister

The prime minister is the head of the government. He or she is appointed by the head of state (the governor-general or the president, depending on the governmental system). The appointment is made on the basis that he or she is:

- leader of the political party that has won an election
- the person best able to command the confidence and respect of the majority of the elected members of the house of representatives.

The prime minister has several powers and functions. He or she:

- determines the size of the cabinet and chooses its members
- recommends the appointment or dismissal of cabinet members to the governor-general
- assigns or reassigns responsibilities to cabinet members
- in a constitutional monarchy, chooses a governor-general and recommends the appointment to the monarch
- chairs cabinet meetings
- advises the governor-general when to dissolve parliament
- fixes the dates for elections
- takes the lead in formulating policies for the country
- coordinates the work of the various ministries.

In some Caribbean countries, the prime minister is able, in consultation with the leader of the opposition, to choose judges to recommend to the governor-general for appointment.

The role of the head of state

The head of state may be a governor-general, an executive president or a titular president. An executive president has full constitutional powers. A governor-general or titular president has mainly ceremonial functions and limited or discretionary powers. He or she uses these discretionary powers to appoint:

- the prime minister
- the leader of the opposition
- independent senators
- members of the local privy council.

The governor-general or titular president also usually acts on the advice of the prime minister to:

- appoint or dismiss ministers
- dissolve parliament
- appoint judges.

ACTIVITY

Carry out some research into the activities of the opposition in your country and decide how effective you think they have been. In making your assessment, you might consider the number of bills they have introduced and the degree to which they have challenged the achievements of the government.

KEY POINTS

1 The different branches of government are the legislature (parliament), the executive and the judiciary.

2 The principle of separation of powers divides power between the three branches of government.

3 A unicameral legislature has one body; a bicameral legislature has two.

4 Parliaments can have appointed senators and elected members.

5 A powerful opposition challenges the government and introduces its own bills.

6 A prime minister is head of government.

7 The head of state can have executive powers or have a largely ceremonial role.

The structure of government 2: the executive

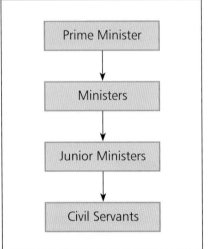

Figure 3.3.1 The hierarchical structure of the executive branch of government

The executive

The executive branch conducts the ordinary business of government and is known as the cabinet. In all independent Caribbean countries, except Guyana, the cabinet consists of the prime minister, who is its chief executive officer, and other ministers of government. The prime minister chooses ministers of government they wish to have in the cabinet, but they are actually appointed by the governor-general. In Guyana, the executive president is the head of the cabinet.

The cabinet is responsible for:

- making policies and programmes for the country
- ensuring that policies and programmes are carried out
- initiating proposals for legislation
- initiating proposals for taxation.

The cabinet is assisted by the civil service, which is responsible for implementing the government's policies and programmes.

How the cabinet system works

The principle of collective responsibility

The cabinet meets to discuss and approve government policy. When a policy is approved it becomes 'cabinet policy', which means that all members of the cabinet have to support and defend it, in public and in parliament. A cabinet member who disagrees with the policy is not at liberty to criticise the policy or express disagreement. The whole cabinet has to take responsibility for any decisions made – this is the **principle of collective responsibility**.

The cabinet has to obtain the approval of parliament for any major policy it wishes to implement. Since the governing party has the majority of **seats** in parliament, getting this approval is often a formality. There are occasions, however, when government ministers will rebel and vote against their party. The ability of members of parliament (MPs), whether from the opposition parties or from the governing party, to challenge proposed cabinet policy is an important element in keeping the power of the executive in check.

Cabinet ministers may be asked by other MPs to give explanations about their ministry's policies.

Ministers

Government ministers are given certain areas of responsibility by the prime minister. This area of responsibility is called the minister's **portfolio**. The minister has individual responsibility for his or her office, which is called a ministry or government department. The minister must promote and defend the ministry's policies and performance in cabinet and in parliament.

The minister may be assisted by a 'minister without portfolio' (or junior minister) who is also known as a 'minister of state'.

The prime minister, or in the case of Guyana, the president, may reassign a minister to another portfolio if his or her work is unsatisfactory or if his or her skills could be better utilised in another area. When ministers are reassigned in this way, this is known as a cabinet reshuffle.

The role of the civil service

Each government ministry has a staff of **civil servants** who are responsible for implementing the government's policies that relate to each particular ministry and who may be asked to advise the minister. Each ministry is headed by a senior civil servant, known as the permanent secretary.

Duties

The permanent secretary and other senior civil servants are expected to use their knowledge and skills to:

- advise the minister on the soundness of the ministry's policies
- devise strategies for implementing policies
- monitor and evaluate policies
- ensure efficient and effective policy implementation.

Standards

Civil servants are obliged to carry out government policy objectively. This means they should not have regard to their own opinions or feelings about the government or its policies, but that they should carry out their duties without any bias in favour of or against any individuals or groups.

A proposed cabinet policy has to win the approval of parliament before it can be implemented. Such approval is often obtained after a debate in parliament.

ACTIVITY

Carry out some research to find out about cabinet reshuffles in your country. Write a report on what happened and why. Answer these questions as part of your report.

- Which ministers had their portfolios changed?
- Were some ministers dismissed from the cabinet?
- Was the size of the cabinet changed and why?
- Were the responsibilities of some ministries being combined?

KEY POINTS

1 The executive (or cabinet) comprises the prime minister and other government ministers.

2 The cabinet is the policy-making arm of government and operates a principle of collective responsibility.

3 Government ministers have individual ministerial responsibility for their ministries.

4 Cabinet is answerable to parliament and has to obtain its approval before its major policies can be enacted.

5 The civil service is a group of non-elected government officials who are responsible for carrying out a government's policies.

3.4 The structure of government 3: the judiciary

LEARNING OUTCOMES

At the end of this topic you will be able to:

- describe the judiciary within the structure of government.

DID YOU KNOW?

The Privy Council in London in the United Kingdom remains the final court of appeal for most English-speaking Caribbean countries.

The judiciary is the legal system through which:

- sanctions can be handed out to individuals or organisations that break laws
- disputes between individuals or organisations can be resolved.

Structure of the court system

The court system in Caribbean countries is shown in Figure 3.4.1.

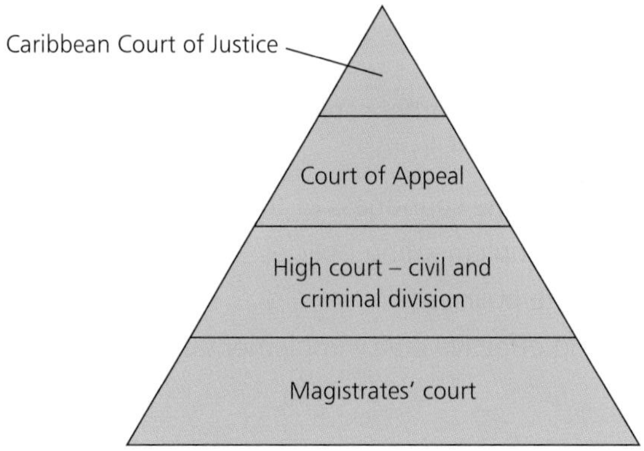

Figure 3.4.1 Structure of the court system in Caribbean countries

Functions of the courts

The functions of the courts in the Caribbean are shown in Table 3.4.1.

Courts	Functions
Magistrates' court	Trials in a magistrates' court are called summary trials Magistrates: • try minor criminal offences • conduct preliminary enquiries into criminal or indictable offences such as murder or rape • conduct (in a coroner's court) investigations into unnatural deaths
High court – criminal division	Tries the serious offences for which the magistrates' court conducted preliminary enquiries
High court – civil division	Settles disputes relating to civil matters such as divorce, libel and property disputes
Court of appeal	Consists of a panel of three judges. An individual who believes he or she did not receive a fair trial in either the magistrates' or the high court may have the case reviewed Any sentence or fine imposed by the lower court may be upheld, reversed, increased or decreased
Caribbean Court of Justice (CCJ)	The final court of appeal for member states of CARICOM who are also signatories of the CCJ The CCJ also functions as an international tribunal, applying rules of international law in respect of the interpretation and application of the CARICOM Treaty

Table 3.4.1 Functions of the courts

How the court system works

Courts hear both civil and criminal cases. In some countries, such as Jamaica, a **justice of the peace** will mediate in certain cases, to attempt to avoid people entering the court system unnecessarily.

Civil cases are brought by one individual, group or organisation against another, if one party feels wronged by another in some way.

Criminal cases are brought by the police against an individual or group if it is believed that the law has been broken. These cases are prosecuted by the state.

Role of the police

Functions of police	Role of police in the court of process
Protect life and property	Investigate offences, bring suspects to trial
Prevent crime	Record statements and provide evidence
Detect and investigate crime	Provide prosecution's witnesses
Apprehend and interrogate suspected criminals	Issue warrants to ensure court appearance
Preserve peace and maintain order	Compile offenders' criminal records
Enforce laws	Act as court prosecutors
Investigate accidents	Provide witness protection
Monitor traffic flows	Maintain order and security of court
Execute warrants	Secure exhibits used as evidence

Table 3.4.1 Role of the police

Role of the prison system

A prison system exists to provide a form of punishment and to act as a deterrent. It also provides victims, potential victims and society protection from convicted criminals. There should be confidence in the judicial system and a sense that justice has been done. A good prison system also provides the possibility of prisoner reform.

ACTIVITY

It is often said police cannot control crime on their own, but are heavily dependent on support from the public in doing so. More successful crime control will follow from gaining public support.

In many countries of the Caribbean, the relationship between the public and the police is not healthy, so successful crime control is jeopardised.

Write a short article for a newspaper suggesting ways in which relationships between the police and the public might be improved in your country. You should establish from research what systems of police accountability exist and what actions are already in place to build up community–police relations.

KEY POINTS

1 The judiciary interprets and administers the law.

2 The court system consists of magistrates' courts, the high court, the appeal court and the Caribbean Court of Justice.

3 The court of appeal may reverse, confirm, increase or reduce sentences passed by lower courts.

4 The police and courts complement the role of one another.

5 The prison system manages the punishment of criminals. Some people believe the system needs to be reformed.

3.5

Functions of government

Upgrading a country's infrastructure is part of a government's responsibilities

A government has to manage the goals and aspirations of a country, implementing policies and regulating activities in such a way as to best serve the interests of its citizens. This section considers some of the areas of government activity.

Taxation

Governments levy taxes to raise revenue that provides for spending on behalf of the citizens of the country, for example on health or education. Tax is raised in two ways:

• Direct taxation, levied at source, such as stamp duty and income tax
• Indirect taxation, levied on goods and services, such as Consumption Tax, Value Added Tax (VAT) and Airport Duty

Social services

Social services provision is about improving the quality of life for as many people as possible, especially those who are least able to help themselves. Through social services, a government provides:

• welfare payments, such as grants to those in poverty
• social security, such as national insurance, unemployment benefits and pensions
• sanitation, namely the provision of clean water and means of sewage disposal.

Infrastructure

The **infrastructure** of a country includes roads, harbours, airports, industrial estates, schools and hospitals, and also the systems that supply such things as fresh water, electricity and gas, or dispose of such things as sewage. Governments are largely responsible for providing such infrastructure since it is an important part of promoting the development of a country.

Managing finances

The raising and spending of government revenue has to be carefully managed and monitored. This is achieved through a government's **fiscal policy**. A government will also have a **monetary policy** which seeks to control the supply of money within a country and so manage such things as inflation.

A government is required to:

• draw up a plan (or **budget**) to show how revenue will be raised and spent
• effectively manage the country's national debt
• ensure goals of **fiscal** sustainability are met

- manage and maintain relationships with international and regional financial institutions, such as the International Monetary Fund (IMF) and the Inter-American Development Bank (IDB).

Law and order

There are several elements to maintaining law and order. The function of government is to:
- pass laws that are intended to enhance lawful and peaceful living
- maintain courts to punish criminals and wrongdoers and to settle disputes
- employ police to enforce laws and to protect people and property.

Employment

A government benefits when most of a county's working-age population is in paid employment, since a large part of its revenue comes from taxation on income. To maximise the number of its citizens who are working, a government will create employment:
- directly – by employing people in the civil service and in statutory organisations
- indirectly – by creating a favourable economic climate in which private enterprises will be established or grow, and so require more employees.

International relations

Governments need to establish and maintain relationships with other countries for many reasons, such as managing potential conflicts and reaching agreements on business, trade and finance. Many Caribbean countries seek financial assistance from other countries as well as making trade agreements concerning the buying and selling of goods and services.

International relations are undertaken by individual countries and as a group within CARICOM. A part of maintaining international relations is to exchange **ambassadors** with other countries.

Defence

Governments are also concerned about the defence of their country from external aggression, and about the country's internal security. To achieve these aims, a country may have its own armed forces or a defence force of some kind.

KEY POINTS

The responsibilities of government are to:
- raise revenue and manage finances
- provide social services
- provide infrastructure
- maintain law and order
- create employment opportunities
- maintain international relations and defend the nation state.

CASE STUDY

The Jamaica Development Infrastructure Programme combines a number of government functions. It is the result of a partnership between the governments of Jamaica and the People's Republic of China. It seeks to significantly improve the island's road network, enhance the quality of life of citizens and stimulate economic development.

The government of China has made US$400m (approximately J$36bn) available for the programme. Work will be done to construct or upgrade roads, bridges, drains and traffic systems over a number of years.

Question

What are the benefits for each of the countries involved in such a programme?

Completed ballot papers are folded so that the vote cast cannot be seen. They are then placed in a ballot box, before they are counted. In some countries voters are required to dip their finger in ink to show that they have voted.

Countries in the Commonwealth Caribbean are **democracies**, where the government is chosen by the citizens in a general election that should be free and fair.

Electoral processes

In a general election, all eligible people get the chance to cast a vote. This happens on a set day and at regular intervals of, usually, no more than five years. The votes cast determine the next government.

Elections are contested between groups known as political parties. Members of a political party share similar political views, beliefs and ideas.

A right to vote is known as a **franchise** or suffrage. When all people who reach 18 years of age are eligible to vote, this is known as **universal adult suffrage**. To exercise the right to vote, a person must register. The **electorate** of a country are all the eligible, registered voters.

Electoral systems

There are two types of electoral system used in the Commonwealth Caribbean.

First-past-the-post

In this system, a country is divided up into constituencies. A **constituency** is a group of voters in a specific geographic area. Each political party will nominate a candidate for election in each constituency. The candidate gaining most votes in a constituency wins the constituency election and becomes the constituency's representative in the lower house of parliament. He or she is said to have won a seat in parliament. This system is used in all Commonwealth Caribbean countries except Guyana.

Constituency boundaries can be altered to favour one party or candidate. This is called **gerrymandering**.

The party that wins the most constituencies wins the overall (or general) election and forms the government. The prime minister is chosen from the winning party and the leader of the opposition is chosen from the party with the second-highest number of seats.

If no party wins an outright majority of seats, the situation is described as a **hung parliament**. The two parties with the most votes may seek to form a coalition government, sometimes with lesser third parties.

Proportional representation

In this system, the whole country is treated as a single constituency. Political parties prepare a list of candidates based on the number of seats in parliament. The list is put in order of preference by the party leader and made public. People vote for a party and not a candidate.

Each party is awarded seats in parliament based on the proportion of votes it gains in the election. A party winning 20 per cent of the votes is awarded 20 per cent of the seats, which will go to the first 20 per cent of candidates on the list.

Advantages and disadvantages

The advantages and disadvantages of both electoral systems are summarised in Table 3.6.1.

Electoral system	Advantages	Disadvantages
First-past-the-post	Guarantees that the election is won by the candidate with the highest number of votes	Constituencies that elect members in opposition may be neglected or victimised by the government.
	Promotes accountability within a constituency from an individual parliamentarian since he or she are responsible to his or her constituency	It is possible for a party with a minority of votes overall to form a government. For example, one party may win more than half the seats in parliament (and therefore form the government) with less than half the total votes
	Constituencies can choose their own representatives	It allows for gerrymandering
	Constituents can appeal directly to their representative regarding services in the constituency	Independent candidates who are not from a political party can struggle to gain votes
Proportional representation	Provides for representation of minority political parties	Too wide a range or too great a number of parties is formed, spreading votes too thinly and running the risk of no party gaining an absolute majority
	Eliminates gerrymandering	May necessitate more frequent coalition governments where no one party wins an overall majority
	Each party is allocated seats in proportion to the votes it receives	Weakens the relationship between voters and parliamentarians – the parliamentarian is representing the country not a local constituency The party leader has a lot of power when compiling the list of preferred candidates

Table 3.6.1 Advantages and disadvantages of first-past-the-post and proportional representation

Managing an election

A country's election system is managed by a government department known as the electoral office or the electoral and boundaries commission. The responsibilities of this department include:

- the division of the country into constituencies
- voter registration
- preparation and amendment of voters' lists and voters' ID cards
- preparation and distribution of election notices, ballot papers and ballot boxes
- registration of candidates on polling day
- supervision of the balloting process on election day
- declaration of results
- auditing candidates' election expenses.

KEY POINTS

1 An electoral system is the set of procedures whereby a country chooses its government.

2 There are two main systems known as first-past-the-post and proportional representation.

3 Universal adult suffrage is the right of all eligible people over 18 years of age to vote.

How political parties prepare for elections

At the end of this topic you will be able to:

• describe how political parties prepare for elections.

An election is the event in which the government of the country is decided. Within the Commonwealth Caribbean, elections are due every five years. A prime minister may call an election at any time in that period. Whenever it is called, preparing for an election is an extremely important activity for political parties since it is during this stage that voters are convinced of which party to vote for.

Important issues

Political parties need to be aware of the important issues in the country. Since individuals and organisations often have conflicting views regarding the priority they would give these issues, the political parties have to gauge the feelings of the people and convince them that their policies will be in the best interests of the country.

Party manifesto

A manifesto is a public declaration of principles or intentions. A political party manifesto sets out the party's beliefs and principles, the changes it believes need to be brought about and the strategies, policies and legislation it would introduce to achieve these changes. It provides the party's assessment of the current situation and sets out the promises it is making to bring about the changes it sees as necessary for improvement.

Candidate selection

Any eligible person may stand as a candidate in an election, either as an independent candidate or as a member of a political party. Anyone wishing to stand must be nominated on an official form and be registered in the nominations office by a given date. All candidates put down a deposit which is lost if they do not gain a specified number of votes.

Local party candidates can be chosen by their local party group or by the hierarchy of the party. The candidate must be approved by the party at a national level.

EXAM TIP

The examination may require you to describe the preparations a political party makes for an election, so make sure you have a good understanding of the various elements.

Fundraising

To run a campaign, a candidate needs funds. Funds can be raised in a number of ways, from simply asking individuals or corporations to donate, through to holding fundraising events.

Election campaign finance laws can be applied to restrict the types of funding a candidate can seek and also to limit the amount a candidate can spend on a campaign. In some Caribbean countries, there is a requirement for candidates to file a report stating their campaign expenditure. These rules exist to avoid the success of election campaigns being determined by the amount of money available.

Campaigning

Campaigning in an election is about convincing eligible voters to cast their vote for a particular candidate or party. When candidates hold meetings, visit homes or speak to people in the streets, this is known as **canvassing**. Political parties run advertising campaigns, which may include broadcasts on television. There is increasing use of communications technology, with candidates having direct access to people through web logs (blogs), social networking sites, emails and text messages to cell phones.

Whichever method is used, all campaigning has to be done in an open and honest way. There should not be any attempt to bribe or threaten individuals into casting their votes for a particular candidate.

Other rules require that officials do not use state-owned resources or media outlets to promote their cause during the run-up to an election. Similarly, all candidates and parties should be free to campaign wherever they choose, without the threat of intimidation by a political opponent.

Monitoring performance

As part of their preparation for an election, political parties monitor their own past performance and that of their opponents. A party in government will want to show how successful they have been while in government. The opposition parties will attempt to prove the opposite.

All parties also monitor their performance during a campaign. They will often use the results of opinion polls to determine how successful or otherwise their campaign efforts are.

Monitoring electoral processes

Elections must be carried out in accordance with regulations, and it is in the interest of political parties to see that the regulations are followed. If an election is not free, open and 'transparent', it can affect how the population views the results, and as a consequence what the attitude is to the party that forms the government. Monitoring the electoral process should ensure that candidates adhere to rules about campaigning, fundraising and expenditure; anyone who wishes to vote is able to do so; each eligible person votes only once; voters are not subjected to any violence, bribery or intimidation; and an open forum for vote counting is provided.

ACTIVITY

Find out about the body responsible for monitoring elections in your country and describe how they fulfil this function.

KEY POINTS

1 Political parties lay out their beliefs and proposals in a party manifesto.

2 Any eligible person may stand as an election candidate.

3 Rules govern campaign fundraising and use of state resources.

4 Free and fair elections require that no threats, bribes or intimidation are used to influence voters.

Posters play an important part during an election campaign

What influences the outcome of elections?

Political parties do all they can to influence voters in the run up to an election, especially **floating voters** who are those not aligned with a particular party. They will also focus attention on **marginal seats**, where the current member of parliament (MPS) has only a small majority and may therefore be unseated. A **safe seat** is one where one political party is considered certain to win.

Campaign strategy

The prime minister of a country calls an election and must give between three and six weeks' notice.

Each political party decides which issues it will campaign on. The party in government will seek to prove that its policies have worked well while the opposition parties will hope to convince voters that it is time for a change of government.

Campaign spending

Campaign expenditure is limited and monitored by a body such as an electoral and boundaries commission. Even with regulation, it is plain that a party with plenty of money to spend on its campaign will have a greater impact and therefore possibly a greater influence.

Media coverage

Political parties and individual candidates use many forms of media to communicate their message. **Mass media** also act as a form of oversight since they could reveal any wrongdoing or failure to follow rules.

Parties use many forms of media to communicate their message

The media have a responsibility to be unbiased, providing balanced and accurate coverage and allowing all parties equal access to advertising opportunities.

Campaign advertising

Paid campaign advertising involves the use of media to communicate with and influence the electorate.

In most countries, there are guidelines concerning the content and use of paid political advertising.

Opinion polls

An opinion poll is a survey of responses to certain questions, given by a sample of the population. The sample group's opinions are then used as an indication of the opinions of the population as a whole. This will inform the messages political parties then give out to the electorate.

Figure 3.8.1 shows the election results from the 2010 elections in St Vincent and the Grenadines. Along the base are the initial letters of the different constituencies.

Questions

1 In which constituency did the ULP have the largest majority?

2 How many constituencies did the NDP win?

3 Which constituencies would you describe as 'marginal seats'?

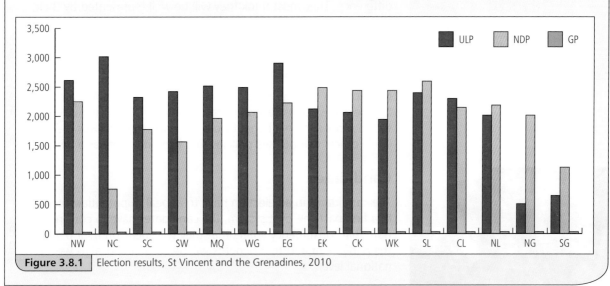

| **Figure 3.8.1** | Election results, St Vincent and the Grenadines, 2010 |

Voter turnout

Voter turnout is the percentage of the electorate who actually cast a vote. An election result based on a high turnout is generally accepted to be a better reflection of the 'will of the people'.

A low voter turnout causes concern because of the fear that this means that a particular section of the population may be under-represented.

Voter attitude to government

Some people will vote for a ruling government because it reflects their own political ideologies and because they feel it has been performing well. People who feel that the current government is not doing a good job or whose political ideologies are different will vote for an opposition party in the hope that a new government will be elected.

KEY POINTS

1 A campaign strategy focuses on what the political parties consider to be the major current issues.

2 Campaign spending and paid advertising is regulated and monitored.

3 Voter turnout is the percentage of the electorate that actually votes.

ACTIVITY

Look at the table below, which shows the percentage of voter turnout in Barbados from 1956 to 2003.

1956	1961	1966	1971
60.3%	61.3%	79.7%	81.6%
1976	**1981**	**1986**	**1991**
74.1%	71.6%	76.7%	63.7%
1994	**1999**	**2003**	
60.9%	63.4%	61.0%	

Source: http://caribbeanelections.com

1 Which year saw the highest voter turnout?

2 Which year saw the lowest voter turnout?

3 How would you describe the trend in voter turnout?

During an election, political parties attempt to stimulate support from prospective voters. They do this by running media campaigns, by having candidates and supporters visit local areas, and by holding larger meetings, known as rallies.

EXAM TIP

The examination may require you to apply knowledge and understanding of these issues by, for example, suggesting strategies to increase voter turnout among younger people.

What makes a person decide whether or not to vote?

Potential voters need to have faith in the political system, must trust the electoral process and must believe that their vote will make a difference. They must think they will be well represented by their constituency candidate and that the party they vote for will govern well.

Campaign issues

Most parties campaign on a range of policies that reflect a concern for the widest cross-section of the population. Some individuals want to see some personal benefit from the party that receives their vote, while others want to see policies that benefit society as a whole.

Candidates

The candidates in an election have to appeal to potential voters. In a first-past-the-post system, the candidates have to convince potential constituency voters that they will speak on their behalf in the parliament and that benefits will be seen at a local as well as a national level.

Voter attitudes towards government

Some people suggest that if people are happy with the performance of an existing government, then they may not vote. Conversely, if people are unhappy with a government, they might be stimulated to vote in order to bring about a change in government.

Voter loyalty to political parties

If a voter wishes their political ideology to be represented in parliament, they will continue to vote for the party that best reflects that ideology. There is a suggestion that as political parties become less distinct from each other fewer people vote.

Voter apathy

Voter apathy reflects people's lack of interest or loss of faith in politics and government, which removes the desire to engage with the process. Why might this attitude arise, and can anything be done to counteract it?

If people lack knowledge and understanding of the functions of government and the role of the voter in elections, they may not see the importance of voting. Apathy may also result if they do not believe their vote will make a difference or they have a low opinion of governments or politicians.

Education

Results of voter surveys often show that there is a link between educational attainment and voting. For example, the percentage of voters among people with degree-level education is greater than the percentage of voters among people whose formal education ended at secondary school level.

Individuals who have received education about the political process and government are also thought to be more likely to want to be engaged in the process.

Age

It is generally accepted that older people are more likely to vote than younger people. This means that the percentage of voters among people aged 18–24 will be less than the percentage of voters from those aged 45–64.

Income

Surveys around the world indicate that people's income level can influence their decision regarding voting or not. In some cases, those on higher incomes are more likely to vote than those on lower incomes. In the Caribbean, this situation tends to be reversed.

A particular political party can come to be more associated with either the richer or poorer sections of a society. If this happens the section that sees a party's policies favouring their interests more will vote for that party.

ACTIVITY

Look at Figure 3.9.1, which shows the proportion of different income groups within a population who voted in a number of elections over a period of time.

1 Which group showed a higher percentage of voters in 2004 than in all previous years?

2 In which year did the greatest proportion of the lower three income groups vote?

3 Taken together, these groups represent total voter turnout. What would you say the chart shows about voter turnout, regardless of income, after the election in 1996?

4 Find out how much this chart reflects the situation in your country and how is it different.

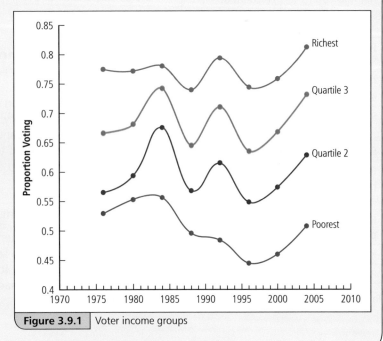

Figure 3.9.1 | Voter income groups

The relationship between citizens and government

At the end of this topic you will be able to:

- describe the relationship between citizens and governments as stated in the constitution.

Rights	Freedoms
Right to life	**Freedom of speech (expression)**
Right to vote	Freedom of association and assembly
Right to security	Freedom of movement
Right to education	Freedom of conscience
Right to liberty	Freedom of religion (worship)
Right to a fair trial	
Right to protection from arbitrary arrest	
Right to own property	
Right to privacy	
Right to work	

Table 3.10.1 Human rights and freedoms

Constitution

A constitution is a set of fundamental principles according to which a country is governed and which includes laws and guidelines that ensure that the constitution is upheld.

The constitution is the supreme law of Commonwealth Caribbean countries and is enforced by the courts. All other laws, rules and regulations have to be consistent with the constitution. If a proposed law is proved to violate the constitution, it is unconstitutional and will be void. The judicial role protects the constitution and the rights of citizens, and limits the power of government.

Provisions within a constitution make it difficult for any government to make any important changes, for example, by requiring a two-thirds majority in parliament in support of the change. Some parts can only be changed through holding a **referendum**, which means every eligible citizen may vote on the proposed change.

A constitution is a contract between the citizens and their government. It outlines:

- the structure of government
- the powers of the executive, legislature and judiciary
- the rights, freedoms and responsibilities of citizens
- the method of choosing a government
- the conditions of citizenship
- the role of the civil service.

Democratic and authoritarian governments

Democratic government

The system of government in Commonwealth Caribbean countries is **democratic**. In a democracy, citizens are allowed to put themselves forward as parliamentary candidates and to freely vote for their representatives from at least two competing parties. Citizens can also criticise the government and challenge its decisions, as well as being involved in consultations.

Authoritarian government

An **authoritarian** government is one in which decisions are made by an individual person or by a small group within government. Citizens do not have an opportunity to participate in government decision-making. Decisions can be made without the knowledge or consent of the citizens.

Human rights and freedoms

The constitutions of Commonwealth Caribbean countries contain a bill of rights that provides the legal protection for the rights and freedoms of individual citizens (see Table 3.10.1). These are based on the Universal Declaration of Human Rights. The bill of rights protects citizens from discrimination on any grounds including race, origin, religion, political opinions, colour or creed.

Citizens' responsibilities

Citizens help promote good governance by:

- obeying laws
- paying taxes
- protecting public property
- assisting police in maintaining law and order
- serving on a jury when requested
- participating in elections
- protecting the environment.

The role of the ombudsman

An ombudsman is an official who is appointed to investigate complaints made by citizens against public authorities and to ensure that citizens' interests are not abused. The ombudsman will investigate any allegations of poor performance in respect of delays, incompetence, loss of documentation, neglect or discrimination against any government officials or departments. The ombudsman's findings are reported to parliament.

The role of the ombudsman also allows for victims of poor performance, if not illegal, to seek redress in a court.

The ombudsman defends human rights, resolves conflicts between citizens and bureaucracy, and ensures transparency and good governance.

Taking part in elections is one of the ways citizens contribute to the governance of their country

ACTIVITY

Find out about the workings of the office of the ombudsman in your country. Find out when the role was created and how many complaints the office of the ombudsman receives each year. Carry out some research into a particular complaint of human rights violation and prepare a brief report.

KEY POINTS

1 A constitution is a set of principles and laws by which people agree to be governed.

2 The judiciary protects the constitutional rights of citizens.

3 In a democracy, citizens have a chance to participate in electing government and in political decision-making.

4 In an authoritarian government, decisions are made by one person or a small group of people.

5 A constitution sets outs citizens' rights and freedoms.

6 The ombudsman investigates allegations of poor performance or administration and reports to parliament.

EXAM TIP

Make sure you are familiar with the rights and freedoms granted in the bill of rights for your country and also be clear about the steps a citizen could take to seek redress if their human rights are violated.

3.11

The essentials of good governance

Freedom of information requests can be made to establish that correct procedures have been followed when applications are made for the construction of new buildings or for major pieces of infrastructure

In relation to a government, good governance has to do with how public affairs are conducted and how public resources are managed in order to obtain the best results for a country's citizens and to ensure that human rights are upheld.

Participation

Good governance relies on citizens' participation. Universal adult suffrage allows for as many people as possible to vote. To encourage voting there should be education about the political process. Citizens should also be given the opportunity to participate in certain decisions through public consultations.

Independence of the judiciary

The judiciary interprets and administers the laws of a country. It may:

- review any law passed by the legislature
- review actions taken by the executive
- deal with challenges on law or policy brought by citizens
- act as a check on the other branches of government.

To do this effectively, it must be independent of other government branches.

Transparency

Transparency in government is:

- to do with openness, good communications and accountability
- assisted by having such things as open meetings, freedom of information laws and independent auditing
- seen as a means of limiting corruption in government.

Accountability

Accountability in government means that the government, its ministers and civil servants are accountable to the public, to parliament and to the judiciary. Certain allegations of wrongdoing or misconduct may be examined in an inquiry.

Governments in the Caribbean have established different structures that have been put in place to ensure transparency and accountability in government. For example, there may be an integrity commission or a parliamentary accounts committee.

Responsiveness to the needs of citizens

A government is given authority to make decisions and to set goals for the good of the country, which should be in line with the wishes of the citizens of that country. Free and fair democratic elections are a way of ensuring that this happens since, if it does not, the government can be voted out.

Access to information

Most Commonwealth Caribbean countries have legislation that gives citizens access to information. The laws usually place an obligation on the government to regularly disclose information to the public and also to provide specific information when this is requested. Freedom of information (FOI) laws often apply to any body or organisation that is responsible for using or spending public money.

Access to information is seen as promoting good governance because it:

- encourages transparency and accountability
- allows for greater public participation in government decision-making processes
- strengthens democracy
- is seen as another means of tackling corruption.

Prudent use of resources

Good governance is evident when the best possible use is made of:

- physical resources – the materials a country produces that allow for the manufacture of products to meet a society's basic needs (e.g. food, clothing and shelter), to enhance citizens' quality of life and to raise foreign exchange earnings through exportation
- **human resources** – the skills, abilities and creativity of the population that can be employed to make the most of a country's physical resources
- financial resources – revenues raised through taxation and loans.

Efficient civil service

Achieving the implementation of government policy uses a large amount of resources and so the functions of the civil service must be carried out efficiently. This can be achieved by:

- making maximum use of new technologies
- employing well-qualified personnel who receive ongoing training
- carrying out regular monitoring of performance.

Consultation

Although a government is elected to take decisions on behalf of the citizens of a country, there are occasions when public consultation is either required by law or seen to be a matter of good practice. The process of public consultation begins with the government drawing up certain proposals. These should then be made available to the public for scrutiny and comment.

Public consultation is another means of encouraging political participation and, therefore, strengthening democracy.

Tolerance of freedom of expression

Freedom of expression is one of the basic human rights recognised in the bill of rights in the constitutions of Commonwealth Caribbean countries.

SECTION 1: Multiple-choice questions

1 A country where the head of state is the president is called a:

  a democracy

  b socialist state

  c republic

  d monarchy

2 In a constitutional monarchy, executive power for governing a country rests mainly with:

  a the prime minister

  b the governor-general

  c the monarch

  d the leader of the opposition

3 A bicameral legislature is made up of:

  a elected members of the cabinet

  b a single body of elected members

  c a single body of elected members of the two main political parties

  d two 'houses' or bodies of representatives

4 When a minister is said to have a portfolio, this means he or she has:

  a large amounts of paper to carry

  b responsibility for running a government department

  c the power to pass legislation

  d the authority to appoint a high court judge

5 A magistrates' court:

  a tries serious offences

  b reviews cases tried by the highest court in the country

  c reviews cases tried by a lower court in the country

  d conducts preliminary enquiries into serious criminal offences

6 A government may raise finances indirectly which means taxes are:

  a paid by one person on behalf of another

  b collected from people who live abroad

  c levied on goods and services

  d passed between government departments

7 Universal adult suffrage means that everyone has the right to vote when they reach the age of:

  a 21

  b 18

  c 16

  d 25

8 The first-past-the-post system means that:

  a the party with the most votes forms the government

  b the votes must be counted as quickly as possible

  c a person who already has a seat in parliament cannot stand again

  d a candidate with the most votes in a constituency wins a seat in government

9 When a constituency MP has only a very small majority, this is called a:

  a marginal seat

  b broad seat

  c safe seat

  d fringe seat

10 Voter apathy may be a result of people:

  a having a large family

  b losing faith in politicians

  c believing their vote is important

  d powerful political advertising

Further practice questions and examples can be found on the accompanying CD.

Country A is a democratic nation that uses the first-past-the-post system of election and a new party is about to begin a term in government.

1 a Describing various elements of the election process, explain how the party comes to be in a position to form the next government.

  b Describe what happens when the prime minister forms a new cabinet.

  c Describe and explain the roles and functions of the three main branches of government you will find in Country A.

  d Say how one of these branches of government may act as a check on one of the other two.

2 The new government of Country A has a number of different functions.

  a Describe some of the steps the government might take to raise and manage finances.

  b Describe some of the social services the government must provide and say how this provision will be achieved.

  c How might the government encourage greater employment, both directly and indirectly?

  d Discuss the different roles the government has in terms of international relations.

3 The new prime minister of Country A has said, 'We have gained a significant majority of seats, which I think is due to our winning over a large number of floating voters. I believe we managed that because we ran a very effective campaign. I am very pleased with the result and with what the high voter turnout indicates.'

  a What do you understand by the term 'floating voter'?

  b Explain what the prime minister might mean by an 'effective campaign'.

  c What do you think the high voter turnout indicates in terms of the people's attitude to politics?

  d What role will the opposition parties in Country A have?

4 The new prime minister of Country A quoted a statement from the United Nations General Assembly of 1946 saying, 'Freedom of information is a fundamental human right and … the touchstone of all the freedoms to which the United Nations is consecrated.' He went on to commit himself and his government to transparency and accountability and to strengthening the role of the ombudsman.

  a What do you think is meant by 'freedom of information' in this context?

  b How will the prime minister ensure that his government is transparent and accountable?

  c What do you think is the role of the ombudsman and do you consider this to be important?

  d How might the relationship between citizens and government be affected if the prime minister is able to deliver on his commitments and why? What other policies and procedures would you recommend the new prime minister adopt if this effect is to continue?

Further practice questions and examples can be found on the accompanying CD.

Development and use of resources

Resources

Concept of resources

Anything that can be accessed, developed and used to satisfy wants and needs, can be counted as a **resource**. Countries have different resources available to them, which are categorised as physical resources and human resources.

Physical resources

Physical resources include the land available for cultivation or the minerals that can be extracted from the earth. They are sometimes called **natural resources** and are the raw materials which can be put to use in the various industries in a country.

Human resources

Human resources include the strength, creativity and mental abilities of the human population, including all the intelligences, gifts, talents, skills and abilities that people possess.

Population and demographics

A **population** is the total number of people living in a given area at a particular time. Demography is the study of populations. Demography reveals the characteristics of a population such as its size, composition, structure and distribution, and considers how these change over time. Demographic information is used by policymakers to assist in making decisions about the allocation and use of resources to meet present and future needs.

Obtaining demographic information

Demographic data is collected in a **population census**. This is an official count of a country's population and also a record of information concerning each household. In many countries it is carried out every 10 years. Census information reveals details about:

• population size
• number of persons of working age
• number of persons employed or unemployed
• gender, age and gender ratios
• individual educational attainment
• marital status
• religion
• ethnicity
• **migration** levels.

The population of a country includes males and females of every age, from different cultural and ethnic backgrounds and with different skills and abilities. The proportion of these different groups is constantly changing, as is the size of the population overall.

DID YOU KNOW?

Some data can also be retrieved from registrations of births, marriages and deaths.

Major characteristics of a population

Establishing the characteristics (or composition) of a population, such as those below, provides information to assist those who are making policies.

Age

Knowing the age structure of a population is important because people have different requirements from such things as health and education services at different stages of life. The age structure is also an indication of the level of development of a country.

Sex

The ratio of males to females might give an indication of the level of procreation within a population. Another use of this information would be determining the degree to which gender-specific health problems may emerge in the future which could determine where health resources need to be focused.

Occupation

Knowing about the spread of occupations across a population helps policymakers determine if there are skills shortages or a lack of skills development. A country needs people working in all areas of the economy.

Ethnicity

Being aware of the number and size of the different **ethnic groups** helps in determining what might need to be in place to meet the different needs of these groups of people. It can also highlight the need for programmes to encourage integration and tolerance.

Religion

A person's religion is an important part of their life and they may expect to see some of the religious **values** they hold reflected in the society in which they live.

Dependency ratio

People in the working-age population, between 15 and 65 years of age, are said to be economically productive. Those outside this age range are dependents. **Dependency ratio** is the term used to describe the ratio of the number of dependents to the number of economically active people. A high dependency ratio means that there are a lot of dependents compared with the working population. In most Caribbean countries, the dependency ratio is quite high.

Population pyramids

Age and sex distribution is often represented in a population pyramid where the relative proportions of age group and gender are clearly shown. The shape of the pyramid can also show, for example, how rapidly a population is growing, the size of the working population and dependency ratio.

ACTIVITY

Use the internet to find the population pyramids for two Caribbean countries and one developed country. Describe some of the similarities and differences between the populations. If a large youthful population is a possible indication of a higher birth rate, decide if any of the countries you have studied might have a rapidly growing population.

EXAM TIP

You should be able to read and interpret population pyramids. Be prepared to suggest the possible implications of a particular age structure, such as a high dependency ratio.

KEY POINTS

1 A population is the total number of people living in a given area at a particular time.

2 The composition of a population includes sex ratio, age distribution, ethnic origin and religion.

3 The term 'dependency ratio' describes the ratio of dependents to economically active individuals in a population.

Factors influencing population change

An increase in the number in a population is known as population growth. The rate of growth is determined by factors such as **natural increase** and migration.

Birth rate

The **birth rate** refers to the number of live births each year for every thousand people in a population. Birth rates are affected by such things as the number of women of childbearing age, norms regarding family size and government policy towards population control, as well as the factors below.

Economic conditions and health care

The economic development of a country affects the level of health care that can be provided, while the economic situation of individuals has implications regarding their access to health care.

Family planning

Family planning is to do with a couple deciding how many children to have and when to have them and usually involves the use of contraceptives. The Caribbean Family Planning Affiliation is devoted to family planning and sexual and reproductive health care in the Caribbean.

Culture and religious attitudes

In some cultures women are traditionally expected to have many children. Similarly, some religions teach that family planning and contraception should only be attempted through natural means.

Education

Governments may run programmes in family planning education and counselling. Links are often made between the level of education an individual has and the ease with which they can access family planning programmes and services.

Women who enter education and consider a career of their own often have fewer children.

Death rate

The **death rate** refers to the number of deaths that occur for every thousand people in a population.

Development and economic prosperity

The level of development and the economic prosperity of a country affect the level of health care provision and therefore the death rate.

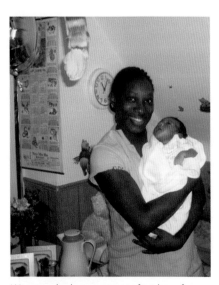
Women who have a career often have fewer children as a result

Medical facilities and health care

Good health care provision and a high standard of medical facilities result in fewer people dying of injuries or treatable diseases.

Nutrition

A key factor in health is an adequate and healthy diet. CARICOM has established the Caribbean Food and Nutrition Institute (CFNI) which aims to attain **food security** and optimal nutritional health for all Caribbean citizens.

Growth rate and natural increase

The growth rate of a country's population is determined by finding the difference between the birth and death rates. If the number of births is greater than the number of deaths, the situation is described as a natural increase.

EXAM TIP

You should be able to explain and calculate birth rate, death rate and natural increase.

ACTIVITY

Find the birth and death rates for five different Caribbean countries. Subtract the death rate from the birth rate to find the rate of natural increase in each country.

Migration

Migration occurs when people move within a country or between countries.

- **Emigration** is when people move away to another country.
- **Immigration** is when they move in from another country.

The effect on the population depends on the relationship between these two types of migration. For example, net immigration occurs when the number of people moving into a country exceeds the number leaving.

Other factors affecting population

Fertility rate

The average number of children born to each woman during her lifetime produces the **fertility rate** of a population.

Infant mortality rate

This is the number of deaths of infants under one year of age for every thousand live births. The **infant mortality rate** is sometimes used as an indicator of a country's level of development.

Life expectancy

This is the number of years a person of a given age in a specific country or region can expect to live. A higher **life expectancy** is sometimes used as an indicator of a country's level of development.

KEY POINTS

1 Birth rate refers to the number of live births each year for each thousand persons in the population.

2 Death rate refers to the number of deaths each year per thousand persons in the population.

3 Population growth rate is obtained by finding the difference between birth rate and death rate.

4 Natural increase is when the number of births is greater than the number of deaths.

5 Migration into and out of a country affects the size of the population.

6 Other important statistics include fertility rate, infant mortality rate and life expectancy.

Population distribution

Population distribution describes the way in which a population is spread out. Within a country, there are areas where many people live close together and other areas where fewer people live with more space between them. The degree of concentration of people living in a given area is called the **population density**. This is established by finding out how many people live within a given unit area of the country, for example within a square kilometre.

Factors influencing population distribution

People settle where they are able to live and to support themselves.

The relief of the land

Flat land is easy to build on and so human settlements can quickly grow in this type of landscape. Where there are steep slopes, development is much harder and so these areas discourage human settlement. Poorer, less fertile soils are generally found on higher ground, which affects the amount of food that can be grown.

Climate

The climatic conditions of an area can make it difficult for human habitation. Areas that experience the following conditions will probably have small populations:

• very heavy rainfall
• very low temperatures
• long periods of drought.

Such conditions generally mean that food is scarce or hard to produce and so the human population that can be sustained is small. In areas of drought, the lack of water also makes it inhospitable for humans. Some countries develop irrigation systems to counteract low levels of rainfall to enable them to continue to produce food.

Fertile areas – agricultural land

Fertile areas attract human habitation and settlement. In these places, food plants grow easily and livestock animals can also be kept. Fertile areas are often associated with the alluvial plains of rivers or flat bottoms of river valleys.

Location of mineral resources

Mineral resources are those that can be extracted from the ground and used in economic activities such as manufacturing. The extraction process provides employment opportunities and so acts as a stimulus for human settlement. Any problems that may be found in such areas, such as a difficult relief or a lack of food, are overcome because of the economic importance of extracting the resource.

EXAM TIP

As well as understanding factors that influence population distribution and affect population density, you should be ready to explain how this type of information might be useful to a government in terms of planning the use of resources and meeting the different needs of its citizens.

Developed areas

As an area develops and expands, the range of facilities and amenities it offers also grows. A large urban area might provide more social, economic and educational opportunities which attract more people. For example, there may be more schools, tertiary institutions, factories and other businesses. The population of the urban area grows as a result, which means it can support more amenities and opportunities, which in turn attract more people. This process leads to continued growth.

Types of vegetation

The establishment and development of human settlements in heavily forested areas is difficult. The large forest areas of Belize and Guyana make large areas of these countries uninhabitable for humans.

Population density

Population density is the number of people living in a given area. The more people living in that given area, the higher the density.

We calculate the population density by finding the total population of an area and dividing by the size of the area. So, if a population of 15,000 people live in an area of 500 square kilometres (km^2), the calculation would look like this:

$$\frac{15,000}{500} = 30 \text{ people per } km^2$$

The population density across a country might seem to be quite low. For example, the population density of the Dominican Republic is approximately 180 people per km^2. This does not provide a particularly accurate picture of conditions in different places. Some areas have less than 25 people per km^2, while other areas, namely the larger cities, have densities of over 1000 people per km^2. In Santo Domingo, for example, the population density is estimated to be almost 1700 people per km^2.

Towns and cities are able to support a wide range of amenities and facilities such as Emancipation Park in Kingston. They also offer more opportunities for employment and for leisure. All of this attracts more people. Although an urban area may spread out as it grows, the population is still concentrated and so population density is usually high.

Migration: causes and consequences

Human migration concerns the movements of people from one area to another. In the Caribbean today, we can see population movements between rural and urban areas, between countries within the region and between the region and the wider world.

Migration can be temporary, which means that the move is only intended to last for a short time. Examples of this are when a person leaves to work on a special project, for a specific time, or to undertake some study. Migration can be permanent, which means that there is no intention of returning. Examples of this are when a person moves to another country, usually for employment purposes, or when the place they are leaving can no longer support them.

Internal migration occurs within a country and external migration occurs between one country and another.

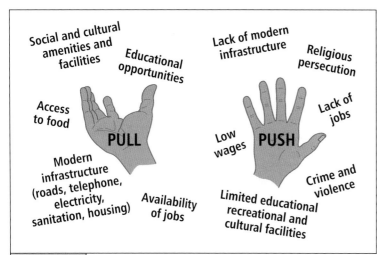

Figure 4.4.1 Push and pull factors

Causes

Push and pull factors

Migration is often understood in terms of push and pull factors. Push factors are the negative aspects of a locality that force people to leave. Pull factors are positive features that attract people to a locality. Figure 4.4.1 shows the common push and pull factors that cause people to migrate. Areas from which people migrate are sometimes known as supply areas. **Depopulation** occurs whenever a population experiences a long-term reduction and is often found in a supply area that has seen a significant amount of outward migration over time.

Internal migration

Rural–urban

People often move for economic reasons, to find work or higher wages. These are often associated with urban areas rather than rural areas, where work might be scarce or seasonal and low-paid. Migration from rural to urban areas is the most common form in Caribbean countries and many governments have strategies to encourage citizens to remain in rural areas. Increasing numbers of people living in cities is known as **urbanisation**.

Urban–rural

Some people dislike living in urban areas, perhaps due to overcrowding, high **pollution** levels, or crime and violence being too common. In some cases, individuals move to a rural area because of an employment opportunity.

Rural–rural

This type of internal migration is not very common within the Caribbean although it does happen. People may move from one farming community to another because the first can no longer sustain them. In some cases, the agricultural land they have been farming is taken over for development or for mineral extraction.

External migration

Between Caribbean countries

When people move between countries within the Caribbean it is usually in response to employment opportunities. There has been some encouragement of movement of workers within the region in an attempt to share the available skills base around the region.

Outside the Caribbean region

Most external or international migration is out of the region to more developed countries such as Canada, the United States and the United Kingdom. Movement out of a country or region is called emigration and movement in is called immigration.

Impact of migration

Internal migration

Negative effects of internal migration include overcrowding of some city residential areas and the development of unplanned settlements. There can be inadequate infrastructure, particularly regarding water and sanitation, and poor health care provision. The hoped-for employment is not always there and there can be a rise in crime and violence. The supply area declines due to the loss of economically active people.

Positive effects of internal migration include new skills being made available to the receiving area. Money may be sent back to the supply area and migrants can return with new skills and funds to assist development.

External migration outside the region

Negative effects of external migration include the loss of qualified and skilled personnel from the region, sometimes known as a **brain drain**; the reduction in the economically productive portion of the population and a greater dependency ratio.

Positive effects of external migration include revenue from those sending money back to their families and individuals return with qualifications or skills acquired abroad.

Net migration

The term **net migration** refers to the difference between immigration and emigration. Where there is greater immigration than emigration in a particular year this produces positive net migration. The opposite situation is called negative net migration.

Many people who move to a city have little money and are forced to live in unplanned settlements. These areas often have inadequate housing, sanitation and health provision. What are the possible consequences of these conditions for the inhabitants and for the government of the country?

KEY POINTS

1 Push factors are negative reasons that force people to move away from a place of residence.

2 Pull factors are positive reasons for people moving to a new place of residence.

3 Rural–urban migration is the movement of people into towns and cities from the countryside.

4 External migration occurs when people move between countries.

5 Migration can have negative and positive effects.

6 Net migration is the difference between immigration and emigration.

Population statistics

At the end of this topic you will be able to:

- outline the sources and uses of population statistics.

Understanding the structure of the population helps a government to decide on the facilities it needs to provide so as to best meet the needs of its citizens. This school will provide for the future needs of the population.

Sources of population statistics

National census

To establish facts about a population, a government will carry out a national census. This is a gathering of information about every man, woman and child in each of the households in the country at a specific time. The information is usually gathered on a specially produced government form that records details about each individual, but also indicates the number of persons living in each household and the relationships between them.

A national census is carried out on a regular basis, which enables comparisons to be made between the data collected in successive years. This allows for trends to be identified, such as an increase in the proportion of older people in a population. The process involves collecting, compiling and publishing demographic, economic and social data.

Registrar's office

The registrar's office collects and publishes data on births, deaths and marriages.

Religious institutions' records

Religious institutions also keep records of events that take place in people's lives. These are records of events such as baptisms or christenings, events marking a coming-of-age, marriages and funerals. Some institutions have a record of membership.

Types of population statistics

Population statistics are concerned with the different characteristics of a population. These characteristics include the age, sex, ethnicity, educational achievement, employment and socioeconomic circumstances of individuals and households.

Uses of population statistics

Simply knowing the size of an existing population helps a government understand the relationship between the resources the country can provide and the needs of the population. Where there are insufficient resources, the country is said to be overpopulated. When the available resources could support a larger population, then the country is underpopulated. If population growth is outstripping the available resources, a government may introduce measures to attempt to control the population.

Population statistics also allow governments to analyse the structure of the current population and to discover if there are any trends in population characteristics. This type of information is useful as the government is responsible for managing and utilising resources for the good of its citizens. Population statistics allow for planning related to a number of fields.

Housing

Governments have to ensure a range of housing is available across the country. The housing needs of a young, single person are not the same as those of a couple with several children. People with different levels of income should be able to find housing to suit their budget. If statistics show a pattern of immigration or of growth over time, then the government may have to respond with a house-building programme.

Health care

Health care provision should respond to the needs of a population and the services required vary according to a person's age. If a government is faced with an ageing population, it may need to consider greater provision of care facilities for older people.

Education

Knowing about the age structure of a population is crucial if a government is going to provide the appropriate kind of educational facilities.

Employment

Population statistics can reveal the state of a country's labour force. The government can determine the number of people who are of working age and the proportion of those who are economically active. There will be implications for the government regarding the dependency ratio or if there is a high level of youth unemployment.

Social welfare

The government needs to have a good understanding of the proportion of the population that requires assistance in the form of welfare payments or services provided by social welfare departments.

Infrastructure development

A developing economy requires a developing infrastructure. Transport, communications and energy links assist in the growth of businesses, which will increase revenues for the government in the form of taxation. A government is also responsible for ensuring that its citizens are living in healthy conditions. Infrastructure systems related to such things as adequate clean water supplies and sanitation are part of that provision.

ACTIVITY

Using material from your country's registrar's office, establish if there are any trends in the number of marriages in your country over the past 10 years. Use the last four census records to see if there are any trends in household size.

KEY POINTS

1 Population statistics are obtained from the national census, the registrar's office and from the records of religious institutions.

2 The census process attempts to collect, collate and publish demographic information on every man, woman and child in a population.

3 Governments use population statistics to assist with the planning of resource management in a number of areas including housing, education, health care, employment, social welfare, and infrastructure development.

Developing human resources 1

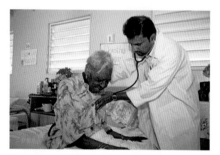

Secondary health care facilities such as hospitals are expensive to build and to maintain. Governments promote preventative health care because it is cheaper to provide and should reduce the need for secondary care among the population, as well as making for a more productive workforce.

EXAM TIP

You need to understand the link between health, productivity and a nation's economy and continued development. You might be required to suggest why a government may spend significant amounts on the health of its workforce.

A country's resources are those things that can be harnessed to generate the nation's wealth. This wealth, in turn, is used to create the economic and social structure on which development is based. Countries have:

- physical resources – the raw materials that can be turned into the things needed by a society
- human resources – the different skills and abilities offered by the population.

Part of a government's role is to develop the human resources by helping individuals reach their full potential and to make a positive contribution to society.

Human health is not simply of concern because of a relationship between health and wealth. In other words, governments and others are not simply interested in maintaining citizens' health and wellbeing simply because healthy, happy people are more productive, but because achieving citizens' health and wellbeing is a worthwhile aim in itself.

The need for developing human resources

Productive workers

Each person has potential skills, talents and abilities which are developed through experience and education. If a country is to grow and develop, it needs to generate wealth and this relies on citizens being willing and able to work in every sphere of life. Access to health and education services will help to ensure the country has a thriving, productive workforce.

Creative and critical thinking

In addition to being productive, people need to develop critical and creative thinking. This kind of thinking allows people to evaluate and assess current situations and circumstances and to decide whether or not any improvements could or should be made. Having identified an area for improvement, the creative thinker is able to suggest what those improvements might be.

Problem-solving skills

If critical and creative thinking identifies areas of deficiency and suggests what improvements might be made, then problem-solving skills are needed in order to put these ideas into practice.

Positive values and attitudes

Positive values and attitudes will encourage people to want to work hard and to make a positive contribution to society. These values and attitudes are often passed on as part of the **socialisation** process that takes place between the generations. They can be reinforced in other institutions, such as schools and universities.

Health care and human development

Primary health care

Primary health care is provided at a national level and is concerned with the prevention of illness and disease, and the promotion of wellbeing and health. Preventative health care includes provision of:

- public education about diseases and conditions or practices that cause them, including the correct handling of garbage
- promotion of good nutritional practices, hygiene routines, exercise and healthy lifestyles
- immunisation
- environmental sanitation
- safe drinking water
- dental and vision care
- care for older people
- recreation facilities
- pre- and post-natal care.

Secondary or curative health

These services are concerned with the detection, treatment and cure of diseases and with the treatment of injuries. Secondary health services provide such things as:

- hospitals, clinics and health centres
- diagnosis of diseases and other ailments
- referrals to specialised services
- administration of medication
- treatment, therapy, counselling, quarantine and rehabilitation services.

All of these are expensive to provide and are a drain on a nation's financial resources.

Mental health

Mental illness can be as difficult to deal with as physical illness and it too can have an effect on individual productivity.

ACTIVITY

Carry out an evaluation of your community in terms of the primary and secondary health provision available. Explain how what you discover might have a bearing on the productivity of the local workforce.

KEY POINTS

1 A nation's human resources are the skills, talents and attitudes of the population.

2 A nation's human resources need to be developed to produce productive workers who can think critically and creatively and who can problem-solve.

3 Health care is a crucial element of developing human resources.

4 Primary health care is about prevention.

5 Secondary health care is about treatment and therapy.

CASE STUDY

Eating food provides nutrients that give the body what it needs to grow, develop, move, repair itself and fight off illness and disease. A good diet also improves cognitive thinking processes. We need to eat a varied and balanced diet because the different nutrients we need come from a mixture of foods. A deficiency in particular kinds of nutrients negatively affects certain functions of the body.

A healthy individual is likely to be more productive. So ensuring that people have a healthy diet and lifestyle is important for a government seeking to achieve national development.

Question

Put the following list into order to show the link between health and productivity:

- Mental and physical fitness
- A healthy lifestyle (adequate nutrition, exercise, sleep, rest and recreation)
- Increased productivity and national development
- Workers who are alert, productive and who have creative and critical thinking skills

Developing human resources 2: education, sports and culture

Developing human resources is about:

- ensuring that the population is as productive as possible in order to create maximum wealth for society
- helping people to develop their potential, to pursue their education and to lead a healthy life
- improving quality of life.

Education

Education is universally acknowledged as the means by which an individual can improve his or her own situation and also make a positive contribution to a country's development. Education is also often linked to improved health, partly because of increased knowledge of nutrition and disease prevention.

In the Caribbean, education takes place at four levels: early childhood, primary, secondary, and tertiary.

Functions of education

In general terms, education has the following functions. It:

- prepares people to function effectively and to meet the challenges of society
- facilitates the continuous development of literacy, numeracy and technical skills
- preserves, transmits and transforms cultural norms and values of society
- contributes to an individual's intellectual, physical, sociocultural, emotional and spiritual development
- prepares individuals for the world of work
- facilitates upward social mobility
- facilitates the development of life skills.

Types of education

Basic education provides teaching and learning about literacy, numeracy and a range of other subjects. This helps people to function in society and gives them a greater awareness of the world and of their place in it.

Moral education is one way of passing on some of a society's **mores** and values. Churches and other religious institutions sometimes have a role in providing moral education along with other community organisations.

Vocational and professional training provides learning that is specifically tailored to prepare a person for their chosen line of work.

Adult education is intended to help adults obtain skills they did not acquire when they were younger, or to gain additional skills and qualifications.

Most Commonwealth Caribbean countries have made significant strides towards the United Nations' Millennium Development Goal 2, which is to achieve universal primary education

Rehabilitation education seeks to improve the quality of life of people with special physical, mental, sensorial, or cognitive needs. Education also plays a part in the rehabilitation of those in prison, and many Caribbean countries have programmes that address inmates' deficiencies in literacy and numeracy, as well as offering the opportunity for gaining skills associated with different types of employment.

Retraining allows for individuals who:

• want to change the way in which they earn their living

• find that the job they are doing is no longer required

• need to update their skills to take account of changes in such things as technology.

Availability and access

Educational institutions cover the three education stages, e.g. primary, secondary and tertiary education. These include school (e.g. infant, primary, junior high, special education, secondary high, technical high), colleges (e.g. community colleges and teachers' colleges) and universities.

Scholarships

Scholarships are payments that cover an element of a person's education. These are usually associated with tertiary-level institutions. A scholarship can be funded by the institution itself or by another organisation with an interest in promoting learning in a particular field. For example, the Caribbean Tourism Organization might offer funds for those wishing to pursue studies in tourism or hospitality.

Sports

Physical and sports education develops a country's human resources in a number of ways:

• Students in schools are taught about aspects of the human body and the health benefits associated with exercise.

• Individuals who are exposed to sports at an early age can develop their natural abilities and refine their skills. They may become sportsmen and sportswomen of national or international significance.

• The Caribbean is a popular destination for sports tourism and citizens trained in sports and health could enhance this type of tourism.

Culture

Cultural education offers the opportunity to develop an understanding of the significance of the heritage and cultural diversity of the region. Promoting understanding and appreciation of these aspects of a country encourages the population to value and appreciate these qualities more for their own sake, and also in terms of their potential as an attraction for tourists or immigrants. Cultural education is also intended to enhance an individual's sense of national identity.

Employment, unemployment and under-employment

At the end of this topic you will be able to:

- explain the factors that influence employment, unemployment and under-employment.

If a person is paid for the work they do, we say they are employed. If a person is available for work but does not have any, they are unemployed. If people are working in jobs that do not fully utilise their skills or qualifications, or if they are not working a standard number of hours, they are said to be under-employed. The **labour force** of a country is all those people of working age, regardless of their employment situation.

Availability and use of capital

Capital is the money or stock available to a company or person when starting a business or that is available to continue or to expand the business. The greater the capital available, the greater the number of employment opportunities that can be created.

Supply and demand in the skills market

At different times, there can be:

- a high demand for certain skills, to the point where individuals are recruited from overseas
- too many people with the same set of skills for the jobs available. This might lead to unemployment and **under-employment**.

Use employment statistics to establish whether most people in your country are employed in the primary, secondary or tertiary sector of the economy.

Types of employment

People have different skills that help them to work in the primary, secondary or tertiary sectors of the economy. Primary industries include mining and agriculture, secondary industries include processing and manufacturing, and tertiary industries include services such as banking and tourism. The number of workers available for a particular sector may not match the availability of work in that sector. If there are more workers than jobs available, this can lead to unemployment.

Markets, trading patterns and preferences

In this context, markets are the potential customers of a business. Markets exist locally, regionally and internationally. Markets can be created, usually through innovation of new products. Trading patterns are the general trends in valuations of stocks, bonds and other **securities** and these valuations will affect the capital available to businesses for employment creation.

Automation may have led to fewer jobs in certain industries, but innovations in other areas such as computing have produced opportunities for new businesses and other types of work

Prevailing economic conditions

If an economy (local, national or global) is contracting, there will be higher levels of unemployment and the population will have less **disposable income**.

Availability and price of raw materials

Employees in all sectors rely on raw materials being produced. If the prices of these rise, this affects businesses' profit margins and their ability to hire or retain workers.

Technology and resource development

Employment can be affected when a business fails to invest in new technology and it loses competitiveness. Equally, those seeking employment need to keep up to date with relevant technological advances to maintain or enhance their employability.

Types of unemployment

Unemployment has different causes, some of which have more serious consequences than others. For example, structural unemployment, which comes about when demand for a particular product or service falls, can result in businesses reducing their workforce or, in some establishments, closing altogether. Many Caribbean countries have faced structural unemployment due to changes in the world markets for sugar and bananas.

Type of unemployment	Cause
Cyclical	A downturn in economic activity in a given area
Seasonal	The end of periods of economic activity such as crop or tourist seasons
Casual/temporary	Casual workers often have periods of unemployment between jobs
Normal	When those normally fully employed are out of work
Structural	Fall in demand for one type of product or service
Technological	Automation, mechanisation, computerisation

Table 4.8.1 Types of unemployment

Causes of unemployment in the Caribbean

- The growth of Caribbean economies is not great enough to meet the demand for jobs.
- Mechanised and capital-intensive businesses are growing; labour-intensive industries are declining.
- Many raw materials are processed overseas, denying work to secondary and tertiary level workers.
- Lack of regional integration makes global competition difficult.
- Young people leave school with insufficient training in new technologies.
- Tourism is not producing the projected number of jobs.
- Importation of foodstuffs and other items reduces the demand for local produce, which affects employment opportunities.
- Some individuals may lack the skills and abilities to enable them to work and they are said to be **unemployable**.

EXAM TIP

You will need to consider the roles of businesses, government and individual workers in regard to addressing issues of employment, unemployment and under-employment, and how each of these groups needs to adapt to changing circumstances.

KEY POINTS

1 Levels of employment, unemployment and under-employment are affected by:
- the availability and use of capital for investment
- the level and range of skills demanded versus those that are available
- the availability and creation of markets for goods and services
- the level of technology available to develop resources.

2 Unemployment can be cyclical, seasonal, casual/temporary, normal, structural or technological.

Preparation for the world of work

At the end of this topic you will be able to:

• describe the factors and procedures to be considered in choosing a job or being self-employed.

DID YOU KNOW?

A CARICOM national who wishes to seek work in another member state must apply for a Certificate of Recognition of CARICOM Skills Qualification (CARICOM Skills Certificate) from the ministry responsible in their home country or from the host country. The certificate is intended to assist in the free movement of labour throughout the region. This is seen as an important part of moving towards regional integration.

EXAM TIP

You should be able to describe the various factors to be considered when choosing a job and also be able to explain why each is an important requirement for making a good choice.

Choosing a career

Your career is the path you take through life and the goals and aspirations you have, as well as the job or profession you might take up in order to meet those goals and aspirations.

What is right for me?

Choosing the career that is right for you means finding the kind of work that suits you as a person. You need to assess your abilities, interests, likes, dislikes, temperament and personality. The career you choose should be challenging and satisfying as well as providing sufficient income. It also needs to relate to your interests and make use of your education.

Career guidance

It is helpful to seek guidance in choosing your career and there are a number of sources for this, including school career guidance counsellors, individuals already working in your chosen field and representatives at employment fairs and seminars. Informal advice can be gained from talking with relatives and friends.

Preparing for the world of work

Collecting job information

When deciding on the suitability of a particular job it is good to consider such things as the availability of work, the hours that are normally worked and the wages or salary the work offers. Other considerations would be accessibility from your home, the benefits available and the prospects for advancement.

Listing and assessing available options

A useful process is the listing of the different job options available within your chosen field and the different routes to take towards that job. For example, one route is to join a company in a junior position and slowly acquire skills and experience to enable you to develop a career. Another way is to undergo education and training to obtain qualifications. This often allows you to begin your career at a higher level.

Working out the consequences

It is impossible to know the future, but it is possible to analyse the information available and to consider the consequences of a choice of career. You need to work out, for example, whether the chosen job will challenge and satisfy you. You need to determine how well the wages and conditions suit the life stages you will enter in the years ahead.

Employed or self-employed?

Many people choose to be self-employed, which means they work for themselves. The benefits of this include independence and the freedom to set your own goals and to work out how these will be achieved.

The disadvantages include bearing all the risks during initial start-up and being responsible for continued success. The hours required are usually longer and there is a constant need for self-motivation, commitment, sacrifice and creativity.

Obtaining resources

Individuals who set up their own business need resources, which may come from severance or redundancy payments, the sale of assets, savings or pension funds.

An individual or group can also approach a bank or other financial institution for a loan or seek a grant from the government.

There are a number of ways to gain experience of the type of work you wish to do. There may be opportunities to visit a business to find out what the work entails. In some cases, offering to do some voluntary work might be appropriate, and some employers may run work programmes.

Rights and responsibilities of workers

Employees are in a formal relationship with their employer. They expect to receive a fair payment for the work they do. In return they are expected to fulfil their duties and do the jobs they are paid for in a satisfactory manner. See Table 4.9.1.

Employees have a right to:	Employees have a responsibility to:
• be paid for any work they do in accordance with agreed terms • be provided with good-quality tools and equipment necessary for their work • a safe and clean working environment. • freely join a trade union • paid holiday periods • agreed maternity leave • equal pay and conditions • a clearly defined job description.	• carry out their duties in accordance with agreed terms • use tools and equipment in a manner that does not damage these or expose other workers to danger • help to keep the workplace safe and clean • use time for which they have been paid solely for work and not any other purpose • avoid using their employer's tools and equipment for personal use or profit • ensure property of the employer does not leave the premises without permission.

Table 4.9.1 Employees' rights and responsibilities

SECTION 1: Multiple-choice questions

1 A population is the number of people:

  a working in industry

  b aged between 5 and 65

  c living in a given area at a particular time

  d who move from one area to another

2 The dependency ratio in a country refers to the ratio of:

  a school-age children to working parents

  b people outside the working-age range to those within it

  c people who need medical care to doctors and nurses

  d people on welfare to people in work

3 The birth rate in a population is:

  a the average number of children in a family

  b the number of live births for every 1,000 families

  c the average time between live births

  d the number of live births for every 1,000 people

4 Population density may be defined as:

  a the number of families with more than four children

  b the average number of people in all households in a country

  c the average number of people in a given area, for example a square kilometre

  d the number of people living in urban areas with populations over 50,000

5 Most internal migration in Caribbean countries is:

  a urban to rural

  b rural to rural

  c rural to urban

  d urban to urban

Further practice questions and examples can be found on the accompanying CD.

6 Under-population exists when:

  a there are insufficient numbers of people to exploit a country's resources effectively

  b the resources in a country cannot support the population

  c the birth rate is not high enough to maintain a population

  d more people are emigrating to live in other countries

7 A government's primary source of information on population characteristics is:

  a an annual opinion poll

  b a national referendum

  c a national census

  d the registrar's office

8 The global demand for a country's agricultural product decreases and a number of people lose their jobs. This type of unemployment is:

  a technological

  b structural

  c seasonal

  d cyclical

9 Most workers in the Caribbean are employed in the primary industries. This means they:

  a work in manufacturing industries

  b help to promote local industries

  c work in tourism

  d produce raw materials for industry and local consumption

10 Which of the following measures is most likely to increase the quality and effectiveness of a country's human resources?

  a Less pollution

  b More day care centres

  c More secondary and tertiary educational facilities

  d Better transport infrastructure

Country A is a developing nation where both the birth rate and death rate have decreased in recent years. Although the country experiences negative net migration, there is still a natural increase in population and the rate of population growth is just above 1 per cent.

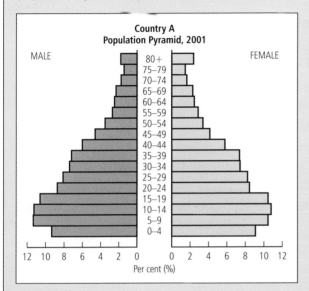

Country A
Population Pyramid, 2001

Many people move from rural areas into the large urban areas, but the people arriving often have inappropriate skills for the kinds of jobs that are available in the cities. There are high rates of unemployment and under-employment. Many of these people live in poverty and in inadequate, overcrowded housing with poor health and sanitation provision.

There has been a drop in demand for some of the country's traditional products on the global market, with a resulting loss of employment in some sectors. The government believes that the forms of industry and the types of occupation available will continue to change as the country develops.

1 a   Give two possible reasons for the birth rate in Country A decreasing.
  b   What role might an improved health care system have in producing an increase in population?
  c   Write two statements about the population of Country A, based on the population pyramid.

  d   What uses might the government of Country A make of the population statistics they have?

2 a   Explain what is meant by negative net migration.
  b   What type of internal migration is most common in Country A and what do you think might be the causes?
  c   What strategies would you suggest to the government of Country A to limit this kind of internal migration?
  d   What impact on health might overcrowding and high population density have? Which types of facilities, amenities and infrastructure might the government have to consider providing if the population of the cities keeps increasing?

3 a   Looking at the population pyramid for Country A, suggest to the government the kind of facilities it needs to be investing in so that the country's human resources can best be developed.
  b   Explain why improving and maintaining the health of the population is a means of developing human resources.
  c   How can individuals in Country A make sure they have the best chance of finding employment?
  d   What options would a highly skilled person in Country A have for finding employment?

4 a   What might cause high unemployment among rural–urban migrants?
  b   What are the effects on Country A's economy if large numbers of people are out of work?
  c   How might the level of unemployment in the large cities be reduced?
  d   What are the possible changes to the forms of industry and types of occupation in Country A as it develops?

Further practice questions and examples can be found on the accompanying CD.

81

Natural resources

At the end of this topic you will be able to:

- identify the location and uses of the major natural resources in the Caribbean region.

Most land in the Caribbean is still agricultural. It is important for the continuing development of the region that agricultural practices are efficient and that the type of crop grown is responsive to the global markets.

A **natural resource** is said to be renewable if it is replaced by natural processes over a long period of time, such as timber, or if it is available as a function of natural processes, such as wind. Non-renewable resources are finite and there will be a time when the resource is exhausted.

Location and uses of non-renewable mineral resources

Main mineral resources

The main mineral resources in the Caribbean are given in Table 5.1.1. Mineral resources contribute to the economy because they provide:

- raw materials needed in the Caribbean
- foreign exchange earnings from export
- employment in the primary, secondary and tertiary sectors.

A number of the mineral resources in the Caribbean provide raw materials for manufacturing processes that are carried out within the region. For example, limestone and gypsum are both used in the manufacture of cement and there are a number of cement factories, including sites in Jamaica and the Dominican Republic. Raw materials not processed in the region are exported to other countries. This may not be best for the region because:

- jobs in the secondary, processing industry are not created
- the revenue from exporting raw materials is less than that available for a processed product.

However, processing raw materials often requires a large amount of energy that may not be available in the countries where they are produced.

Resources	Uses	Country
Limestone	Construction, cement manufacture	Barbados, Jamaica, Trinidad and Tobago
Bauxite	Aluminium production	Guyana, Jamaica
Gypsum	Cement manufacture, ingredient in plaster, food additive, fertiliser component, soil conditioner	Jamaica, Trinidad and Tobago
Petroleum	Fuel	Trinidad and Tobago, Barbados, Belize
Natural gas	Fuel	Trinidad and Tobago
Diamonds	Jewellery, industrial applications	Guyana
Gold	Jewellery, artefacts, industrial applications	Guyana
Asphalt	Road construction	Trinidad and Tobago
Marble	Flooring, construction	Jamaica

Table 5.1.1 Location and uses of non-renewable mineral resources in the Caribbean

Location and uses of renewable resources

Renewable resources are available throughout the Caribbean in varying concentrations.

Agricultural land

Agricultural land is used for the production of crops or for rearing livestock animals. Agricultural production takes place on:

- a commercial basis, involving large-scale production of produce for sale in the local markets or for export
- a subsistence basis, involving small-scale production which allows individuals and families to be self-sufficient and to have some excess produce available for sale.

Agriculture is important in the Caribbean because it:

- contributes to food security
- raises foreign exchange earnings through exportation of produce
- provides employment directly in production and in secondary and tertiary industries.

Major commercial crops include sugar cane, bananas, citrus fruits, rice, coconuts, coffee, cocoa, spices and ground provisions. The markets for some traditional crops have decreased in recent years and so farmers have diversified, which means they grow more non-traditional crops.

Marine life

The Caribbean Sea supports a rich variety of marine life. Consumption of fish, crustaceans and molluscs provides an important source of animal protein. Fishing and aquaculture industries provide employment in all three economic sectors and in certain cases provide foreign exchange revenue through export. Marine life also contributes to the economy through ecotourism and sports fishing activities and events.

Water

Water resources are important for many reasons. Humans use water to:

- keep themselves and any livestock animals they tend alive
- supply moisture to crops
- perform domestic tasks such as washing and cooking
- generate power, as in hydroelectricity.

Forests

Forests are especially useful resources since a wide range of products are made using material from trees. Wood is used in construction, furniture-making, charcoal and paper production, and as fuel.

Certain trees provide food and others provide materials used in the production of items ranging from medicine to rubber gloves. Forests provide wildlife habitats, help to prevent soil degradation and erosion, contribute to a healthy atmosphere and are tourist attractions.

The export of timber products is important for the economies of Caribbean countries such as Belize and Guyana.

Beaches

Beaches are popular with tourists and also provide access to the seas for fleets of fishing boats. They are also a source of sand, which is a useful material in construction.

ACTIVITY

Prepare a table showing the uses of water in domestic, industrial, agricultural and recreational situations. Explain why a reliable supply of water is important for a country's development.

EXAM TIP

You should be familiar with the natural resources of the Caribbean and their uses. You should also be able to explain the links between the resources and the economy of a nation and the region.

KEY POINTS

1. Non-renewable resources cannot be replaced.

2. Renewable resources are replaced naturally over a long period of time or result from natural processes.

3. The main mineral resources in the Caribbean provide raw materials for use and export, and employment in all sectors.

4. Agriculture contributes significantly to the economic and social wellbeing of the region.

5. Forests are very valuable resources both for products and for aesthetic and health reasons.

6. The Caribbean is well placed to take advantage of renewable energy resources.

Natural energy resources

Wigton Wind Farm in Manchester, Jamaica, has been a successful endeavour in rerenewable energy for the country

Location and uses of non-renewable fuel resources

Main fuel resources

Barbados and Trinidad and Tobago have deposits of oil and Trinidad also produces natural gas. Trinidad and Tobago is the only Commonwealth Caribbean country self-sufficient in these fuels – most Caribbean countries spend a large amount importing these products. The Caribbean region is still very reliant on these non-renewable **fossil fuels** for supplying its energy needs.

There are many calls to reduce the use of fossil fuels because burning them produces **greenhouse gases**. These form part of the Earth's atmosphere and prevent some of the heat radiating from the Earth's surface passing through and out into space. The heat is re-radiated back to the planet's surface, causing the temperature to rise. This is called the **greenhouse effect** and is producing **global warming** and the associated **climate change**. If fossil fuel consumption is cut, those countries that rely on imported fuel will reduce expenditure, but a declining market could have adverse effects on exporting countries such as Trinidad and Tobago.

Renewable energy resources

Solar energy

Solar systems convert energy from the sun into electricity or use it to heat water. Solar water heaters are in use in most Caribbean countries in domestic, government and commercial buildings. Photovoltaic (PV) systems, which use specialised panels to produce electricity, are largely small in scale and are stand-alone projects. This means that they are used to supply a premises directly rather than feeding into a national grid. However, as the technology improves and system costs decrease, there are more instances of using PV systems to produce electricity on a commercial scale for sale to a supplier.

Wind energy

Wind turbines generate electricity using the power of the wind. Turbines of various sizes are in use throughout the Caribbean. Small turbines are useful for domestic situations or on smallholdings. A commercial wind farm consists of a collection of large wind turbines from which electricity is fed into a country's national grid, for example Wigton Wind Farm in Jamaica.

Geothermal energy

Geothermal energy is derived from the natural heat within the Earth. For commercial purposes, a geothermal reservoir that can provide a constant supply of hot water or steam is needed. The reservoir must be close enough to the surface to be easily accessible through the sinking of a well. In some cases, the heated water and steam finds its way to the surface to appear as geysers or hot springs.

There are some drawbacks to geothermal energy. Firstly, it is difficult to know whether there are sufficient resources at a given site to warrant exploration and development. Secondly, the exploration and development both require highly specialised technical knowledge and experience, and both are expensive.

Exploitation of geothermal energy is being explored in several Caribbean countries.

Biogas

Biogas results from the anaerobic decomposition of organic matter. Sources include animal waste on farms and also landfill sites that contain mostly domestic waste. The gas is mainly methane, the second most significant greenhouse gas. Capturing it prevents it from entering the atmosphere and it is also used as a fuel. When captured at a landfill site, it is known as landfill gas (LFG).

Solid biomass

Biomass fuels are non-fossil, carbon-based fuels. Some biomass materials available in the Caribbean are:

- wood, including forest wood, waste from logging and milling operations
- agricultural waste from various food-processing activities, such as bagasse, nuts and shells, husks and straw
- crops and trees grown especially for use as fuel, such as miscanthus and reed canarygrass.

Hydroelectric power

Hydroelectric power stations use the energy available in moving water to turn turbines that drive electricity generators. Small-scale, low-volume continuous flow systems could have made significant contributions in many Caribbean countries. However, poor agricultural practices and inadequate forest management, resulting in such things as the degradation of watershed areas, have limited this potential.

CASE STUDY

The Caribbean Renewable Energy Development Programme (CREDP) was founded in 1998 when 16 Caribbean countries set about preparing a regional project to remove barriers to the use of renewable energy and to foster development and commercialisation.

Questions

1 Explain the links between the development of renewable energy and the economy of your country.

2 In what ways do the situations vary in different countries and what effect might this have on cooperation?

3 How can regional and national renewable energy projects support one another?

4 What are the environmental and economic consequences of developing renewable energy projects?

KEY POINTS

1 Non-renewable sources of energy used in the Caribbean include coal, oil and natural gas.

2 Renewable sources of energy available in the Caribbean include solar, wind, geothermal, biogas, biomass and hydroelectric.

3 Using renewable energy will decrease amounts spent on fuel imports and increased energy security.

4 Reducing use of fossil fuels will help to combat global warming and climate change.

5.3

Sustainable development 1: use of resources

LEARNING OUTCOMES

At the end of this topic you will be able to:

- describe proper and improper practices related to the sustainable development and use of natural resources, and their effects on the environment and the population.

EXAM TIP

You should understand the role of government in educating members of the public and businesses about the sustainable use of resources and in providing incentives to encourage such use.

ACTIVITY

Identify the contribution made to the economy of your country by the extractive industries, agriculture and forests. How do these figures compare with other countries in the region, with an established economy, such as Canada, and an emerging economy, such as China? Decide on some of the issues facing the Caribbean region and your country in particular, in regard to exploiting these resources sustainably.

Proper practices in resource development

Proper practices are to do with managing the safe and sustainable use of resources. This is sometimes referred to as **conservation**, which seeks to make the best use of resources for current and future generations.

The extraction or production of raw materials should be performed in ways that avoid waste and damage to the local and global environment.

Agricultural land

The effects of proper farming practices

Proper practices ensure that agricultural land is as productive as possible. Techniques such as ploughing following the contours of a hill help to conserve water. Regularly adding organic matter to the soil maintains the levels of plant nutrients and improves soil condition.

These techniques ensure that yields are high and contribute to a country's food self-sufficiency. High yields of export crops mean that greater levels of foreign exchange earnings can be achieved.

Improper practices

The negative effects of improper farming practices are mostly to do with degrading the condition of the soil and soil erosion. Poor soil condition means levels and quality of production are low and chemical fertilisers need to be added. Soil erosion results in the removal of fertile top soil. Some poor practices result in the threat of pollution.

Improper farming practices include:

- overgrazing, overcropping, deforestation and vertical slope ploughing, all of which lead to loss of nutrients and soil erosion
- slash-and-burn techniques, which risks fires and air pollution
- the overuse of chemicals, which risks water supply contamination.

Forests

The effects of proper forestry practices

A properly managed forest continually produces resources. Forest management usually involves limiting the number of trees that are removed and ensuring that new trees are planted to replace those felled. This is known as reforestation, and has taken place in several Caribbean countries, both in response to gradual loss of forest through normal usage and because of the effects of natural disasters.

Forests are important because they provide benefits at three levels:

- locally, for example by regulating water supplies, by supplying useful materials and by generating employment

- nationally, for example by providing opportunities for development of industries, by providing a source of renewable energy and by enhancing environmental stability
- globally, for example by helping to limit the amount of certain greenhouse gases entering the atmosphere and by helping to maintain biodiversity in plants and animals.

Improper practices

Improper practices in regard to forests are associated mainly with deforestation. This is the indiscriminate removal of trees without replanting. When areas of forest are removed, the surface is likely to experience soil erosion and a useful resource is gone. In Caribbean countries, deforestation occurs when large areas are cleared for development.

Mined and quarried resources

The effects of proper practices

One aspect of good practice in mining areas is the rehabilitation of land. To achieve this, a layer of top soil is removed and stored, ready to be replaced when mining operations have ceased. Former mined lands have been returned to forest or for agricultural use. However, some argue that the reclaimed land lacks the fertility of the original and other qualities are altered, such as the ability to retain water.

Improper practices

The negative issues surrounding **extractive industries** include the loss of agricultural land and animal habitats, air and noise pollution, waste production, possible contamination of water supples and disruption to or relocation of rural communities.

Mining and quarrying operations have significant negative impacts on the environment. When granting licences, governments have to balance these negative impacts with the positive benefits of employment creation and large amounts of foreign exchange earnings.

CASE STUDY

The rugged Cockpit Country of Jamaica is recognised as an area of significant environmental and ecological significance. New animal and plant species are constantly being discovered and there is significant potential for plant-derived medicines and for a growing ecotourism market. The area is also the source of headwaters for five principal rivers and five parishes obtain water directly or indirectly from the area. Areas of Cockpit Country are also sites of major bauxite deposits.

Questions

1 What arguments might be put forward by environmental groups against the use of the area for bauxite mining?

2 What are the arguments for granting mining licences?

KEY POINTS

1 The extractive industries have significant negative environmental effects.

2 Good practices can return land to other uses once a mineral resource is exhausted.

3 Improper practices in mining produce land pollution.

4 Good farming practices maintain healthy soil, ensure high crop yields and contribute to food security.

5 Improper farming practices lead to soil erosion, lower crop yields, air and water pollution.

6 Proper forestry practices ensure the survival and regeneration of forests.

7 Improper practices in forestry lead to deforestation.

8 Forests are an essential resource in the Caribbean.

Sustainable development 2: marine, river and wetland resources

Coral reefs are an important, but extremely fragile, feature of Caribbean coastal waters. This coral reef has died. What are the threats to coral reefs and what are the links between healthy coral reefs and a country's economy?

ACTIVITY

You have been asked to give evidence to a planning committee that is considering an application to build a new tourist hotel and resort by draining an area of wetland. Your presentation needs to explain:

• the value of the natural functions of the wetland

• the ways in which it currently contributes to the economy

• the negative impact of draining the wetland.

Marine life and environment

The effects of proper practices

The major effect of following proper fishing practices is that the stocks of marine life are maintained and the resource is used sustainably. We rely on marine life for much of the animal protein in our diets and fishing provides income for **artisanal fishers** and employment for those involved in the larger commercial ventures. There are also employment opportunities in secondary and tertiary sectors of the economy. Certain species of marine life are very popular overseas and so there are potential foreign exchange earnings.

A well-maintained marine environment also offers attractions to tourists.

Improper practices

A major problem in the Caribbean is overfishing. This is the taking of a large number of fish of a particular species, or taking fish before they reach maturity, to the point where the fish population cannot reproduce itself in sufficient numbers to be sustainable. As a consequence, the number of fish declines and the species may disappear from some areas altogether.

Another improper practice is the use of destructive fishing techniques where, for example, people use explosives to kill fish. The explosions damage the marine environment at the same time as killing the fish, which means loss of marine animal habitat.

Illegal fishing is another improper practice which threatens sustainability. Laws govern:

• the granting of licences
• the establishment of sanctuary areas and closed seasons
• the right to fish in territorial waters.

Improper practices that affect the marine environment also include such things as:

• the disposal of untreated sewage into the sea
• ships washing out tanks at sea
• improper practices associated with rivers and wetlands (see below).

Many actions that pollute and damage rivers eventually have harmful effects on the sea since this is the final destination of river water.

Rivers and wetlands

The effect of proper practices

The proper use and maintenance of rivers and wetlands means that they will remain as useful resources. Rivers and wetlands provide natural habitats for wildlife, some of which is food for humans. Wetlands are important as breeding grounds for many fish species, some of which are commercially important. They have a vital role in maintaining ecological balance, helping to protect the shore from storm damage, and marine environments, such as coral reefs, from damage caused by soil washed from eroded hillsides.

Improper practices

Rivers and wetlands suffer from pollution due to:

• the careless disposal of garbage, paint and oil
• factories dumping toxic waste
• farm chemicals running off the land or seeping through the ground
• toxic waste from mining operations seeping through the ground
• soil from poorly managed farmland running off into the rivers
• people using chemicals to kill fish.

Many of these eventually have a negative impact on the marine environment.

Wetlands are threatened because of:

• poor management
• pressure for development of tourist hotels and facilities
• clearance for use as farmland.

Rivers are sometimes subject to river mining. This is the removal of materials such as sand and gravel. Taking too much material can change the course of a river and affect its natural development and flow with the consequence that it is more likely to flood.

Beaches

The effects of proper practices

Beaches that are carefully managed and monitored will be long-lasting natural resources. Beaches are useful resources in the Caribbean because they are a major attraction for tourists, both within the region and from overseas, and income from tourism has a positive impact on the economy of the region.

Improper practices

The removal of sand from beaches has been happening on a small scale for many decades without causing too much damage. More recently the demand for sand has increased, along with growing populations, national development and the demand for tourist facilities. Sand mining on a commercial scale has serious environmental consequences and can mean that a beach no longer functions as a useful resource.

Garbage and other pollutants contaminate beaches and reduce their quality.

SECTION 1: Multiple-choice questions

1 The two CARICOM countries that are major gypsum producers are:

  a   Dominica and St Vincent

  b   Belize and Barbados

  c   Jamaica and Trinidad

  d   St Lucia and Grenada

2 Food security means:

  a   stopping illegal fishing in a country's territorial waters

  b   ensuring that a country has sufficient food to feed its population

  c   erecting fences to protect crops and livestock

  d   ensuring food is properly packaged and labelled

3 Of the following practices, the one most likely to prevent soil erosion is:

  a   clearing an area of all its tree cover

  b   allowing livestock animals to remove all vegetation

  c   ploughing furrows up and down a steep slope

  d   cutting terraces for cultivation around a hillside

4 Geothermal energy is produced using heat from:

  a   within the Earth

  b   burning agricultural waste

  c   the sun

  d   burning gas produced in landfill sites

5 In CARICOM countries, most energy is produced by:

  a   hydroelectricity

  b   burning fossil fuels

  c   solar power

  d   wind power

6 Commercial agriculture in the Caribbean has diversified recently. This means farmers:

  a   use land in wetland areas

  b   cut down trees to create agricultural land

  c   grow crops to sell to hotels

  d   grow more non-traditional crops

7 Reforestation involves

  a   allowing agricultural land to slowly return to forest

  b   limiting the number of licences granted to logging companies

  c   implementing a programme of tree planting to replace those removed

  d   planting trees around a tourist resort

8 The improper farming practice most likely to lead to water pollution is:

  a   overcropping

  b   overuse of chemicals

  c   overgrazing

  d   slash and burn removal of natural vegetation

9 The proper management of available resources for the present and for the future is known as:

  a   preservation

  b   heritage

  c   integration

  d   conservation

10 Over-fishing means that:

  a   so many fish are taken that the fish population cannot replace itself

  b   fish are caught within a closed season

  c   fish are caught outside territorial waters

  d   more fish of a certain species are caught than can be sold

Further practice questions and examples can be found on the accompanying CD.

1 Investigations carried out by a mining company in Country A have revealed large deposits of a valuable mineral underneath land that is currently owned and farmed by members of a small rural community and that is also partly covered by natural woodland.

   a What are the arguments in favour of exploiting the newly discovered mineral resource?

   b What reasons might people have for objecting to the development of mining in this area?

   c Suggest some conditions that would be placed on the mining company before it would be granted a licence to begin operations.

   d Explain how and why internal migration within Country A might result from the development of mining in this rural community.

2 Country A is a Caribbean nation with no oil or gas resources available for exploitation. Consequently it relies heavily on expensive imported fuel oil for energy. The prime minister has urged citizens to conserve energy and stated that new forms of energy must be developed.

   a Describe some of the ways in which energy might be used in Country A by businesses, industries and individuals.

   b What do you think energy conservation means? How might individuals and larger organisations achieve this?

   c Suggest two new forms of energy production that may be available for Country A. Explain the advantages of these new energy sources.

   d Which factors will be most important in determining how successful Country A will be in achieving the prime minister's goals on energy?

3 Country A has a rich and varied marine life, living in a beautiful but fragile marine environment.

   a Explain two ways in which the marine life and marine environment might contribute to the economy of Country A.

   b Fishing in Country A suffers because of a number of improper practices. Describe two improper fishing practices and explain the short- and long-term consequences they might have.

   c What strategies and legislation can the government of Country A employ in order to maintain fish stocks in their territorial waters?

   d If a sanctuary area in a marine park was established how might this be used to promote marine conservation and how it could contribute to the economy?

4 Some farmers have been using slash-and-burn techniques to clear the way for agricultural land use and some illegal logging has also taken place. The area is now subject to soil erosion and farmers struggle to produce a high crop yield.

   a What action might be taken to help the area to recover?

   b What strategies might the government implement to prevent these kinds of practices being used in the future?

   c If the area concerned was a watershed, what would be the possible implications for the water supply in Country A?

   d How might soil erosion lead to damage to coral reefs and what could be the consequences for Country A's economy?

Further practice questions and examples can be found on the accompanying CD.

6.1 Regional integration 1: challenges facing the Caribbean region

The concept of regional integration

Regional integration involves the unification of a number of nation states into a larger whole. The degree to which the separate states are willing to share and unify indicates the degree of integration.

Purposes of integration

The fundamental purpose of regional integration is to enhance the development of the region. This is achieved in part through:

• developing human resources

• providing improved education facilities

• improving health standards

• helping businesses to thrive through policies of free trade, free movement of labour and tariff reduction or elimination.

Regional integration is an important issue in the Caribbean because the region faces a number of significant challenges.

Major challenges facing the Caribbean

Small island nations

The Caribbean is a region consisting of small **developing countries**. They can be described as small because this definition is not only to do with land area but also considers the size of the population and the economy. Small nations have particular challenges when it comes to providing for all the functions of government, pursuing continued development of the country, and improvements in standards of living and quality of life.

Education is a crucial element of developing a country's human resources

Governments are needed to manage the **resources** of society and to oversee the provision of education, health care, housing, hospitals and all necessary infrastructures. All of this activity requires huge investment and in a small country the **per capita** costs are very high.

Small nations also struggle to compete in markets that are increasingly open as a result of globalisation. Their small size means that business and economic expansion is not easy and so they cannot benefit from **economies of scale**.

Countries are known as **underdeveloped countries** if they have not reached their full potential of development.

Human resources

The greatest resources available to Caribbean nations are its **human resources**. Although there is an abundant supply of labour, the region faces a number of challenges regarding developing human resources. There are still high rates of illiteracy and many people lack other basic skills that would increase their employment opportunities and lead to greater productivity.

There are frequent problems with supply and demand in the labour markets. Demand for skilled workers can sometimes not be met from the local population. At other times, skilled workers have difficulty finding suitable work locally and so they look elsewhere.

Unemployment and under-employment

Challenges also arise when there are too many people for the number or type of jobs available. This results in unemployment or **under-employment**. These have a negative effect on those concerned and also on a country's economy through low productivity, a decrease in tax revenue and a potential increase in state-dependency.

Unemployment and under-employment among young people is also a particular concern across the Caribbean as it has been linked to increases in antisocial and criminal behaviour in this age group.

Migration

In many Caribbean countries, a large number of those with tertiary qualifications leave to live and work elsewhere, usually in a **developed country**. This has positive effects when money is sent back in the form of remittances, since these often represent a significant portion of a country's **gross national product (GNP)**.

However, this form of migration also represents a **brain drain**, where these high-level skills, and the capacity for productivity that they represent, are lost. There is also concern that many migrating professionals have been trained at public expense.

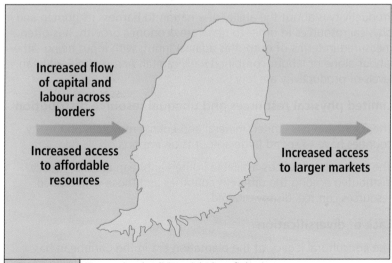

Increased flow of capital and labour across borders

Increased access to affordable resources

Increased access to larger markets

| **Figure 6.1.1** | How regional policies might benefit business |

ACTIVITY

1 Find statistics for your own country to establish the number of professional people who have migrated to work out of the region. If you can find figures covering a number of years, see whether you can identify any trends.

2 What strategies would you suggest should be put in place to stem the flow of this kind of migration?

EXAM TIP

You need to be able to explain how the challenges facing the Caribbean countries limit their ability to expand their economies and to compete in a global market.

KEY POINTS

1 Regional integration is the bringing together of nation states into a larger whole.

2 Regional integration seeks to provide economic and social benefits.

3 The nations of the Caribbean are small.

4 Human resources in the Caribbean are not well developed.

5 There are high levels of unemployment and under-employment.

6 Many skilled and professional persons migrate out of the region to work.

Regional integration 2: major economic challenges

At the end of this topic you will be able to:

- describe the major challenges facing the Caribbean region.

Major natural disasters have serious negative effects on the economy of the country where they occur and on the region as a whole

Carry out some research to establish the short- and long-term economic effects of a recent natural disaster in the region.

Economic challenges

Debt burden

Countries borrow money from various sources, including:

- commercial financial institutions
- regional institutions, such as the Caribbean Development Bank
- international financial institutions, such as the World Bank or the International Monetary Fund.

These borrowings, or debts, have to be repaid and this is known as a country's **debt burden**. A country's debt burden is often expressed as a percentage of the market value of all goods and services, known as the **gross domestic product (GDP)**.

A debt is classified as sustainable as long as a debtor country is able to:

- meet its current and future debt obligations in full
- avoid seeking any debt relief
- avoid accumulating any arrears
- maintain an acceptable level of economic growth.

Shortage of capital

Entrepreneurs and businesses need capital investment if they are to establish new businesses or expand existing operations. The small economy of Caribbean nations generally means that there are severe restrictions on the availability of public and private capital so this investment is not available locally. When capital is obtained from external sources, it can result in increased foreign debt or simply lead to an increase in foreign-owned companies.

Productivity

Productivity is about the ability of a nation to harness its human and physical resources in order to generate economic growth. It is often measured in terms of output as against input, with input being either labour alone or labour combined with capital. Across the Caribbean, levels of productivity are low.

Limited physical resources and unequal resource distribution

The Caribbean has limited mineral and energy resources and many counties have to spend large amounts on imports.

The **natural resources** available in the Caribbean are not equally distributed among the different countries and those with limited resources can feel disadvantaged.

Lack of diversification

The agricultural legacy of the plantation era in the Caribbean has seen a tendency towards **monoculture**, which is the growing of a single crop, and a consequent reliance on sales of one or two

commodities. Any commodities traded on the world markets are subject to fluctuations in price and demand. An over-dependency on a limited range of these puts a country's economy in a vulnerable position. In response, agricultural production needs to diversify so that a wider range of goods is available.

It has also been necessary to apply diversification to tourism, which has historically concentrated on cruise ship and resort-based products. New forms of tourism, such as ecotourism and adventure tourism, need to be developed further in order to continue to attract tourists using the unique features on offer in the Caribbean.

Imports and exports

The commodities and resources that most Caribbean countries need to import from outside the region are high value, while those they are able to export are low value. This results in a negative **balance of payments**. This is the balance of the economic transactions between the residents of a country and the rest of the world.

Markets in developed countries

Selling to markets in developed countries is challenging for Caribbean countries, partly because it is difficult to keep production costs down, which would allow products to be offered at competitive prices. Also the small size of the country and inefficient production methods means that the quantity required by the international market cannot be produced.

Technology and infrastructure

Inadequate technology

A 2009 report by the World Bank recognised that access to high-speed and reliable internet and mobile phone services was a key feature of economic growth and job creation. The use of mobile phones is widespread in the region, but internet usage is very low. Part of the reason for this is that personal computers are still a comparatively expensive item for most households. A key to further development is the provision of high-speed broadband services and the availability of cheaper computers.

Transport

Effective transport is a particularly important issue in the Caribbean since most nations are islands, physically separated from their neighbours. For example, Haiti in the north of the region is just over 900 miles from Trinidad in the south.

Natural disasters

The region faces challenges because it is susceptible to a range of natural disasters caused by extreme weather conditions, such as hurricanes and droughts, and other phenomena such as volcanic eruptions, earthquakes and landslides. All of these have devastating effects on societies and their economies. There are losses to business and a drop in productivity, and at the same time there is an increased need for expenditure to repair damage, rebuild infrastructure and to enable people to return to work.

KEY POINTS

1 All countries have debts that need to be paid off.

2 The Caribbean suffers from a shortage of available capital.

3 There is generally a low level of productivity in the Caribbean.

4 Physical resources are limited and unevenly distributed.

5 The transport and communications infrastructure needs to be developed.

6 Natural disasters cause immediate problems and discourage investment.

The road to regional integration

The CARICOM Secretariat building is in Georgetown, Guyana

West Indies Federation

The West Indies Federation was an attempt at political union amongst a group of British colonies whose aim was to seek independence from Britain as a single state. It was established by the British Caribbean Federation Act of 1956 and when it was formed in 1958 it comprised the following states: Antigua and Barbuda, Barbados, Dominica, Jamaica, Grenada, St Kitts-Nevis-Anguilla, Montserrat, St Lucia, St Vincent and the Grenadines, Trinidad and Tobago.

A federal government was established and there were moves towards centralised planning and taxation. Jamaica held a **referendum** on membership in 1961, the results of which were overwhelmingly in favour of withdrawal. Jamaica left and the federation collapsed in January 1962.

Caribbean Free Trade Association (CARIFTA)

The CARIFTA was founded in 1965 with the signing of the Dickenson Bay Agreement. Original members were Antigua and Barbuda, Barbados, Guyana, and Trinidad and Tobago.

Dominica, Grenada, St Kitts-Nevis-Anguilla, St Lucia, and St Vincent and the Grenadines joined in July 1968, Montserrat and Jamaica in August of that year and by Belize (then British Honduras) in 1971.

CARIFTA was established to unite the economies of these countries and to give them a more powerful, joint international presence.

CARIFTA became the Caribbean Community (CARICOM) in 1973.

CARICOM

CARICOM members are shown in Figure 6.3.1.

Associate members are: Anguilla (1999), Bermuda (2003), British Virgin Islands (1991), Cayman Islands (2002), Turks and Caicos Islands (1991).

CARICOM promotes economic integration and functional cooperation among its members.

Organisation of Eastern Caribbean States (OECS)

OECS is a grouping of LDCs of the Commonwealth Caribbean. It was established in 1981, following the signing of the Treaty of Basseterre in the previous year.

The British Virgin Islands joined the organisation in 1984 and Anguilla joined in 1995.

Association of Caribbean States (ACS)

The convention establishing ACS was signed on 24 July 1994 in Cartagena de Indias, Columbia and brought together a number of

Caribbean and Latin American states. The main objectives of ACS concern strengthening the processes of regional cooperation and integration and promoting **sustainable development** across the Greater Caribbean.

Associate member states include Aruba, France (on behalf of French Guiana, Guadeloupe and Martinique), Netherlands Antilles, and Turks and Caicos Islands.

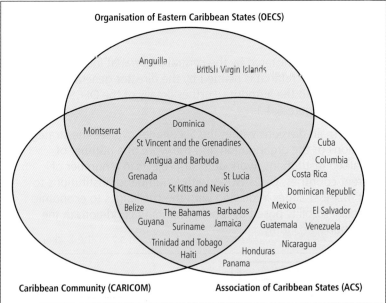

| Figure 6.3.1 | Membership and relationship of Caribbean organisations (excluding associate member states) |

CARICOM Single Market and Economy (CSME)

The CARICOM Treaty was revised in 2002 with the intention of establishing a **single market** and economy. The resulting CSME is an arrangement that establishes a single large market among the participating member states.

The organisation is in part a response to the challenges and opportunities of **globalisation** and **trade liberalisation**. Part of trade liberalisation is the removal of **protectionist** policies that restricted trade through the imposition of tariffs and the application of quotas.

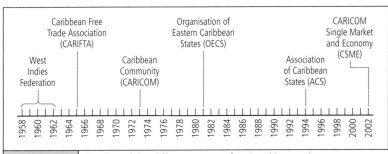

| Figure 6.3.2 | Timeline of the different stages of regional integration |

Organisation of Eastern Caribbean States (OECS) Secretariat

The OECS is administered by the central Secretariat located in St Lucia. The Secretariat is headed by the director general, who is responsible to the authority. Further details of the OECS structure is shown in Figure 6.4.1.

The four main divisions within the Secretariat oversee the strategic operations of the organisation and the work of a number of specialised institutions, work units or projects in a number of different countries. OECS works with a number of institutions to assist member states in dealing with the challenges to economic and social stability posed by rapidly changing conditions in the international economy.

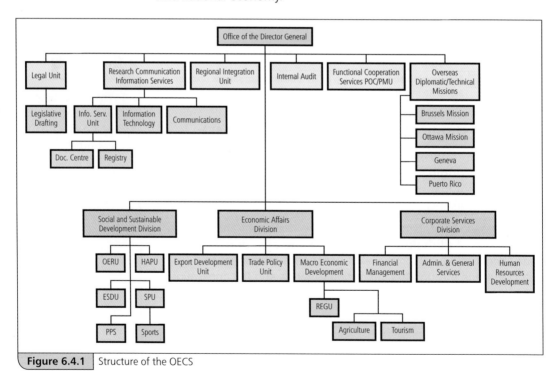

Figure 6.4.1 Structure of the OECS

CARICOM Secretariat

The CARICOM Secretariat is the principal administrative organ of the Community. It is headed by the secretary general who is the chief executive officer of the Community. The executive management of the organisation consists of the offices of the secretary general, deputy secretary general, and general counsel, and the Directorates of Foreign and Community Relations, Human and Social Development and Trade and Economic Integration. The executive management is responsible for the strategic management and direction of the organisation.

The main functions of the Secretariat are to:

- initiate and develop proposals for consideration and decision by the relevant organs
- initiate, organise and conduct studies
- provide services to member states on Community-related matters
- service meetings of the organs and bodies of the Community and take appropriate follow-up action on decisions taken
- collect, store and disseminate relevant information to member states
- assist Community organs in the development and implementation of proposals and programmes
- mobilise resources from donor agencies to assist in the implementation of Community programmes
- prepare the draft work programme and budget of the Secretariat for examination by the Budget Committee
- provide, on request, technical assistance to the national authorities to facilitate implementation of Community decisions
- conduct, as mandated, fact-finding assignments in member states.

Conference of Heads of Government

The Conference of Heads of Government consists of heads of government of the member states. Other designated ministers or persons may represent a head of government at any meeting of the conference.

The conference is the supreme organ of the Community and determines and provides policy direction for the Community. It is the final authority for the conclusion of treaties on behalf of the Community and for the entering into relationships between the Community and international organisations and states, except where otherwise provided by the revised Treaty of Chaguaramas.

The conference may:

- take decisions in order to establish the financial arrangements necessary to defray the expenses of the Community
- establish such organs or bodies as it considers necessary for the achievement of the objectives of the Community
- issue policy directives of a general or special character to other organs and bodies of the Community
- consider and resolve disputes between member states, notwithstanding any other provisions of the revised treaty
- consult with entities within the Caribbean region or with other organisations.

The conference regulates its own procedures and may decide to admit at its deliberations observers of non-member states of the Community and other entities.

The Conference of Heads of Government meets annually in different states within CARICOM

ACTIVITY

Read about some of the statements issued by the Conference of Heads of Government or another organ or body of CARICOM. What issues were covered by these statements and why was it appropriate for them to be made at a regional level?

KEY POINTS

1 The OECS is administered by the OECS Secretariat.

2 The CARICOM Secretariat is the administrative body of CARICOM.

3 The Conference of Heads of Government is the supreme organ of the Community, determining and providing policy direction and also the final authority in finalising treaties and establishing the basis for regional and international relationships.

6.5

The OECS, CARICOM and the CSME: the objectives

LEARNING OUTCOMES

At the end of this topic you will be able to:

- outline the objectives of the Organisation of Eastern Caribbean States (OECS), CARICOM and CARICOM Single Market and Economy (CSME).

Objectives of the OECS and CARICOM

CARICOM

CARICOM has three objectives, which are to promote:

- economic cooperation through the Caribbean **Common Market**
- the coordination of foreign policy among independent member states
- the establishment of common services and cooperation in functional matters such as health, education, culture, communications and industrial relations.

OECS

The major objectives and functions of the OECS are to:

Freedom of movement of persons, labour and skills is an important feature of attempts at full regional integration

- promote cooperation among the member states at regional and international levels
- promote unity and solidarity among member states and to defend their sovereignty, territorial integrity and independence
- assist the member states in the realisation of their obligations and responsibilities to the international community
- seek to achieve the fullest possible harmonisation of foreign policy among member states to adopt common positions on international issues and arrange joint overseas representation
- promote economic integration among the member states.

Objectives of the CSME

The economic objectives of the CARICOM CSME are:

- free movement of goods and services through measures such as eliminating all barriers to intra-regional movement and harmonising standards to ensure acceptability of goods and services traded
- improved standards of living and work
- full employment of labour and full exploitation of other factors of production
- accelerated, coordinated and sustained economic development and convergence
- expansion of trade and economic relationships with third states
- enhanced levels of international competitiveness
- organisation for increased production and productivity
- the achievement of a greater measure of economic leverage
- enhanced coordination of member states' foreign and extra-regional economic policies.

ACTIVITY

Choose one of the economic or functional objectives from CARICOM, OECS or CSME and research the measures that have been put in place to achieve this objective.

CSME also has objectives concerning functional cooperation, including:

- more efficient operation of common services and activities for the benefit of its peoples
- accelerated promotion of greater understanding among its peoples and the advancements of their social, cultural and technological development
- intensified activities in areas such as health, education, transportation and telecommunications.

One strategy for achieving full employment is providing for the free movement of labour through measures such as removing all obstacles to intra-regional movement of skills and labour and the harmonisation and transfer of social security benefits.

Other measures that are intended to encourage business growth and job creation include:

- a right of establishment, whereby any CARICOM-owned business can establish in any member state without restriction
- free movement of capital, through measures such as eliminating foreign exchange controls, convertibility of currencies and an integrated capital market
- free circulation, which allows for the free movement of goods imported from extra-regional sources which would require collection of taxes at first port of entry into the region and the provision for sharing of collected customs revenue
- a common trade policy, which is an agreement among the members on matters related to internal and international trade, together with a coordinated external trade policy regulated on a joint basis.

CSME economic, monetary and fiscal policies

CSME also has economic, **monetary** and **fiscal policies** to support its proper functioning.

CSME economic policies

Economic policies include coordinating macroeconomic policies and harmonising foreign investment policies. Monetary policies include coordinating exchange and interest rates and the commercial banking market, and fiscal policies include coordinating indirect taxes and national budget deficits.

The CARICOM Development Fund

The revised Treaty of Chaguaramas established the CARICOM Development Fund, the objective of which is to assist member states to engage equally with one another. The fund is used to assist certain member states to attain a particular economic level so that they are able to effectively enter into, and benefit from, the integration process.

The capital for the fund comes from contributions of member states, from the Caribbean Development Bank and from friendly states.

KEY POINTS

1 OECS and CARICOM represent arrangements to promote economic integration and functional cooperation among Commonwealth Caribbean countries.

2 CSME is a response to the challenges and opportunities of globalisation and trade liberalisation.

3 Economic integration is achieved through the creation of a single regional market which is protected against outside competition.

4 Freedom of movement of labour goods and services is a key component of meeting the objectives of full employment in the region.

Promoting regional integration

Integration is partly a response to the fact that the many countries in the region, while being separate entities, also share a number of common characteristics which ought to help them come together and work together. There are factors that naturally draw countries together and also common challenges, which they can face more effectively if working as a larger, single unit.

Domestic factors

Common language

With the exception of Haiti and Suriname, member states of CARICOM use English as the official language, which makes communication much easier.

Common history and cultural heritage

The diversity of cultures within the region actually reflects a common history and heritage which informs the establishment of **values** and goals that can be shared across territorial boundaries.

Small population and economy

The small populations in the individual countries do not provide a sufficiently large market to support continued development. Cooperation and integration in trade produces a larger, regional market. A country with a small economy finds it difficult to influence international organisations or larger, more developed nations and to avoid exploitation by large, international businesses. Working together as a region helps to overcome these challenges.

Limited physical resources

There are limited physical resources in the region and more effective use of these could be made through seeking integration.

Underdeveloped human resources

There are high levels of illiteracy and under-achievement in education across the region. It is hard for individual countries to address these issues because of the difficulty in financially supporting education through all the levels. Working together as a region means that some facilities can be provided on a region-wide basis and be available for individuals from any member state.

In 1995, the Soufrière Hills volcano on Montserrat began erupting. It eventually buried Plymouth, the former capital and major port, under 12 metres of mud and destroyed the airport and docking facilities. More than half the population left the island as a result of economic upheaval and a lack of housing. Montserrat is a British Overseas Territory and a member of the Organisation of Eastern Caribbean States (OECS) and receives a good deal of funding from the Department for International Development (DFID) in the UK. How does regional integration help a small country like Montserrat cope with such a natural disaster?

Common social issues

There are common social issues, such as teenage pregnancy and drug and alcohol abuse, which can be more effectively tackled on a regional basis due to joint funding and functional cooperation.

External factors

Globalisation

Globalisation is a process that sees national economies, cultures and societies being drawn together through transportation, communication and trade. Economic globalisation is usually associated with the reduction or removal of barriers to the flow of goods, services, capital and labour across national boundaries. This can result in some companies becoming multinational, doing business around the globe and having access to the whole world as their market. Caribbean businesses need to be able to function across the region if they are to meet this challenge and compete in this global market.

Trade liberalisation

Trade has been liberalised around the world. Caribbean governments are no longer able to restrict imports from outside the region in order to protect local producers and manufacturers. The peoples of the Caribbean need to be encouraged to support these local and regional producers and manufacturers so that they survive and continue to contribute to the region's economic development.

The difficulties with trade liberalisation arise because smaller, poorer countries have to compete in the same markets with and on the same terms as larger, richer, more industrialised and developed countries. The economies of scale utilised by these larger countries are not available for small countries. The hope is that regional integration will help in this regard.

Trading blocs

Trading blocs are institutions made up of a number of countries, who share the same economic and political aims, which are linked by a system of special trading arrangements. The European Union (EU) and the Free Trade Area of the Americas (FTAA) are two examples of such trading blocs.

Economic shocks

The countries of the Caribbean are vulnerable to economic shocks, which are unexpected or unpredictable events from outside an economy that affect that economy. An example might be a sudden or dramatic fall in demand for a particular product or a rapid rise in price of, or a restriction to supply, a basic commodity such as oil.

Natural disasters

The Caribbean is also vulnerable to natural disasters on a scale that can have a devastating effect on a society and an economy. A country is unlikely to be able to overcome the problems caused by such disasters alone and the recognition of this need for cooperation should encourage moves to integration.

ACTIVITY

Research some recent news stories about the effects of globalisation and trade liberalisation on your country. Use this research to explain how regional integration will help counter these effects.

FXAM TIP

You should be able to identify common characteristics of Caribbean countries that lead to a natural level of integration. You must also be able to explain why the small size of the countries in the region makes it difficult for them to overcome certain challenges and how regional integration will help.

KEY POINTS

There are a number of factors that promote integration including:

- common language
- common history and heritage
- small populations and economies
- limited resources
- common local and international challenges
- globalisation, trade liberalisation and trading blocs.

Benefits of regional integration

Figure 6.7.1 Increased efficiencies in production can lead to cheaper prices of goods within the region, helping to keep the cost of living down, which will benefit all the region's inhabitants

Regional integration is a process that seeks to bring economic and social benefits to the countries of the Caribbean by facilitating cooperation, support and pooling of resources.

Reduction in unemployment and under-employment

Unemployment and under-employment are serious and widespread problems within the region. They are caused, to some degree, because most of the individual states are small and therefore have:

• a limited range and supply of natural resources
• a small population
• a small economy.

If the region is considered as a whole, then it offers:

• a wider range of resources, which could be exploited and that would generate more job opportunities in the secondary manufacturing sector
• a larger population, which can potentially be more productive
• a larger economy, which will be stronger, attract more investment to feed growth and be more robust.

An integrated region produces possibilities for employment creation because it overcomes the challenges and limitations faced by the individual countries.

Better response to implications of globalisation and trade liberalisation

Integration offers better prospects for the region when dealing with the implications of globalisation and trade liberalisation because the greater economies of scale produced would result in more competitive costs of production and more competitive prices for goods on the world market. At the same time, the region would become a bigger local market for Caribbean producers, making them less reliant on the market in a single country or on trade with richer, more powerful nations.

Improvements in the quality of life

Economic stability and growth are not simply goals within themselves but are means to achieving a greater goal. Raising **revenue** and capital within the region would mean more money being available to address issues that affect the quality of life of the population. Quality of life depends on many factors, but would include provision of decent housing, health care and sanitation and, in terms of individuals fulfilling their potential, education.

Reduction in the inequality of wealth distribution

Inequality of wealth distribution, or **wealth disparity**, is concerned with the income available to different sections of the population of a country or region. It results in the concentration of wealth with a small group within a population and the distribution of whatever is left across a larger impoverished group. Access to education and health is often a key to people escaping from poverty. If integration can bring about better provision of, and wider access to, these services, as well as increasing the opportunities for jobs, then it will contribute to reducing the gap between the rich and poor.

Free movement of goods, labour and capital

Successfully growing the economy and improving employment levels depends largely on the ability to move goods, raw materials, labour and capital around the region.

Increased market size

Having the Caribbean region as an accessible market opens up many opportunities for businesses that would be unable to generate sufficient revenue if they relied solely on the market represented by the population of their home country.

Improved levels of international competitiveness

Pooling resources, sharing expenditures and avoiding duplication are some benefits of integration that will help to lower production costs for Caribbean producers, manufacturers and service providers. This will help them to offer their goods and services on the world market at competitive prices.

Expansion of trade

Trade expansion, where there is diversification of products available to broader markets, is often seen as a key to greater economic growth. Regional integration will contribute to the possibilities of trade expansion because:

- the region as a whole becomes a market for goods and services originating from within the region
- the region is able to trade more effectively on the world market.

Increased cooperation among member states

Regional integration will result from, and contribute to, increased cooperation. Cooperation between nation states is necessary if the objectives of greater coordination and less duplication of effort are to be achieved.

KEY POINTS

Regional integration will help the region tackle unemployment and under-employment, improve provision of, and access to, education and health services, strengthen trade and business, and reduce wealth disparity.

CASE STUDY

A devastating earthquake struck Haiti on 12 January 2010. The region's initial response was spearheaded by Jamaica, which has responsibility for the northern geographic zone of the Caribbean Disaster Emergency Management Agency (CDEMA), and took the form of search and rescue, medical, security and engineering teams. Subsequent intervention by CARICOM included emergency response coordination, medical assistance and logistics, including the distribution of relief supplies.

Within a month of the quake, over 300 persons from 11 member and associate member states had been involved in the comprehensive response, including those experienced in emergency operations management, members of fire services and defence forces.

Question

Explain how the objectives of regional integration were clearly shown in the response to the disaster in Haiti.

Barriers to regional integration

LEARNING OUTCOMES

At the end of this topic you will be able to:

• describe the factors that hinder regional integration.

The US dollar is often used as a benchmark when people are converting currency within the CARICOM region. Some people fear that it will become the default common currency.

ACTIVITY

Carry out a survey of the involvement of multinational corporations in your country. Find out which areas of the economy they are currently operating in and identify positive and negative effects on the economy.

Geography

The region consists largely of small island states and so some aspects of integration, such as the movement of labour, goods and services, are more difficult since an effective transportation **infrastructure** is needed.

Distribution of power and connection to high-speed broadband networks are both keys to economic growth and both rely on physical links between the islands, such as submarine cables, which are expensive to provide.

Absence of common development model or strategy

Caribbean countries have tried different strategies to overcome some of their difficulties, such as import substitution and the deregulation of international trade. To gain the maximum benefit from such strategies for the largest number of people, the appropriate policies need to be applied on a region-wide basis.

Different stages of growth and development

There is some concern that the more developed countries in the region will attract more business and become more developed, leaving the less-developed further behind. Those in favour of integration argue that the development of a market economy can actually enable smaller economies to catch up.

Another barrier can be that the more developed countries feel they may have to bear a larger part of the responsibilities associated with integration.

Competition

Countries within the region are in competition with one another when an industry is looking for a new location, the same goods, such as bananas, or services, such as tourism, are being offered.

Conflict between territorial and regional demands and loyalties (insularity)

National governments have a historic duty to implement policies that best serve the people of that nation. Sometimes they seek to protect jobs, manufacturers and suppliers in their own country, which can be in conflict with the goals and objectives of regional integration.

Absence of common currency

It is thought that a common currency in the region would bring a number of benefits, such as including reduced transaction costs of intra-regional trade, investments and remittances, increased price transparency, reduced uncertainty in exchange rates, enhanced efficiency of financial markets and a greater sene of regional identity.

These benefits would, in turn, lead to more investment, greater trade, better prices for goods and services and easier movement of people both for commerce and tourism.

While eight Organisation of Eastern Caribbean States (OECS) territories share the Eastern Caribbean dollar as a single currency, the establishment of a single currency for all of CARICOM remains a long-term goal.

Unequal distribution of resources

The countries with fewer resources feel that they would be at a disadvantage when trading with countries that have greater resources.

Lack of diversification in production

Production of similar products across the region has limited trade between Caribbean countries and produced competition in extra-regional markets.

Influence of multinational corporations

Individual Caribbean countries are often unable to fully exploit the resources they may have. As a result, **multinational corporations** become involved in the process. Although this may keep an industry alive and even see it expand, the strategy of the corporation is likely to best serve the corporation, rather than the country in which the resource is found.

A long-term goal would see local businesses, workers and producers playing a greater role in growing a country's economy, rather than seeing further reliance on multinational corporations.

KEY POINTS

Hindrances to regional integration include:
- geographical features making transport and communication difficult
- the lack of a unified development strategy
- different stages of growth and development
- competition between countries
- the conflict of national and regional demands and loyalties
- the lack of a common currency
- unequal distribution of resources
- the lack of diversification of goods and services
- the influence of multinational corporations.

CASE STUDY

In a statement to the Barbados Chamber of Commerce and Industry in January 2011, Prime Minister Freundel Stuart said that the government had made the point that 'because you are committed to freedom of movement and because you are committed to the realisation of a single market and economy, it does not mean that you give up your sovereignty as a nation and it certainly does not mean that you turn a deaf ear or a blind eye to issues of national security.'

Questions

1 What fears do you think the prime minister is reflecting concerning freedom of movement?

2 Do you agree with the prime minister's remarks?

3 Do you think freedom and regulation can work side by side?

Facilitating the integration process

At the end of this topic you will be able to:

- examine the role of individual citizens, business organisations and government in the integration process.

Role of citizens

Entrepreneurship

An entrepreneur is a person who has an idea for a new business venture or enterprise and who accepts responsibility for launching, running and developing it. Entrepreneurs hope to provide an income for themselves and also to build up their business to create employment opportunities for other people. Individuals in the Caribbean who have the skills, attitudes and personality to become entrepreneurs need to be encouraged to do so in order to stimulate local and regional economies.

Supporting regional producers

All citizens of the region can contribute by choosing to support local producers. For example, this would mean choosing to buy a commodity from a local producer rather than from an overseas producer.

Showing solidarity and mutual support towards regional fellow citizens

One aspect of showing solidarity is through welcoming and accepting workers from other CARICOM islands and treating them with dignity and respect.

Investing in local and regional businesses

Businesses often rely on other individuals or organisations for investment. This is an injection of capital that allows a business to be established or for an existing business to expand or modernise. To assist with integration and development of the region, those with money to invest are encouraged to place this with local or regional businesses rather than in overseas companies. This will help these businesses to grow and, therefore, to provide job opportunities and to make a more significant contribution to the economy.

Being informed

Citizens have a responsibility to be aware of the issues associated with integration in relation to their country and in the region. An example of this awareness would be when citizens understand the importance of buying products from local or regional suppliers.

Role of business organisations

Improving competitiveness

The degree of competitiveness achieved by a business is usually considered in terms of its ability to supply and sell goods and services within a given market. In order to be competitive, a business must be able to match others in terms of price, quality and reliability. These aspects will be related to efficiency, lowering production costs and maintaining high productivity levels. Improving these aspects of business in the region will contribute to success when competing in global markets.

To help the regional economy, it is important for consumers to support local businesses by buying local goods whenever possible

Increasing range and quality of goods and services

Businesses have an important part to play in creating a diversity of products and services that the region can provide.

Providing opportunities for investment and employment

The establishment, expansion or modernisation of a business requires investment. Investors usually hope to get a good return but this will be dependent on the success of the business. A successful business will be generating income for employees and investors and also for the government through taxation. Expanding businesses also provide more employment opportunities.

Successful multinational companies within the region

A number of companies have operations in different countries within the region in all sectors of the economy. For example:

- TCL Group – cement, ready-mixed cement products, packaging
- Sandals – all-inclusive resorts and vacations
- Grace – food processing and financial services
- Sagicor – financial and investment services.

Role of government

Enacting enabling legislation

Enabling legislation is legislation that gives another entity, which usually relies on the legislating body for authority or legitimacy, the power to take certain actions. The legislation may also indicate functions, roles and responsibilities of the entity. Enabling legislation might also be used to give legislative functions and powers to a supernational body, for example the heads of government of CARICOM.

Harmonising policies

Harmonising policies within the region is to do with agreeing on the rules and regulations that will apply to a particular area. The ultimate aim is to ensure that each member of the region is treated in a similar way, is given no particular advantage nor suffers any unique disadvantage. This seeks to improve efficiencies in the function of government through reducing bureaucracy and duplication. It also seeks to stimulate business and to promote economic growth through making trade more straightforward.

Honouring protocols

Governments sign agreements and conventions which often include protocols. For example, the Convention for the Protection and Development of the Marine Environment of the Wider Caribbean Region contains a protocol regarding Specially Protected Areas and Wildlife (SPAW). The convention is about protecting, managing and developing coastal and marine resources for the benefit of the region. Individual governments are legally bound to follow the rules in the convention.

Educating citizens about the objectives and benefits of integration

Citizens need to be made aware of the issues regarding integration so that they will understand the role they have and be able to take a full and active part in the process.

This topic considers some examples of the many regional agencies that demonstrate functional cooperation between CARICOM countries.

Agriculture

Caribbean Agricultural Research and Development Institute (CARDI)

CARDI provides for the agricultural research and development needs of the region by producing technical information for crop and livestock farmers, assisting with business planning for individuals and encouraging development on an industry-wide basis.

Sport

West Indies Cricket Board (WICB)

The WICB is the governing body for professional and amateur cricket in the West Indies and organises domestic cricket, test tours and one-day internationals against countries from overseas. The board aids the regional development of cricket as part of the International Cricket Council's development programme.

Confederation of North, Central American and Caribbean Association of Football (CONCACAF)

This confederation is part of Fédération Internationale de Football Association (FIFA). It is the administrative body for 40 national football associations in the region.

OECS Sports Desk

The OECS Sports Desk contributes to the development of sport in member states by:

• establishing links with tertiary and specialised training institutions at regional and international levels
• assisting in regional championship coordination
• promoting physical education in schools in member states
• contributing to improvement of sports administration, programme development, planning, marketing and regional organisation
• accessing resources in support of sports development initiatives from local, regional and international sources.

Health

Caribbean Public Health Agency (CARPHA)

CARPHA was formed in July 2011 as an umbrella organisation integrating the functions and administrations of the five existing Caribbean Regional Health Institutions (RHIs). The phased transition is due to be complete by 2014. The existing RHIs are:

Caribbean countries are subject to natural disasters such as hurricanes. Having a regional organisation like the Caribbean Disaster Emergency Management Agency (CDEMA) means that more resources are available to manage and provide a coordinated response.

- the Caribbean Environmental and Health Institute (CEHI)
- the Caribbean Epidemiology Centre (CAREC)
- Caribbean Food and Nutrition Institute (CFNI)
- the Caribbean Regional Drug Testing Laboratory (CRDTL)
- the Caribbean Health Research Council (CHRC).

Emergency response

Caribbean Disaster Emergency Management Agency (CDEMA)

This agency is responsible for disaster management. Its main function is to facilitate an immediate and coordinated response to disastrous events in any participating state. Other functions of CDEMA include:

- securing and collating comprehensive and reliable information on disasters affecting the region
- mitigating or eliminating the effects of disasters
- establishing and maintaining adequate disaster response capabilities
- mobilising and coordinating disaster relief.

Media

Caribbean Media Corporation (CMC)

CMC is a multimedia organisation working in radio, television, print, satellite and new media.

Education

University of the West Indies (UWI)

The UWI is a regional institution, dedicated to regional development through the training of its human resources by the provision of tertiary education and research facilities.

Caribbean Examinations Council (CXC)

The CXC conducts examinations and awards certificates and diplomas, provides services of curriculum and syllabus development, training and professional development and statistical research and analysis.

Justice

Caribbean Court of Justice (CCJ)

The CCJ is the regional **judicial** tribunal that acts as the final court of appeal of the CARICOM countries that are signatories. It has a critical function in determining how the Caribbean Single Market and Economy (CSME) operates.

Security

Regional Security System (RSS)

The RSS is a security force of military and police personnel from participating members who are all part of the Organisation of Eastern Caribbean States (OECS). The main function of the RSS is to bring stability to the region of the Eastern Caribbean in order to achieve economic and social development and to maintain principles of democracy, liberty of the individual and the rule of law.

SECTION 1: Multiple-choice questions

1 A major reason for the formation of the Caribbean Community was:
   a the creation of a single people
   b economic cooperation between member states
   c the promotion of cricket
   d greater acceptance of multinational corporations

2 A major challenge facing Caribbean countries is:
   a their small size
   b the lack of fresh water
   c litter on beaches
   d a loss of native tree species

3 The Caribbean Free Trade Association (CARIFTA) became CARICOM in:
   a 1956
   b 1968
   c 1971
   d 1973

4 CARICOM is an organisation of:
   a all Caribbean countries
   b Caribbean territories formerly colonised
   c independent Caribbean territories
   d former British colonies in the Caribbean

5 Trade liberalisation means that:
   a shops can open 24 hours a day
   b goods can be sold at any price
   c goods can be feely traded across national boundaries
   d regulations on product labelling are removed

6 The Caribbean Single Market and Economy (CSME) is an example of a:
   a trading bloc
   b unilateral agreement
   c protectionist policy
   d system of trade barriers

7 The fund that helps CARICOM member states enter the integration process is:
   a the CARICOM Monetary Fund
   b the Caribbean Development Fund
   c the CARICOM Development Fund
   d the Caribbean Regional Fund

8 One factor that drives the need for integration is the process of globalisation, which results in:
   a people being able to talk to one another in different countries
   b everybody eating the same food
   c people being able to access the internet
   d movement of goods, services, labour and capital across national boundaries

9 Skilled workers in the Caribbean will benefit from regional integration because they will be able to:
   a work more flexible hours
   b travel freely within the region to find work
   c demand higher wages
   d have longer holidays

10 Lack of diversification of agricultural production results in:
   a people in the Caribbean paying more for bananas
   b there being a smaller market for regional produce
   c exporting Caribbean countries being in competition in the world markets
   d high prices for traditional crops

Further practice questions and examples can be found on the accompanying CD.

1 The Caribbean region faces a number of challenges.

  a Explain why the small size of Caribbean nations is a challenge to economic development.

  b Suggest two reasons for the need to develop human resources and the ways in which the region's human resources are currently underdeveloped.

  c Explain why diversification in agriculture and tourism is needed and what positive effects this diversification might have.

  d Suggest what CARICOM leaders might do to address one of the challenges identified in a–c.

2 Many people see that the future success and sustainability of the Caribbean region relies on the policy of regional integration.

  a Describe what is meant by regional integration.

  b Outline three factors that promote regional integration.

  c Describe three factors that hinder regional integration.

  d Suggest one activity that CARICOM leaders could promote that would allow Caribbean states to integrate more effectively.

3 Governments, businesses and individual citizens all have roles to play in the process of integration.

  a Give two examples of different types of goods that are produced in your country and outline two benefits to your country when you choose to buy locally produced goods.

  b Explain how regional integration will help producers through access to a regional market.

  c Suggest three ways in which manufacturers have to improve their products in order to compete successfully.

  d Suggest one strategy that governments could adopt in order to educate citizens about the benefits of regional integration.

4 Many important steps have been taken towards achieving regional integration and using integration to address some of the challenges facing the region.

  a Name three members of CARICOM and state three main functions of the CARICOM Secretariat.

  b Identify two regional agencies that address different aspects of society. Explain the role they play in integration and the benefits this brings to the region.

  c Explain what a trading bloc is and give two benefits that might arise to members of such a bloc.

  d Define globalisation. Describe the negative effects of this on trade in CARICOM and how integration can reduce these negative effects.

Further practice questions and examples can be found on the accompanying CD.

7.1 Forms of communication and media

Concept of communication

Communication is about sending and receiving information and ideas. Communication requires that a sender sends a message that is received by a recipient (or receiver). The sender might be an individual, a group or an organisation. The message is the content and, for communication to be effective, the recipient must be able to understand the meaning of the message and provide feedback. Any device or means used to transfer a message can be referred to in several ways. It may be called a mode, a medium, a means or a channel of communication.

We use non-verbal and verbal forms of communication and the means of communication ranges from a printed page to mobile phones. Much of our communication is interpersonal, that is, it takes place between people. This can happen in face-to-face meetings or in situations where messages travel by various means over distance.

There are many other uses for communication in addition to interpersonal situations. Governments, organisations and institutions communicate information for many different reasons. In today's world we have **mass media**, which use communication networks to transmit information around the world. The mass media informs us of events but is also capable of influencing our opinions and decisions.

As well as the purely functional uses of communication, we are also very familiar with ideas, feelings and emotions being communicated through the visual arts, music and dance.

Even though societies are increasingly dependent on cellular communications, many people dislike telecommunications masts and towers, saying that they spoil the visual environment

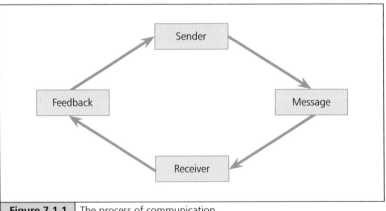

| **Figure 7.1.1** | The process of communication |

Forms of communication

Verbal

Any form of communication that uses words is called verbal communication. It includes songs, books, newspapers, information signs and drama.

Non-verbal

Any form of communication that does not use words is called non-verbal. Non-verbal communication includes facial expressions, gestures, screams, cries, sighs, pictograms, signals, signs, postures, mime, painting, sculpture, dance and clothing.

Communication using expressions, gestures and postures is known as body language. This is sometimes used to emphasise or even to replace spoken words.

Media of communication

There are numerous media of communication including messengers, mail, telegraph, telex, telephones, courier, radio, television, newspapers, magazines, books, satellite, facsimile (fax), computers, video recorders, cell phones, portable music players, internet sites and email.

Transmission

Transmission is the process of passing one thing on to another place. In the context of communication, messages and information are passed or transmitted by a number of means. It is most common to find the words 'transmit' and 'transmission' associated with electronic communication media such as radio and television. During such a transmission, signals are sent out from a radio or television station and picked up by a receiver within a radio or television set.

CASE STUDY

Non-verbal communication is widely used in the Caribbean, as elsewhere.

Questions

1 What is the message transmitted by each of the examples of non-verbal communication above?

2 Explain why these non-verbal forms of communications are particularly effective in these situations.

3 What are the advantages of avoiding the use of words in these and similar signs?

Factors influencing forms and media of communication

LEARNING OUTCOMES

At the end of this topic you will be able to:

- explain how forms and media of communication are influenced by geographical, sociocultural and technological factors.

The form and medium of communication that may be used are influenced by the:

- urgency of the information being transmitted
- nature of the information
- degree of confidentiality required
- geographical conditions in the location of the sender or receiver
- sociocultural background of the sender or receiver
- available technology
- size and geographical distribution of the audience.

Geographical factors

A number of geographical factors influence the choice of form and medium of communication.

- The physical distance between a sender and receiver may make face-to-face communication impossible.
- Physical features such as rivers, gorges and mountains hinder communication because the movement of people and the provision of associated infrastructure is more difficult.
- Transmissions for radio, television or mobile phones can be interrupted or distorted by certain weather conditions or by physical features such as mountains.
- At certain times, the signals being transmitted from satellites can be overwhelmed by microwave radiation from the sun. This is called sun outage or sun fade and results in degradation or complete loss of signal.

Sociocultural factors

Sociocultural factors can affect the choice of form and medium of communication in a number of ways.

- Languages differences can be a barrier to communication.
- Countries have their own cultural **norms** and expectations, which may affect the way in which communication happens.
- Socioeconomic factors can influence or determine the type of communication media a person is able to afford.
- An individual's level of educational achievement, physical or mental ability may be an influence.
- A person's religious beliefs may prohibit the reading of secular magazines or newspapers, the use of the radio and television, and engaging in certain forms of art.
- Some people are concerned about the possible harmful effects of using such things as computers and cell phones.

ACTIVITY

1 Carry out some research to establish the level of usage of cell phones in your country.

2 Explain the effect on social and business communication that this technology has had, comparing it to the situation when people could only use land-based telephones.

3 Describe the factors that prevent there being 100 per cent cell phone usage.

Technological factors

For people to be able to make use of the latest technology, they need to have access to the equipment and an understanding of its operation. Some recent developments in communications technology are given below.

- The internet is a system of interconnected computer networks that serves billions of people worldwide. The system allows people to provide and access huge amounts of information and resources and also supports electronic mail.

- Electronic mail (email) is sent between computers via phone lines, dedicated cabling systems and wireless networks.

- Teleconferencing allows people to see and talk to one another through the use of specialised video equipment connected to a computer network.

- Telecommuting is working from home or in another location away from a usual place of work, which is made possible through computer links with employers, colleagues and clients.

- Voicemail is a computer-based answering service.

- Facsimile (fax) machines are used to send printed textual or graphic information between users. Many of the features of fax machines are now available through computers but they are still favoured in some circumstances where they are felt to offer higher levels of security.

- Mobile or cellular phones (cell phones) offer freedom of movement and convenience for users, since they will operate anywhere within range of a transmitter.

- Communications satellites make instant long-distance communication possible.

KEY POINTS

1 The form and medium of communication is influenced by geographical, sociocultural and technological factors.

2 Choice of communication is sometimes determined by the characteristics of the information to be transmitted, for example, confidentiality or urgency.

CASE STUDY

The International Telecommunication Union organises World Telecommunication and Information Society Day. The event helps to raise awareness of the possibilities offered to societies and economies through use of the internet and other communications technologies. As the illustration shows, one idea promoted in 2011 was that information and communication technologies (ICTs) could produce a better life in rural communities.

Questions

1 Say how you think modern ICTs can reach rural communities in ways that other modes of communication cannot.

2 Explain how you think life in rural communities might be improved through the use of ICTs.

3 What benefits to Caribbean countries might such improvements bring about?

WTISD
World Telecommunication and Information Society Day, 17 May 2011

Better Life in Rural Communities with ICTs

www.itu.int/wtisd

What causes communication to break down?

Human communication is about transmitting information in one form or another between a sender and a recipient. Communication is effective if the sender conveys the information accurately and it is received and interpreted accurately by the recipient. If any of these steps in the process does not happen, there is a failure (or breakdown) of communication.

A person may actually receive a message but either not understand it or misinterpret it. If this happens, the response that the original sender hoped for will not result. If there is no response or an unexpected response, the sender may begin to feel negatively about the recipient and communication between them will become increasingly difficult.

Every effort should be made to ensure that any message sent is clear, has been received and is properly understood. Even so, there are many factors that can lead to a breakdown in communication.

Human factors

Human factors in communication breakdown are given in Table 7.3.1.

Communication between people can be difficult at times of stress or anxiety

Technical factors

Failure of equipment or systems

If the equipment or systems allowing the communication to take place fails, then the communication will obviously cease and, in effect, break down. Such a breakdown can result from anything, from running out of credit on a cell phone to there being a postal strike.

Geographical factors

Communication also breaks down if geographical factors cause an interruption to the transmission of signals.

ACTIVITY

1 Identify some occasions in which you have experienced a breakdown in communications because of human factors.

2 Prepare an outline for a talk you would give to members of a youth club explaining the possible human causes of communication breakdown and how this breakdown can be avoided.

Factor	Results and responses
Lack of clarity	Poorly chosen words and poor sentence structures are more likely to make a message difficult to understand or interpret. Choosing words well limits the chances of misinterpretation.
Age differences between sender and receiver	The **generation gap** sometimes sees people from across generations operating from different viewpoints and sets of **norms**, **mores** and **values**. They can use different language and also interpret things differently.
Gender differences between sender and receiver	In some cases, men and women have different priorities and different approaches to communication, which can lead to misinterpretation.
Language differences	Communication between people speaking different languages is extremely difficult.
Prejudices	If a sender is prejudiced against an intended recipient, the tone of the message may be affected and may be negatively received.
Beliefs and ideology	A person's beliefs and ideology are very important to them. When communicating to a recipient with different beliefs, it is important not to make any assumptions about what they understand about the sender's beliefs. Showing respect for different beliefs and ideologies is equally important.
Status	Each person has a status that gives him or her certain levels of responsibility and authority. The form and content of communications should acknowledge and respect a person's status.
Unresolved conflict and strained relationships	Difficulties in human relationships can mean that open and effective communication is a struggle. Senders may transmit messages in a manner that is intended to hurt or upset the recipient. A recipient may be too ready to be hurt and upset by a message that is intended to do neither of these things.
Mistrust	A lack of trust results in communication that is not open and honest. A sender may not be willing to convey certain information if they do not trust the recipient to deal with it appropriately.
Stress	Senders under stress may communicate things they regret. Recipients under stress may not wish to receive the message or may feel they do not have the time or energy to consider it properly and carefully.

Table 7.3.1 Human factors in communication breakdown

KEY POINTS

1 Communication can break down due to human factors that can affect an individual's ability to send a clear message or ability to receive a message properly.

2 Failure in equipment or interruptions to transmission through geographical factors can also lead to a breakdown in communications.

How can the mass media promote regional integration?

Mass media

Communication that reaches large numbers of people is called mass communication. The forms or media used to transmit the information in this way are known as the mass media. Mass media include radio, television, the internet, newspapers, magazines, books, posters and billboards.

• Many different agencies, businesses and organisations are involved in mass communication.

  • Publishing and printing establishments produce newspapers, magazines and books.
  • News agencies, such as the Caribbean Media Corporation (CMC), gather, edit and broadcast news.
  • Telecommunications companies assist radio and television stations in broadcasting their programmes.
  • Internet service providers (ISPs) enable other organisations to transmit webcasts, which are accessible around the globe.
  • Government information services and departments of information use mass media to provide information to the public.

Daily newspapers are still a very popular mode of mass communication in Caribbean countries

Functions of mass media

The mass media are able to transmit information to large numbers of people but at the same time they have the ability to influence and even shape public opinion. Mass media are relied on to:

• keep people informed by providing news and comments on the news
• transmit public service announcements regarding such things as disaster warnings
• provide a variety of entertainment
• provide public education through documentaries, debates, lectures and access to distance learning
• provide the public with facts and opinions about social issues or current events, such as national elections
• act as a watchdog for society by alerting people to any threats to their rights or to any improper behaviour in government, businesses and in wider society
• reflect the best and warn against the worst values of society
• provide information about products and services
• provide opportunities for citizens to express opinions through, for example, letters to newspaper editors or by participating in phone-in programmes on radio or television.

Access to information

Communications technology means that the world is moving towards a situation where information will be universally available. However, there will probably always be some factors limiting accessibility for some people, including the geographical, sociocultural and technological factors previously considered in topic 7.2.

Since the mass media have this tremendous potential audience and can reach so many people, they have the potential to play a very significant role in promoting regional integration.

The role of mass media in regional integration

The mass media are well placed to spread **propaganda** about the desirability of promoting Caribbean culture and about the aims, objectives and benefits of regional integration.

Radio and television stations

Radio and television stations are able to transmit programmes beyond country boundaries and so have the ability to provide for regional links and discussions.

Regional news agencies

A news agency is a news organisation with journalists based in several countries who collect, write and edit news and information for transmission to media houses for printing or broadcasting.

Printing establishments

Although newspapers and magazines are predominantly produced in a particular country and aim to produce news of direct relevance to that country, they are also able to carry reports of regional issues.

Regional departments of information

Departments of information or government information services serve the citizens of their own country but can also provide information to other nationals and to their own nationals about other countries in the region.

Promoting integration

Each form of mass media has the potential to present information about the similarities and differences in the cultures of the Caribbean people that will help to foster insight and understanding between nations and encourage a sense of belonging to the region as well as to a particular territory. Each should be able to:

- provide Caribbean people with reports on events and issues from across the region
- help to promote the Caribbean internationally through provision of material to international media
- promote cooperation between media houses within the region by sharing and exchanging information.

Using communications technology to promote regional integration

The cell phone has become an essential part of life for many people throughout the Caribbean

Information and communications technology (ICT) has become a part of our everyday life and impacts on almost every aspect of life. ICT is used for talking, shopping, managing money, arranging loans and booking vacations. The ease with which communication takes place today may lead to the development of better relationships and improved efficiencies for businesses and governments.

Information technology, and the access to information that this allows, has also long been recognised as a crucial factor in the development of modern nations.

Cellular phones

Cellular (cell) phone technology has revolutionised personal and business communications across the region. The advantage of cell phones over static or landline phones is that they operate wherever a signal is available and so individuals can be reached wherever they are.

Cell phones are becoming increasingly sophisticated and can be used to access the internet, to send and receive email, to undertake internet banking, to obtain e-tickets for air travel and to check-in online.

Such ease of communication can assist regional integration in regard to such aspects as business, economics, finance and disaster response.

Internet

The internet can promote regional integration by allowing people to:

• access websites of regional newspapers and broadcasters
• access government websites in different countries
• take part in video-conferencing
• arrange travel between the different countries
• buy and sell products and services across the region.

The possibilities for building a successful internet industry in the region are greatly enhanced when businesses, governments and specialists are able to work together.

Internet exchange points (IXPs)

An internet exchange point (IXP) is a physical structure that allows different internet service providers (ISPs) to exchange internet traffic across their networks. This is achieved through mutual 'peering' agreements which allow the exchange to take place without cost. The development of a Caribbean IXP network would allow for more content to be developed and hosted locally and may encourage more local ISPs to enter the market.

Electronic transfers

Electronic funds transfer (EFT) involves the transferring of funds from one bank account to another using computer-based systems and networks. EFT allows for:

- people to use a payment card to make purchases
- payment of wages and salaries direct to employees' bank accounts
- direct debit (or automatic payments), where a business or organisation deducts payments directly from a purchaser's account
- payment of bills using internet banking.

Electronic mail

Electronic mail (email) works via the internet. It allows for almost instantaneous communication from one computer to another, anywhere in the world. Using email, it is possible to transmit text, photos, video and audio files.

Telecommunications networks

Telecommunications networks facilitate voice, data, image and multimedia communications and are an important part of the overall ICT system. The Caribbean Association of National Telecommunication Organizations (CANTO) was formed in 1985 to provide a forum for operators to exchange information and expertise. In 2009, there were 113 members from 31 countries.

CASE STUDY

CARICOM recognises that ICT is probably the single most important facilitator of the integration process. Within CARICOM, there is a focus on using ICT to achieve the United Nations Millennium Development Goals, particularly those related to income poverty reduction, education, health, the environment and gender equity through:

- creating economic opportunities and contributing to poverty reduction
- managing the process of providing basic services (for example, health care and education) at lower cost and with greater coverage
- facilitating access to information and the involvement of regional organisations and stakeholders through greater transparency and support to networking at every stage
- enhancing the capacity to measure, monitor and report progress on the goals and strategies.

Source: www.caricom.org

Question

Take each of these bullet points and decide the role ICT will play in achieving these objectives.

KEY POINTS

Information and communications technology (ICT) is a crucial factor in the development of modern nations.

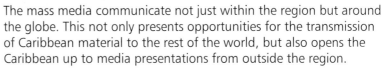

The effects of global media on Caribbean society

The mass media communicate not just within the region but around the globe. This not only presents opportunities for the transmission of Caribbean material to the rest of the world, but also opens the Caribbean up to media presentations from outside the region.

We have previously considered that mass media can influence our ideas, opinions, values and actions, including how we choose to spend our money and our leisure time. The ability to present a positive image of the Caribbean to the rest of the world is to be welcomed. It is important to be aware of the possibility that negative influences can also be imported from outside the region.

Global media and Caribbean society

Some people express a number of concerns about the possible negative effects of global mass media on certain aspects of Caribbean society.

Identity

The Caribbean has a rich and varied history and from this a unique culture has developed which has its own identity. Some fear that Caribbean people are influenced to adopt lifestyles from elsewhere, particularly North America which provides much of the content for television programmes, films and advertisements. This influence is seen in the way people choose to dress, how they speak, the food they choose to eat and the music they listen to. If a good deal of output focuses on North American values, news and issues, then there is little reinforcement and celebration of the Caribbean identity.

Global brands are able to penetrate every market thanks to global advertising

Values, attitudes and behaviour

The **values**, attitudes and behaviours that are acceptable in the Caribbean are not necessarily those presented by elements of global mass media. Some people fear that the presentation of violence, promiscuity and other behaviour can have a negative influence on Caribbean people, especially the younger members of society.

Perceptions

The perceptions presented by programmes from the developed world are obviously reflecting the viewpoint of people in the developed country. We should be aware of this potential influence and make efforts to form our own perceptions of the world.

Creativity

The popularity of foreign programmes means that advertisers and sponsors are more likely to support them rather than local productions. Raising the funds for local productions, which will foster talents in many creative fields, is therefore more difficult to achieve.

Nationalism and regionalism

Nationalism seeks to promote the best interests of a country or nation and foster a sense of pride and belonging in citizens. **Regionalism** seeks to achieve the same for a particular region. Both of these are hindered by foreign programmes because they do not address, or promote understanding of, national or regional issues.

Mass media and positive contribution to the development of Caribbean society

Mass media could help to bring Caribbean people closer together and therefore promote regional integration by:

- providing opportunities for Caribbean people to share their ideas, thoughts and feelings through regional radio and television link-ups
- presenting information on the way of life of the people of the different Caribbean territories to highlight the similarities and differences in the culture of the Caribbean peoples
- preserving our Caribbean identity by promoting Caribbean culture and the Caribbean way of life
- providing detailed, accurate and unbiased information on events and issues in the Caribbean in order to develop people's understanding
- promoting acceptable moral values to develop good attitudes and behaviour
- encouraging cultural creativity by producing and broadcasting local films, drama and music and by covering local artistic events and exhibitions
- promoting freedom of expression by providing opportunities for nationals to air their views and opinions on national issues and events to ensure responsive government actions
- promoting nationalism and national pride by focusing on a nation's achievements
- explaining governments' social and economic programmes to encourage popular support.

Reducing the influence of global mass media

The presence of global mass media in the Caribbean is a reality and is, perhaps, unlikely to change. The influence of these media could be reduced if:

- citizens are educated regarding the importance of preserving national cultures
- the possible negative effects of foreign television programming on Caribbean society are highlighted
- local programme producers and directors are encouraged to create more local music, dance, drama and films
- local businesses are encouraged to support and sponsor locally produced programmes and events
- funding is provided to encourage more local production
- there is good provision of education and training for preparing for work in the media.

ACTIVITY

1 Use television schedules to draw up a chart comparing the hours of transmission of television programmes produced outside the region and those produced locally.

2 Identify any programmes you think might be making a positive contribution to the development of Caribbean society and explain how they achieve this.

EXAM TIP

You should be able to explain how global mass media may affect the social development of Caribbean media consumers.

KEY POINTS

1 Mass media can have a strong influence on values, attitudes and behaviour.

2 Mass media present opportunities for presenting the Caribbean to the rest of the world, but also allows for ideas and values to be transmitted into the region from outside.

3 Mass media can make a positive contribution to the development of Caribbean society.

4 It is possible to limit the influence of foreign mass media.

Transmitting and transforming Caribbean cultural heritage

The language, ideas, beliefs, religion, music, dance, art, dress, **norms**, values and technologies we have inherited from our ancestors all contribute to our cultural heritage. It is reasonable to say that they are a part of who we are as people – they help to make us the people we are, to give us a sense of identity as individuals and a feeling of belonging to a wider society. When people express concerns about the negative influences of global mass media, they are often worried that our own cultural heritage will be lost or drowned out by the ideas, norms and values that will inevitably be reflected in the material transmitted.

Festivals are an important part of the culture in many Caribbean countries

At the same time, people are also keen to see our own cultural heritage communicated, celebrated, developed and transmitted. This can be done in a number of ways by different groups and individuals.

Individual artists, artistes and cultural groups can use the visual arts of drawing, painting, photography, sculpture and architecture or the performing arts of storytelling, music, drama and dance to preserve and transmit different elements of culture. The performing arts are often used to pass on oral traditions, which are not available in written form.

Cultural groups

Cultural groups seek to preserve a country's uniqueness and cultural identity by:

• helping people to understand their historical and cultural background
• providing cultural knowledge and information
• encouraging young people to develop pride in their own culture
• providing alternatives to the foreign cultures from global mass media.

Cultural groups would include all those seeking to preserve and promote an aspect of Caribbean culture as well as those representing the indigenous peoples of the region, such as the Kalinago people of Dominica.

Artists and artistes

Those working in the visual or performing arts are able to communicate more than straightforward information about our culture and heritage. The arts are a valuable way of expressing and passing on the ideas and values of a community. Groups such as the Kalinago may concentrate on producing traditional art, crafts and dances in order to preserve their heritage. Equally important is the interpretation of Caribbean culture by contemporary artists and artistes.

Institutions

A number of institutions exist to preserve and transfer aspects of Caribbean culture. The facilities are often open to the public and the institutions sometimes organise lectures and exhibitions.

National trusts

These preserve buildings of national, historical, architectural or artistic importance, as well as the paintings and furniture that they may contain.

Museums

Museums store and display historical and cultural items, artefacts and works of art, which are important elements of cultural heritage.

Art galleries

Art galleries acquire, store and display important works of art that reflect local talent and creativity. The works of art may reflect traditions and cultural heritage or may be representations or interpretations of contemporary Caribbean culture.

Archives

Archives store historical material such as official documents, maps, photographs and letters, which can be used to find out about aspects of life and culture.

The role of government

Governments recognise the importance of preserving and upholding national culture and there is usually a department or ministry responsible for cultural matters. A major role of a government is to provide financial and other resources to institutions, groups and individuals to support the work they do in regard to promoting cultural heritage.

Governments can assist the promotion of cultural heritage by:

- supporting the construction or development of arts centres, museums, art galleries and archives
- enhancing the place of arts and culture in education through the curriculum and the provision of scholarships
- enabling artists and artistes to move and work freely within the region
- including regional arts within tourism promotions.

Mass media

Just as the mass media from outside the region can influence us with the ideas and values their programmes contain, so our regional mass media can promote and preserve our cultural heritage. This would be achieved, for example, by producing more local material and through encouraging citizens of the region to take pride in local culture.

EXAM TIP

You should be able to identify forms in which traditional Caribbean cultures are presented and how the cultures can be transformed or interpreted today. You may need to suggest how the culture can be best transmitted and what policies or strategies should be in place to promote this.

KEY POINTS

1 Cultural heritage includes practices, ideas and beliefs that have been passed on to us from our ancestors.

2 Individual artists and artistes, as well as cultural groups, transmit our cultural heritage through various visual and performing art forms.

3 Institutions such as national trusts, art galleries, archives and museums collect, store and display artefacts, works of art and historical records, which help to reveal our cultural heritage.

4 Governments provide assistance to individuals, groups and institutions involved in transmitting our cultural heritage.

Mass media: ownership and control

The mass media can reach people in almost every situation and therefore have a huge potential to influence the lives of many people. For this reason, the ownership of the media and the influence that those owners have over media content is an extremely important issue.

The mass media can be owned and operated:

• privately, by a local or foreign individual, group, company or corporation
• publicly, by a government or statutory organisation (the state)
• jointly, by governments and private enterprise.

The type of ownership can influence the content of the media.

Effects of forms of ownership

Private ownership

Private ownership of mass media is usually carried out for profit. It is often easier and cheaper for radio and television stations to buy in and transmit programmes from outside the region rather than fund locally made productions. As a result, a large proportion of television programming is imported from abroad, notably from the USA.

The possible negative effect of all this foreign programming is a loss of cultural identity within individual countries.

An important advantage of private ownership of mass media is that such media has freedom to transmit any material, within the law, even if that material is critical of a government.

Public ownership

Public or 'state' media ownership, exists when that media is owned, operated or funded by a government.

State ownership allows governments to:

• promote national development by presenting information to help citizens understand its social and political policies
• present accurate and reliable information on government policies
• provide services of importance to the nation but which may not be profitable for private enterprise.

Arguments against state ownership include the ideas that governments could:

• exert undue influence on staff to promote a good image of the government
• prevent access to the facilities for sections of the population, for example opposition parties and other government critics
• prevent the presentation of a variety of views on particular issues or events
• use large amounts of public resources in an inefficient or unprofitable manner.

Joint ownership

When issues of freedom of expression and editorial control are resolved agreements can be reached, and a successful public/private partnership allows for governments to support media companies who are producing regional programmes and promoting such things as regional integration.

Community and social media

Communications technology has brought the possibility of mass communication to many more people, both individuals and organisations.

It is possible for eyewitness footage of events to be seen via the internet almost as soon as they have occurred.

Cable and satellite television technologies have brought about the possibility of small-scale television stations run by people in a community, producing programmes aimed at an audience within that community. Such community programming allows for the expression and celebration of the cultural diversity which is such an important element of Caribbean life.

Freedom of the press

Freedom of expression is the right to express oneself freely in speech or in writing without violating any existing relevant laws.

It is illegal to print, publish or broadcast any statements about an individual that are known to be untrue, with the intention of damaging the reputation of that person. This is known as **libel**.

It is illegal to speak any untrue statements about an individual with a view to damaging their reputation. This is known as **slander**.

Freedom of the press (newspapers, radio and television and all print and electronic media) establishes the right, working within the law, to gather and transmit information, ideas and opinions freely, without government or any organisation influencing what is broadcast or published by censoring or vetting information to determine which parts are made public and by coercing journalists, editors or producers to present a particular viewpoint or opinion.

KEY POINTS

1 Different parts of the mass media can be owned by:
  • private individuals or companies
  • the government
  • both government and private enterprise.

2 The form of ownership of the mass media can influence:
  • the choice and quality of the content
  • the flow of information
  • access to transmission facilities.

3 Access to facilities will affect the range of opinions broadcast.

CASE STUDY

The Caribbean Broadcast Media Partnership on HIV/AIDs (CBMP) was launched in 2006 and is a coalition of private and public broadcasters from across the region that expand programming and public education activities related to HIV/AIDs across the Caribbean.

Questions

1 In what ways will the CBMP be able to transmit information and provide education to the public?

2 What are the advantages of having a partnership or coalition of many regional broadcasters when addressing an issue, such as HIV/AIDs, which affects the whole region?

Regulatory practices and protecting creative work

It is often very difficult to tell if a DVD or CD is an unauthorised copy. Consumers need to be educated about the problems of piracy and of ways to avoid purchasing pirated material, such as purchasing only from reputable dealers.

Material that is transmitted through the media is regulated for reasons ranging from privacy to security. Legislation also exists regarding creative and artistic works that seeks to protect the rights of those responsible for the creation of such works.

Media regulation by government

Media needs to be regulated to protect privacy and reputation, maintain state security, prevent sedition and promote moral standards. Government can regulate the media in a number of ways.

Broadcasting Commission

The Broadcasting Commission may determine the proportion of local and foreign material that locally owned radio and television stations may transmit. It also sets guidelines or establishes codes of conduct in relation to accuracy, impartiality, public taste and product or political advertising.

Censorship boards

Censorship is a form of regulation of the press that involves examining material, with the aim of removing anything that is considered morally harmful, offensive or politically dangerous.

Legislation

Broadcasting legislation prohibits the transmission of any material that is profane, indecent or incites violence against any person or group. Defamation laws cover such things as libel and slander.

Licensing

In most cases an individual or company needs a licence to transmit material via mass media.

Such licences can be refused to individuals or companies that are perceived to be critical of the government. A licence can also be withdrawn or revoked if any relevant legislation is violated.

Media regulation by professional associations

There are accepted codes of conduct for those working in the media to deal with issues such as fairness and accuracy in reporting, privacy and public morals.

The Association of Caribbean Media Workers was established in 2001. One of its aims is to collaborate with national media associations and related organisations in promoting professional and ethical standards.

Mediating in disputes

Organisations that are licensed to broadcast should have a simple and responsive complaints system. Where a complaint is not dealt with to the satisfaction of a complainant, then a regulatory body might become involved. A broadcaster can be required to air an apology, it might face having its license revoked and it could even face prosecution.

Protecting artistic and creative work

An artistic or creative work of visual or performance art is a creation of someone's mind. It is owned by the creator of the work and known as **intellectual property**.

Creators of such works often hope to earn an income, which can be affected if other persons copy the work and sell it without the original creator's permission. This known as media piracy. When pirated works are available outside the country of origin, revenue for that country is lost.

Another threat to a creative person's rights occurs due to **plagiarism**. This is where one person tries to pass off another person's creative work as their own.

Copyright laws

Creators or owners of literary, musical and artistic works can have a **copyright** on them. A copyright grants the holder a monopoly on the use of their work in regard to copying, selling or publishing. Copyright holders can receive payment from others for the right to reproduce the work.

Rights under copyright law

Copyright law grants the holder economic rights and moral rights. Economic rights allow a creator to benefit financially from the work by:

- copying or reproducing the work
- issuing or distributing copies to the public for sale or rent
- performing, broadcasting or displaying the work in public
- adapting or rearranging the work for accessibility by a different audience
- exacting payment in the form of royalties from authorised users
- suing any persons who carry out any of the above without permission.

Moral rights are usually retained by the author or creator and allow him or her to object to any distortion or alteration of the work that may negatively affect his or her reputation.

Obtaining copyright

A work that is to be copyrighted must exist in tangible form. So, for example, a literary work must be in printed or electronic form.

Copies of a publicly distributed work must be registered and deposited with the relevant copyright organisation and must contain the word 'copyright' and the © symbol, the year in which the work was first published, and the name of the copyright owner.

ACTIVITY

1 Carry out some research into the institutions in your country that are responsible for the preservation and protection of creative or artistic work, for copyright administration and for the collection and distribution of funds to original creators.

2 What laws exist to address the issue of piracy of music and video materials?

KEY POINTS

1 Freedom of the press is the right to gather, write, edit and distribute or broadcast information, ideas or opinions within the limits of the law.

2 Press freedom is regulated by government and by self-regulation so that the freedom is not abused.

3 Abuse of press freedom might invade a person's privacy, threaten the security of the state, encourage sedition, damage the reputation of individuals or organisations, or threaten moral values.

4 Creators of literary or artistic works can protect their work by applying copyright.

5 Copyright gives creators of work economic and moral rights.

6 A person who copies, sells or distributes another person's work without their permission is guilty of piracy.

LEARNING OUTCOMES

At the end of this topic you will be able to:

- differentiate between the categories of consumers.

For most people obtaining their own home involves some of the hardest decisions and largest financial commitments of their lives. Most people have to secure a mortgage in order to buy or build their home.

Concept of consumer affairs

A **consumer** is any individual, group or organisation that acquires and uses goods and services provided by a **supplier**, who might be another individual, group or organisation. A consumer is usually, but not always, the purchaser or buyer of the goods and services they consume.

Consumer affairs concern the relationship between supplier and consumer and are largely about establishing rules and codes of conduct that:

- safeguard the rights of consumers
- make the marketplace fair for competing businesses.

Consumer protection concerns such things as ensuring that a consumer receives accurate information about the goods or services to be acquired and that a fair price is being asked.

Goods and services

Goods and services have different characteristics that allow them to be separately defined. Both are sometimes referred to as **commodities**.

Goods

A good is a product that can be used to satisfy a need or a desire. A good is usually considered to be a tangible product that can be physically delivered from a seller (supplier) to a purchaser (who may be the eventual consumer). The ownership of the good is also transferred from the seller to the purchaser.

When a good commands a price, it is known as an **economic good**. Goods that have utility but have no value are known as **free goods** and include such things as air and sunlight.

Consumer goods are those available directly to the consumer in the form in which they are intended to be used, for example bread, vegetables, shoes and televisions. Consumer goods that last for a long time, such as a television, are **consumer durables**.

Producers' goods are those that are used to make other goods, for example the components bought by a television manufacturer.

Services

A **service** is provided to meet a need or desire. It is distinguished from a good in that it is intangible, which means that it is not something that can be touched or physically measured.

A service provider uses a range of knowledge, skills, expertise and aptitudes to perform the service offered. The service has economic value if and when a consumer of the service is willing to pay for it.

Service providers generally carry out work that their customers do not have the time, skills or resources to do themselves.

When services such as education or health care are paid for with taxation revenue and provided by a government, this is known as a **public service**.

Categories of consumers

A consumer can be an individual, a group, a business or other organisation.

Consumers of credit

Credit is deferred payment of a debt. The debt may be due to a financial arrangement, such as a loan, or to the provision of a good or service for which the consumer has insufficient funds available.

Personal loans

Individuals can apply for a personal loan from a bank or similar financial institution. The loan will usually be taken out over an agreed period and at a given rate of interest.

Credit cards

A credit card is used when an individual sets up a credit account with a bank or similar institution. The card can be used as a form of payment for goods and services and the cardholder pays off a certain amount of the outstanding debt on a regular basis.

Hire purchase

Hire purchase allows people to have the use of goods for a fixed period of time in return for a percentage deposit followed by regular payments. The hirer does not own the goods and a vendor can repossess them if there is a default in payments. When the amount of payments reaches the original sale price, plus interest, the buyer has the option to purchase the goods.

Mortgages

A mortgage is a loan particularly associated with housing. A homebuyer or home builder can secure a loan with a bank or other financial institution which will be secured against the value of the property for which the loan is being made.

CASE STUDY

Stan had thought that getting his television on hire purchase was a smart move. He could barely watch it now as he thought about the almost-empty food cupboard. He realised that if he continued his payments, the television was going to cost him more than twice the cash price. If he didn't, then the company could take it back, even though he had been making payments for months. He wished he had never signed that agreement.

Question

What advice would you give to someone like Stan who is thinking of buying a product using hire purchase?

Influences on consumer demand

At the end of this topic you will be able to:

- assess the factors that influence consumer demand for goods and services.

Goods and services are bought and sold in a **market**. In economics, 'market' refers to any structure that allows for transactions to take place, where buyers purchase goods, services or information from sellers.

The term can also be used to describe the transactions that take place in regard to a particular good or service. We can talk about the 'housing market' or the 'market for cell phones', for example.

Markets differ in structure and in the numbers of buyers and sellers they contain. They all operate to some extent on the notion of supply and demand.

- Supply is the amount of a product that producers are willing and able to sell at a particular price.
- Demand is the willingness and ability to buy a product at a given price at a given time and this can be affected by many factors.

Factors that influence demand

Size of income

A person's **disposable income** is that money available after tax. The larger a disposable income a person has, the more likely they are to purchase.

Taste patterns

Consumers buy goods or services to satisfy a need or want. Some products are particularly desirable for some individuals and the greater the desire, the greater the willingness to buy.

Savings

A person considering buying an expensive good may save money over a period of time in order to make the purchase. The amount of money saved will determine their willingness and ability to do this.

Credit facilities and conditions

If people are not able to save, they may seek credit in one way or another and their ability to purchase will be determined by success in obtaining credit.

Fluctuations in supply

In economics, there is understood to be a relationship between supply and demand. In a competitive market, it is assumed that the price of a good will eventually settle at a point where the quantity demanded by consumers at a given price will be equal to the quantity

When people spend on luxury goods and services, mainly for the purpose of displaying wealth or status, this is known as conspicuous consumption

supplied by producers at that given price. If the supply is altered, this can affect demand. If, for example, supply decreases and demand remains the same, then the unit price of a good will rise. This may eventually produce a decrease in demand.

Quality

Consumers require a certain level of quality of product at a given price. A decrease in the level of quality will decrease the demand for that product at that price.

Pricing

Generally speaking, an increase in price produces a decrease in demand and a decrease in price produces an increase in demand. Demand that shows these characteristics is known as elastic.

Most basic foods, which people have to buy in order to survive, show inelastic demand. Luxury items show greater elastic demand since people do without them when prices are high and their budget is stretched.

Price of related goods

Related goods that are complementary are those that are essential for obtaining the utility from the primary good. For example, gasoline is a related good to a car. If the price of gasoline rises, this may cause potential car purchasers to decide against it.

Related goods can be substitute goods and these act as an alternative to the primary good. If the price of a substitute good goes down, demand for the primary good falls.

Access to information

Knowing a lot about a product is important, especially if it has a high price.

Advertising

Advertising is the act of presenting a product or event to the public. Advertising can be informative or persuasive.

- Informative advertising seeks to provide information on availability, uses, price and content.
- Persuasive advertising seeks to persuade consumers to purchase a particular product or service or to attend a particular event. Persuasive advertising predominantly focuses on people's desires and seeks to enhance the desirability of the product being advertised. Successful advertising will produce an increase in demand.

Consumers' future expectations

If consumers think that the price of a good will rise in future, they are more likely to purchase at the present time. If they feel the price might fall, they will defer purchase to a later date.

How consumers use modern technology

At the end of this topic you will be able to:

- explain how consumers use modern technology to conduct transactions.

Use of modern technology in transactions

Commercial transactions involve buying and selling goods or services. Financial transactions involve the movement of money, for example making a deposit into an account or obtaining a loan from a financial institution.

Commercial and financial transactions have previously largely involved face-to-face contact. Other means of making a transaction have included mail order, the telephone and facsimile (fax). The way in which modern technology has revolutionised commercial and financial transactions means that many transactions are possible today without any form of human contact or communication.

Telebanking

Telebanking services are provided by financial institutions. The systems allow customers to use an automated phone service which responds to phone keypad inputs or uses voice recognition. Once a customer has been verified by correctly providing identification information and passwords, he or she will be able to perform many actions, such as requesting account balance details and transaction histories, paying bills and arranging for the transfer of funds between accounts.

ATM

An automated teller machine (ATM) allows customers of a financial institution access to a number of services 24 hours a day. Customers can usually make cash withdrawals, check account balances, check recent transaction history and obtain cell phone credit. Access to the services is made possible through the use of a special card.

The financial institution issues a card to a customer together with a personal identification number (PIN) which is to be used with the card. The card is inserted into the machine and the PIN is entered on the keypad.

An ATM allows customers to access many banking facilities in a public space outside of normal banking hours

E-commerce

E-commerce can be used to describe all the financial and commercial transactions that take place electronically, including credit and debit card purchases and transactions that involve electronic funds transfers from the consumer's account to the seller's account. It has more recently been associated with the transactions in which consumers, both individual and corporate, make use of the internet to place orders and pay for goods and services.

Internet shopping (or shopping online) allows businesses to display goods and services on websites which potential customers can browse at their leisure. If the customer has a credit or debit card, they are usually able to pay through the website.

Internet banking

Internet banking allows customers of a financial institution to carry out a number of financial transactions and related activities on a secure website. Customers can make fund transfers, loan applications or payments, and arrange payments to third parties. They can also access balances and statements, allowing them to keep track of recent transactions.

Debit and credit cards

Debit cards allow a person to pay for goods at a point of sale without having to use cash. The card is linked through the telephone system to the person's bank account and the money is deducted from this and transferred to the seller's account. The card is placed in a machine at the point of sale and correct ownership is verified by the use of a PIN.

Credit cards can be used to buy goods and services in a similar way to a debit card. The main difference is that the amount will not be deducted from the buyer's account immediately but rather on the given date in the month when a payment is due. The credit card holder can elect to pay off the full balance each month or to pay a set amount, with any outstanding amount attracting interest.

Benefits of modern technology

Increased security

One perceived advantage of the use of modern technology in commercial and financial transactions is the reduced use of cash, which can be more easily stolen.

Convenience

Using modern technology allows people to carry out commercial and financial transactions at any time of day or night from any location. People with access to such facilities no longer need to physically visit a bank or shop in order to carry out the transaction. The advantage for those selling goods online is that their shop is effectively open 24 hours of every day.

Time-saving

The fact that people do not need to actually visit a bank or shop in person means that all the travelling time associated with this is saved.

Accessibility

Provided a person has a computer and internet access, the many online services available are accessible to them regardless of their level of personal mobility and the availability of suitable transport.

Disadvantages of modern technology

Possible disadvantages of modern technology are:

- consumers who do not handle actual cash find it harder to keep track of transactions made and therefore become inclined to overspend
- unpaid balances on credit cards have high interest rates
- customers may be subject to fraud if their card is lost or stolen
- consumers may be open to fraud and identity theft.

ACTIVITY

1 Establish how widespread the use of modern technology for transactions is in your local retail area.

2 Which retail outlets face competition from online shopping?

EXAM TIP

You should be familiar with the various uses of modern technology in financial and commercial transactions and with any relevant precautions consumers would be advised to take.

KEY POINTS

1 Modern information and communications technology has revolutionised the way commercial and financial transactions are carried out.

2 E-commerce describes commercial and financial transactions that are carried out electronically and increasingly refers to internet shopping.

3 Modern technology can help consumers by reducing the need for them to carry cash.

4 There are potential disadvantages to using modern technology for financial and commercial transactions.

The role of government and other agencies in consumer protection

CASE STUDY

In November 2007, the government of St Kitts and Nevis introduced a price control order affecting basic food items such as chicken, meat, fish and rice, as well as some non-food items such as toothpaste. The action was taken to moderate the cost of living, which was spiralling upwards. One reason given for this was import inflation, where imported goods were becoming more expensive.

Questions

1 If the goods a retailer imports are becoming more expensive, what might the effect of a price control order be on the retailer's business?

2 What can a small country do to offset the effects of import inflation?

Consumers can be exploited by manufacturers, wholesalers, retailers and service providers. Consumer protection seeks to avoid such exploitation and to safeguard consumer rights.

How do governments offer consumer protection?

Consumer rights

CARICOM member states are required to enact legislation that provides for a consumer's rights. These rights are largely to do with fairness and honesty in trading and with keeping consumers safe, educated and informed of their rights.

Consumer protection legislation

Governments enact legislation to protect consumers, for example:

- The Sale of Goods Act states that goods must fit the purpose for which they are sold.
- The Hire Purchase Act gives consumers the right to:
  - information about the credit and cash price of the good and the terms and conditions of a credit agreement
  - withdraw from the agreement
  - retain possession of the goods.
- The Trade Descriptions Act prohibits manufacturers and sellers from making false or misleading statements about products they make or sell.

The government department responsible for trade can limit or ban the importation of certain dangerous or poor-quality products.

Consumer protection agencies

Governments establish agencies to monitor consumer issues in many areas.

Prices Commission

One way in which governments seek to protect consumers is through policies of price control. Price controls usually set out a maximum and a minimum that can be charged for the specified goods or services. Price controls have been introduced in recent times within the Caribbean, with the intention of keeping the cost of essential items of food at an affordable level.

The Prices Commission:

- controls prices by fixing the legal maximum percentage wholesale and retail mark-up on some basic food items and some basic consumer durables such as refrigerators, stoves and furniture

- publishes the controlled prices in the official gazette and in newspapers, and requires the price schedule be displayed by wholesalers and retailers
- monitors and enforces the controlled prices through price control inspection and possible prosecution of offenders who exceed them.

Public Utilities Board or Utility Regulation Board

This board fixes prices that can be charged for utilities such as water, electricity or telephone services.

National Standards Institute or Bureau of Standards

These agencies are responsible for:

- determining the quantities, quality and types of ingredients that manufacturers should include in their products, thereby establishing the overall level of quality of the finished product
- issuing compulsory and voluntary standards
- issuing standards for product labelling and packaging
- testing goods for quality and safety
- certifying locally produced products that meet acceptable standards by authorising the use of the institute or bureau's mark of approval on the product.

Fair Trading Commission

The Fair Trading Commission administers and enforces laws relating to utility regulation, consumer protection and fair competition. These functions may be achieved by:

- monitoring rates charged and standards of service provided by service providers to ensure compliance
- reviewing commercial activities
- receiving and responding to consumer complaints
- educating and assisting consumers in making and resolving complaints
- investigating possible anti-competitive business practices.

Consumer affairs division

This will often be the Ministry of Consumer Affairs, which would:

- handle consumer complaints and help consumers obtain redress
- initiate action for consumer legislation
- provide consumer rights education
- coordinate activities of other government consumer protection agencies
- promote fair trade practices to enhance relationships between consumers and business.

Food and drug inspection

The Food and Drugs Division of the Ministry of Health tests food items, drugs and cosmetics to ensure they are safe for human use.

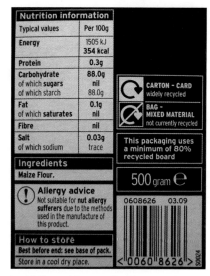

Legislation exists regarding the correct labelling of food and drink, which should be clear and easily read. It should show such things as the net weight of the contents, a list of the ingredients and the date by which the product should be used.

EXAM TIP

You should be able to evaluate efforts of governments and other agencies to protect and educate consumers and be ready to offer strategies to make these efforts more effective.

KEY POINTS

1 Consumer protection is about guaranteeing consumer rights.

2 Governments introduce legislation and establish consumer protection agencies.

3 Other non-government agencies are involved in consumer protection.

The role of government, agencies and business in consumer protection

Supervision of credit facilities

Regulatory authorities are concerned to protect a consumer's interests including when they desire to obtain credit. Regulations will require those institutions that are considering extending credit to an individual to take all possible measures to ensure that the consumer is in a position to repay the credit without undue hardship.

The authorities will also be concerned that banks and other lending institutions are not exposing themselves to bad debt by lending to people who cannot make the necessary repayments. If this happens on a large scale, there can be serious consequences for the economy of a country or many countries.

Regulations will also limit the percentage rate of interest that can be charged for extending credit facilities. It is advisable to obtain any credit from authorised lenders since unauthorised lenders can charge extremely high interest rates and are not subject to other official regulations.

Protection offered by regional agencies

Regional institutions that assist with consumer protection include:

• Caribbean Food Corporation (CFC)
• Caribbean Public Health Agency (CARPHA)
  • Caribbean Agriculture Research and Development Institute (CARDI)
  • Caribbean Regional Centre for the Education and Training of Animal Health and Veterinary Public Health Assistants (REPAHA)
  • Caribbean Poison Information Network (CARPIN)
  • CARICOM Competition Commission (CCC)
  • CARICOM Regional Organisation for Standards and Quality (CROSQ)
  • Caribbean Consumer Council (CCC).

Protection offered by businesses

Some businesses offer protection to consumers beyond that which is required by law or regulation. Such protection is offered since it is good for customer relations. Some businesses:

• voluntarily recall defective products
• provide accurate and reliable information on labelling and other information sources
• establish customer service departments to handle complaints and queries and to facilitate redress where this is necessary.

Apple One-Year Limited Warranty

Apple's warranty obligations for this hardware product are limited to the terms set forth below:
Apple Computer, Inc. ("Apple") warrants this hardware product against defects in materials and workmanship for a period of one (1) year from the date of original purchase ("Warranty Period").
If a defect arises and a valid claim is received by Apple within the Warranty Period, at its option, Apple will (1) repair the product at no charge, using new or refurbished replacement parts, (2) exchange the product with a product that is new or which has been manufactured from new or serviceable used parts and is at least functionally equivalent to the original product, or (3) refund the purchase price of the product.
If a defect arises and a valid claim is received by Apple after the first one hundred and eighty (180) days of the Warranty Period, a shipping and handling charge will apply to any repair or exchange of the product undertaken by Apple.
Apple warrants replacement products or parts provided under this warranty against defects in materials and workmanship from the date of the replacement or repair for ninety (90) days or for the remaining portion of the original product's warranty, whichever provides longer coverage for you. When a product or part is exchanged, any replacement item becomes your property and the replaced item becomes Apple's property. When a refund is given, your product becomes Apple's property.
EXCLUSIONS AND LIMITATIONS
This Limited Warranty applies only to the hardware product manufactured by or for Apple that can be identified by the "Apple" trademark, trade name, or logo affixed to it. This Limited Warranty does not apply to any non-Apple hardware product or any software, even if packaged or sold with the Apple hardware product. Non-Apple manufacturers, suppliers, or publishers may provide a separate warranty for their own products packaged with the Apple hardware product.
Software distributed by Apple under the Apple brand name is not covered under this Limited Warranty. Refer to Apple's Software License Agreement for more information.
Apple is not liable for any damage to or loss of any programs, data, or other information stored on any media contained within the Apple hardware product, or any non-Apple product or part not covered by this warranty. Recovery or reinstallation of programs, data or other information is not covered under this Limited Warranty.
This warranty does not apply: (a) to damage caused by accident, abuse, misuse, misapplication, or non-Apple products; (b) to damage caused by service performed by anyone other than Apple; (c) to a product or a part that has been modified without the written permission of Apple; or (d) if any Apple serial number has been removed or defaced.

Product guarantees are a form of consumer protection. A guarantee will often state that a product will be repaired or replaced if is found to be defective or ceases to operate properly within a given timescale.

Consumer groups and organisations

Consumers can form groups to help to protect themselves. Such groups may:

- highlight unfair business practices
- lobby for and have input to consumer protection legislation
- educate consumers about rights and **thrift**
- monitor price increases and lobby for reasonable prices
- advise consumers and assist in gaining redress
- form consumer cooperatives
- organise boycotts of businesses that exploit consumers
- provide feedback to government on its consumer affairs policies.

A black market

A **black market** is a system that people use to illegally buy or sell goods that might be difficult to obtain through legitimate channels. Goods for sale on the black market might also have been illegally imported. A black market does not operate in favour of governments because taxes associated with legitimate commercial transactions are avoided. Similarly, there are negative effects on legitimate businesses which may suffer a loss in sales if black market goods are available at cheaper prices. Consequently, it is in the interests of government and business to limit black market activities. A consumer is also more vulnerable to exploitation if purchasing through the black market since they will not have the consumer rights protection offered for legitimate business.

EXAM TIP

You should be able to define terms such as 'black market' and 'dumping' and explain some elements of these.

Dumping

Part of consumer protection is about ensuring that the marketplace in which businesses operate is fair. One practice that is often considered to be unfair competition practice is known as **dumping**. This can refer to any form of **predatory pricing**, which is the practice of selling a good or service at a very low price, usually with the intention of driving a competitor out of the market or making it difficult for any potential new competitors to enter the market.

Dumping is the term usually applied when a manufacturer in one country exports products to another country at a price that is below the price it would charge for the product at home and that is likely to be cheaper than products already available in the importing country. This can have a negative effect on consumers if it affects competition in the market.

KEY POINTS

1 Consumer protection extends to regulation of credit services.

2 A number of regional institutions exist to offer different aspects of consumer protection.

3 Some businesses offer elements of consumer protection.

4 Consumers are able to form groups to pursue consumer protection issues.

5 Black markets are systems of illegal trading.

6 Dumping is an anticompetitive action and a form of predatory pricing.

ACTIVITY

1 Find out about any examples of dumping that have affected producers or manufacturers in your country.

2 Investigate the government strategies that are in place to prevent this activity.

At the end of this topic you will be able to:

• describe the ways consumers can protect themselves

Types of exploitation

Consumers and businesses are in a relationship in which they have rather different objectives. A consumer wants to be able to obtain the best quality goods and services at prices that they consider to be reasonable. Most businesses exist to make maximum profit, usually by obtaining the highest practical price for a good or service. Normally, a business succeeds because it is able to balance the desire for profit with the desires of the consumer. A business, therefore, seeks to offer a good or service at a fair and competitive price, which will result in a strong and steady demand.

Occasionally, a business might seek to maximise profit through unscrupulous means. For example, they may:

• overcharge the consumer
• sell poor-quality or substandard goods
• use incorrect weights and measures so a consumer does not get all that they have paid for
• sell goods that are not fit for purpose
• place unfair conditions in contracts that seek to deny consumer rights
• deny consumers a right to return goods and receive refunds
• lure consumers into spending money on items they do not need.

To avoid these types of exploitation, a consumer should:

• be aware of appropriate prices for goods and services
• check items thoroughly prior to and following purchase
• read carefully through contracts, warranties and hire purchase agreements
• be familiar with their rights regarding refunds and exchanges
• demand and keep receipts as proof of purchase
• have a clear idea of items needed and resist pressure to buy more
• refuse to buy items on the black market.

Although there is a good deal of customer protection offered through legislation and regulation, it is important for consumers to take all reasonable steps to protect themselves from exploitation. A consumer has responsibilities as well as rights and part of this responsibility is remaining informed about the different kinds of exploitation that can be encountered.

Consumers should be aware that not all sales are genuine

Being well informed

Consumers should make sure that they are well informed in areas of consumer affairs.

Consumer rights and responsibilities

Consumers International is a not-for-profit company and is the world federation of consumer groups. It was founded in 1960 and has members around the world, including many in the Caribbean region. Consumers International has identified eight consumer rights that consumers should be familiar with. These are:

- the right to satisfaction of basic needs – to have access to basic, essential goods and services: adequate food, clothing, shelter, health care, education, public utilities, water and sanitation
- the right to safety – to be protected against products, production processes and services that are hazardous to health or life
- the right to be informed – to be given the facts needed to make an informed choice, and to be protected against dishonest or misleading advertising and labelling
- the right to choose – to be able to select from a range of products and services, offered at competitive prices with an assurance of satisfactory quality
- the right to be heard – to have consumer interests represented in the making and execution of government policy, and in the development of products and services
- the right to redress – to receive a fair settlement of just claims, including compensation for misrepresentation, shoddy goods or unsatisfactory services
- the right to consumer education – to acquire the knowledge and skills needed to make informed, confident choices about goods and services, while being aware of basic consumer rights and responsibilities and how to act on them
- the right to a healthy environment – to live and work in an environment that is non-threatening to the wellbeing of present and future generations.

Source: www.consumersinternational.org

Factors influencing consumer decisions

Consumers should understand the various factors that influence their decision-making. Many of these were considered in topic 8.2. For example, being aware of the prices of comparable products will help to avoid being overcharged.

The extent of individual control

Individual consumers have to be able to exercise control of their spending and purchasing. Some people are compulsive shoppers who find themselves drawn to buying items, almost as a form of leisure activity, rather than because the goods or services are actually needed. A consumer exercising self-control will also be better able to resist all the influences such as the pressure of advertising.

Uses of modern technology

Modern technology has transformed the way commercial and financial transactions are carried out (see topic 8.3). Consumers need to exercise caution when using such technology as the systems are open to abuse. For example, consumers should:

- ensure that internet shopping sites have secure payment methods
- never give out personal information, bank details or PINs
- be aware of internet and email scams.

ACTIVITY

Carry out some research into food labelling and packaging. Consider any examples where you feel that the consumer might be misled into thinking something about the product that is not true. For example, can you find any products that appear to be locally produced within the Caribbean but that are in fact from outside the region?

EXAM TIP

Be familiar with the ways in which a consumer can be exploited and the available strategies of consumer self-protection.

KEY POINTS

1 Consumers can be exploited in many ways.

2 Consumers can protect themselves by being well informed and knowing their rights and responsibilities.

3 Consumers should be aware of their own level of self-control in spending.

4 Consumers need to know how to protect themselves from fraud or identity theft when using modern technology.

The thrifty consumer

At the end of this topic you will be able to:

• describe the ways consumers practise thrift in the Caribbean.

Leaving lights on when they are not needed means money is spent unnecessarily on utility bills and the resources needed to produce the electricity are wasted

ACTIVITY

1 Make an assessment of the thrifty practices in your household, including reuse and recycling.

2 Find out about the initiatives in your community that encourage recycling. Say how effective you think these have been and what you would suggest that might improve them.

A person who practises thrift is able to use the money and possessions they have to gain the maximum use from them. Thrift is particularly important for people with limited income and savings, but it is a sensible approach for all to adopt.

Ways of practising thrift

Managing your income

Gross income is the money received from all work or investments earned before any taxes or other compulsory payments are deducted. Disposable income is the money that remains after these deductions.

A person decides how to use their disposable income on regular expenses such as utility bills, on basic needs such as food, and for savings.

Budgeting

In order to use their disposable income wisely and well, consumers need to prepare a budget. A budget is an estimate of income and expenditure over a given period of time. Table 8.7.1 shows a budget for a disposable income of 3000 Eastern Caribbean dollars.

Items	$EC	Percentage
Food	1200	40
Clothing	150	5
Rent	450	15
Savings	300	10
Transport	150	5
Entertainment	90	3
Utilities	300	10
Life insurance	60	2
Hire purchase payment	300	10
Total	**(3000)**	**100**

Table 8.7.1 A budget for a disposable income of 3000 Eastern Caribbean dollars

Budgeting helps an individual to become more disciplined in financial matters. It also enables him or her to:

• know how much disposable income can be saved
• know the amounts spent in different categories
• plan for the future
• avoid unplanned debt by keeping within the budget
• prioritise needs and wants.

Shopping wisely for goods and services

Good shopping also helps consumers to get the maximum benefit from their money. Such practices include:

- distinguishing between needs and wants
- comparing prices and quality between stores and between substitute goods
- knowing when certain fruits and vegetables are in season and therefore plentiful and cheaper
- buying items in bulk to obtain the best price
- preparing a shopping list and adhering to it
- avoiding impulse buying
- avoiding false economies of buying very cheap goods that do not last
- examining items carefully before purchase
- keeping receipts and warranties in case goods need to be returned
- checking the expiry dates on perishable items before purchasing.

Using and caring for possessions well

This is part of a consumer's responsibilities. Items should only be used for the purpose for which they are intended and in the manner recommended by a manufacturer. Guarantees and warranties are usually void if a consumer has used an item in any other way.

Conservation and recycling

Conservation and recycling strategies can reduce expenditure and in some cases earn an income. Such strategies include:

- using leftover food to create new dishes
- reducing wastage around the home, including food and utilities
- passing on clothes to younger siblings
- reusing items within the household, for example using bottles as storage containers
- maintaining possessions in accordance with manufacturers' usage and care instructions.

Benefits of thrift

To individuals

Adopting thrifty patterns of behaviour benefits individuals because they will limit spending and increase saving potential, have money available for daily needs and unexpected expenses and limit their reliance on credit. They will also know they are receiving good value for money, enjoy a better standard of living and feel a sense of achievement when accumulating savings.

To society

Thrifty behaviour among citizens results in less wastage of a country's resources. This is especially important in Caribbean countries where so much of what we consume is imported. Thrift can curb some of the exploitative behaviour of certain business people.

KEY POINTS

1 Thrift is the wise and careful use of money and possessions in order to obtain the maximum benefit from them.

2 Disposable income is the money that consumers have available to spend.

3 A budget helps an individual decide how much money to spend, save or invest.

4 Thrifty practices include careful shopping, correct use and maintenance of possessions, conservation and recycling, and regular saving.

5 Thrifty consumers save more, get value for money, waste less, become more responsible and enjoy a better standard of living.

6 Thrifty behaviour results in less wastage of a country's resources and acts as a check on business practices.

When people are said to be saving, it means they are keeping some of their disposable income for use at a later stage. People can keep their savings in the form of cash at home or in a commercial bank, a credit union or other savings institution.

Reasons for saving

People save for many reasons, including the possible need to:

• finance unexpected or unforeseen expenditure such as medical bills and car repairs
• finance the purchase of expensive items such as a house or car
• provide **collateral** for a loan
• improve their education or pay for their child's education at tertiary level
• invest in securities, such as company shares, government bonds and treasury bills, to earn income
• provide for financial security following retirement or loss of work.

Benefits of saving

For individuals

The main benefits of regular saving for individuals are being better able to satisfy needs and wants and having a greater sense of security. An individual may also develop greater self-control and discipline and may even be able to consider early retirement.

For a country

Savings can directly benefit a country if individuals are investing in local companies or in such things as government bonds and treasury bills, which provide the government with funds to invest in the country.

For the region

Investing savings in local businesses benefits the region, since this allows regional businesses to expand and so create employment.

Factors influencing saving

In order to save money, an individual must have a personal commitment to the idea that it is worthwhile. To save money, a person has to limit his or her present spending and consumption and this will happen only if there is a belief that saving will bring greater benefits in the future.

An individual's ability to save is largely to do with the size of disposable income and this will be affected by trends in prices of such things as food, housing and utilities.

People are encouraged to save for their retirement so that they have money available when income from other sources is reduced

Forms of saving

People can save money in many ways. Some simply put money aside and keep it as cash in the home. The disadvantages of this are that the money is vulnerable to theft and does not attract any interest.

Table 8.8.1 shows some of the organisations that provide savings facilities and the kinds of savings plans offered.

Institutions	Types of savings plan
Commercial banks	Savings deposits, term deposits, retirement savings plans
Life insurance companies	Retirement savings plans, endowment plans
Finance houses	Term deposits
Credit unions	Shares, savings deposits
Friendly societies	Savings deposits
Investment trusts, unit trusts	Term deposits, mutual funds
Building societies	Savings deposits

Table 8.8.1 Savings organisations and savings plans

Credit unions

Credit unions are financial cooperatives that are owned and controlled by their members. A credit union usually has a common bond, such as membership of a group or organisation, which determines the people who can join.

Benefits of credit unions to consumers

Credit unions promote thrift among members and provide loans and other financial services including counselling. They are usually not-for-profit organisations where excess earnings are used to reduce fees or to provide free services. Credit unions can give saving members a sense of self-reliance and can also promote community development.

Informal saving groups

Sou-sou is a form of saving where a group of people contribute an equal amount of money to a common pool for a period of time (for example, a month) and after that time is up, one group member gets all the money. This is repeated until each member has had a turn and received the full lump sum at least once. Sou-sou allows members to purchase larger commodities while only having to make manageable contributions to the group.

ACTIVITY

Find out about the differences between commercial banks, credit unions and investment trusts. Explain some of the different facilities they offer. Explain the different circumstances in which a consumer might choose to save with each of the different institutions.

EXAM TIP

You should be able to explain the main functions of credit unions and how they bring benefits to their members and to a country as a whole.

KEY POINTS

1 Savings are the unused portion of disposable income.

2 People save for different reasons, which are usually concerned with increasing a sense of worth and security.

3 Saving brings many benefits to individuals, a country and the region.

4 There are many institutions offering savings facilities including commercial banks, life insurance companies, credit unions, friendly societies and building societies.

5 Credit unions offer many benefits to members.

6 Sou-sou is a popular informal savings arrangement in the Caribbean.

Devaluation and inflation

Growing food to help meet a family's needs is a practical way of reducing expenditure

All countries have a currency, which citizens and governments use to buy goods and services. This is the domestic (or local) currency. Imports have to be paid for using an **international currency**, such as US dollars or British pounds sterling, which are accepted by other countries. Caribbean countries usually pay for imports using US dollars.

Local currencies have a fixed relationship to international currencies in terms of their respective values. This is known as the **exchange rate**. For example, one US dollar might be equal to approximately two Barbados dollars.

A Caribbean country can earn international currencies by exporting goods to other countries. A country's stock of international currencies is known as its **international reserves**. These can be accumulated and used to pay for imports or to make repayments on foreign loans.

Devaluation is a reduction in value of a currency in relation to other currencies with which it can be exchanged.

If a country's imports exceed its exports or if it has large loans to repay, then it loses international currencies and reserves. If such losses persist, a country will struggle to pay for the goods and services it wishes to import. The government may be forced to devalue its currency against the international currency. This means that it would cost more of a local currency to buy the same amount of the international currency. The intention of devaluation is to reduce the level of imports.

Inflation is the sustained rise in the general level of prices over a given period of time. Inflation means that each unit of a given currency buys fewer goods and services.

Effects of devaluation and inflation

Higher prices

When a country devalues its currency, local consumers have to pay more for imported goods and services. Locally produced goods may become more attractive, but if these rely on imported raw materials then the price of these will go up and affect the price of the manufactured product.

Higher prices and reduced purchasing power

A major reason for devaluing a currency is to reduce a country's persistent losses caused by too much spending on imported goods and services. If local consumers' income remains the same, they will experience a reduction in their buying power for imported goods and goods that contain imported materials. The money they have does not go as far as it did before devaluation. People who are on a fixed income which remains the same during a period of inflation and who are not able to negotiate a wage increase are especially hard hit.

Retrenchment

As a result of falling incomes and rising prices, some businesses, particularly those producing goods and services solely for the local market, will experience a fall in demand and income. A shortage of international reserves may also mean that some businesses struggle to import the raw materials they need. Both of these situations can mean that businesses are forced to reduce staff levels, sometimes referred to as the retrenchment of workers.

Lower standard of living

The overall effect of these factors is to produce a lowering in the standard of living of consumers, as you can see in Table 8.9.1. The effect will vary depending on the income level of the consumer.

Income level	Effect of inflation
Low income	Fewer goods can be afforded including basic necessities. Consumers buy lowest-priced goods available.
Fixed income	A fall in the value of money and purchasing power means people spend more and save less.
High income	Less income is spent on luxury goods. Cheaper alternatives may be sought out or such goods may not be purchased at all. People may spend more and save less.

Table 8.9.1 Effects of inflation

Strategies to deal with the effects

Individual consumers

Consumers can employ a number of strategies to help them deal with the effects of devaluation or inflation, including:

- producing more of their own food
- prioritising their needs so that expenditure is reduced to only purchasing essential items
- recycling and reusing household items
- maintaining consumer durables well so that they last a long time
- offering a service locally, for example carrying out garden maintenance
- engaging in a profitable hobby to supplement their income or to produce goods for their own use
- considering retraining to widen employment opportunities
- establishing a business and being self-employed.

Groups and organisations

Some agencies provide micro-loans to assist in establishing small income-generating enterprises. Financial help can also be found through cooperative arrangements and traditional and informal ways include a box, sou-sou and a partner or meeting turn.

Money can be made to go further through a consumer cooperative. This is a business owned, formed and controlled by a group of individuals who share a common bond, with the aim of providing foodstuffs and household items at fair prices by purchasing in bulk and selling directly to members. Members receive a patronage refund in proportion to the business that they do with the cooperative each year.

Globalisation and trade liberalisation

Globalisation is the process where the economies, cultures and societies of different nations are drawn together. It has been brought about through advances in technology, communication and transport and through business and trading practices. For businesses, it has meant that the world has become a global market. **Trade liberalisation** is the relaxation or removal of laws and guidelines regulating trade. This has made the potential for global commercial activity a reality.

Cheaper goods and services

Globalisation has increased the availability of cheaper goods and services. Goods and services can be cheaper to produce in one country than another for a number of reasons. For example:

• workers may receive lower wages
• other costs of production are lower
• less money is spent on providing good working conditions
• costs of raw materials are lower
• businesses are able to make use of **economies of scale**.

Cheaper goods may seem a good thing for consumers, but cheapness does not always represent value for money. Cheaper goods may be substandard or inferior quality and they may not provide the level of service or durability of more expensive items. A thrifty consumer will determine whether an immediate purchase of a cheaper good is preferable to delaying the purchase of a superior product.

Globalisation and trade liberalisation has meant that Caribbean markets are increasingly open to foreign producers. Caribbean consumers must sometimes choose between imported goods and those produced locally.

Wider choice of goods and services

Globalisation results in the availability of a wider choice of goods and services. At face value, this would seem to be a good thing for consumers. If the good or service is also available locally, local consumers need to consider the importance of purchasing from a local producer, even if this is not the cheapest option.

A wider choice of goods and services often presents further challenges to the desire or need to be thrifty. Part of being thrifty is distinguishing between needs and wants. Many of the goods and services offered following globalisation meet people's wants rather than their needs.

More widespread use of technology for transactions

Part of globalisation is the increasing use of communications technology for commercial transactions. The major technological development in this regard has been the internet, which has the advantages of presenting a huge range of products and services without the consumer needing to visit a store or service provider in person. Possible disadvantages are that the products cannot be physically assessed before purchase and there may be costs, such as delivery charges, which consumers may overlook when making price comparisons.

Technology is also making it easier for consumers to pay for goods and services without having to deal with cash or cheques. Such payments are made using a debit or credit card and the consumer needs to keep a careful record of such transactions in order to keep track of their financial situation.

Internet technology and improved communications also means that consumers have access to a great deal of information about the products and services being offered. Making good use of this will help in making sound purchasing decisions.

Competition from developed countries for available markets

Globalisation and trade liberalisation have meant that producers and service providers from developed countries have gained access to markets everywhere. For the Caribbean consumer, this means that they sometimes have a choice between buying locally produced goods and services and those provided by foreign companies.

Exposure to competition might mean that:

• local producers and retailers who fail to compete will either reduce their workforce or go out of business, both of which would lead to unemployment

• local products become unavailable, effectively limiting consumer choice

• increased outflow of foreign exchange to purchase unrestricted imported goods may eventually result in devaluation and consequent economic hardship.

KEY POINTS

1 Globalisation is the coming together of world economies, cultures and societies through improved communications, transport and trade liberalisation.

2 Globalisation and trade liberalisation have introduced a wider range of cheaper goods and services to Caribbean markets.

3 New technologies have made commercial transactions possible on a new scale.

4 Local markets are open to competition from developed countries.

ACTIVITY

Assess the impact of globalisation and trade liberalisation on your local community. What are the goods and services available as a result of these trends? How have local businesses been affected and are there signs that local consumers are supporting local producers?

The role of the consumer in sustainable regional development 1

At the end of this topic you will be able to:

• explain how consumers can contribute to the sustainable development of the region.

People in paid employment provide revenue for the government which helps towards the development of the country and the region. If consumers make use of local businesses and help them to grow and prosper, they may need to increase their workforce, which will have further beneficial effects on regional development.

Awareness of integration objectives

For the efforts to achieve regional integration to succeed there must be popular support among the populations of the different Caribbean countries. Regardless of the number of policies put in place by the governments of the different Caribbean nations, if Caribbean citizens do not support integration, it will not happen.

One barrier to people supporting regional integration could be a lack of understanding of the objectives of the movement. Governments and consumers both have a role to play.

• Governments are responsible for providing information about the integration movement, its goals and objectives. Citizens have a duty to make themselves aware of these objectives and to understand the contribution they can make to bringing them about.

• Consumers have the greatest role to play in the development and sustainability of regional businesses, which is a vital part of the overall integration process.

Preference for regional goods and services

One of the main aims of CARICOM is to promote economic integration among member states through a common market arrangement (Caribbean Single Market Economy). This is intended to remove trade barriers between the states and encourage the free movement of labour, goods, services and capital.

These strategies are intended to make it easier for business people to access the workers they need and also to open up their businesses to a larger, regional market, rather than a market based within a single country.

Although these may have some impact, it is important for consumers within the region to support manufacturers and service providers from within the region if the idea is going to work. Consumers may not support local manufacturers because:

• they believe that the quality of imported goods is superior to locally produced substitutes

• the prices of some locally produced goods are higher than the imported substitutes

• some local producers may fail to provide a reliable supply of goods of a consistently high quality

• advertisements are successful in convincing consumers to buy foreign goods

• the high penetration levels of foreign mass media result in a strong influence towards foreign values and tastes.

Investment in local and regional businesses

Consumers might be able to make direct investments in local and regional businesses. Businesses often rely on other individuals or organisations making an investment in order for them to expand or improve production. Consumers who manage to make some savings can always choose to invest in a local or regional business.

Consumers might also be able to influence investment from other organisations. For example, they could lobby government to increase the amount of investment it provides to local and regional businesses. Consumers who use commercial banks could also choose their bank on the basis of how much regional investment the bank is committed to.

Choosing to support local and regional businesses through directly buying their goods and services or by making investments will potentially lead to job creation, which will have a positive effect on the region's economy.

Conservation of the region's resources

If the region is to develop in a sustainable way, consumers have to make the best possible use of the available resources.

Energy resources are a particularly important aspect of Caribbean economies since the vast majority rely on imports of fuel to produce the energy they need. Adopting energy conservation practices, such as turning off lights and electrical equipment when they are not in use or installing alternative forms of electrical production such as photovoltaic solar panels, could bring benefits to the economy since less money will need to be spent on importing fuel. Consumers might be encouraged to adopt energy conservation strategies if they could see that it would reduce their own fuel bills. Spending a smaller proportion of disposable income on fuel means that more is available for other goods or for saving.

CASE STUDY

'We use lots of onions in our products,' said the CEO, 'and the cheapest way to get them is for us to order a containerload from overseas.'

'What should we do with any we don't need?' asked a colleague.

'We can simply sell them on the local market – and they will all sell because we can offer them much cheaper than the local producers.'

Questions

1 What will be the effect on local onion growers of this idea?

2 What arguments could you suggest to encourage him to buy local produce?

3 What could local consumers do to encourage the use of local ingredients in food products produced in the Caribbean?

4 How will buying local products help in the sustainable development of the region?

The role of the consumer in sustainable regional development 2

Prudent use of foreign exchange

When products and services are bought from overseas companies, the money is going to support the economies of those countries and is not available to support economies within the Caribbean. In many cases, money spent with overseas companies is on non-essential items. Consumers, both individuals and businesses, need to limit the amount of money that is spent as foreign exchange and increase the money that is spent in domestic and regional markets.

Leading a healthy lifestyle

The largest resource available to the Caribbean region is the **human resource**. A healthy population is necessary for the sustainable development of the region for two important reasons:

• Firstly, a healthy population is more productive. Individuals have higher energy levels and are more able to meet the physical and mental challenges presented in working, training and educational environments. There are also fewer incidences of health-related absenteeism from work.

• Secondly, a healthy population puts less demand on health and welfare services.

The Caribbean has a rich tradition of food dishes made using locally produced ingredients

Increased agricultural production and a conscious choice on behalf of consumers to buy and consume healthy fresh foods could have a marked effect on the general health of the population and consequently a positive influence on sustainable regional development.

Some health issues facing the region include a level of malnutrition and vitamin deficiency in certain sectors and growing levels of obesity and related health concerns in others. Obesity is often attributed to over-nutrition (or overeating), especially of the wrong types of foods (which are often imported), combined with a lack of physical exercise and a sedentary lifestyle.

Creative use of regional agricultural products

The agricultural sector makes a significant contribution to the economy of the region, partly through foreign exchange earnings but also through provision of food for local consumption and large amounts of employment. Continued growth and diversification of the agricultural sector is essential for the sustainable development of the region and for rural areas in particular.

Regional consumers have an important role to play in that they provide the most easily accessible market for much of the food that is locally produced.

Consumers can be persuaded by advertising to consume foreign-style foods, created using foreign ingredients, in preference to traditional Caribbean dishes using local ingredients. To counteract this trend, consumers need to be aware of interesting ways of using local foods and to promote the use of local ingredients.

Some agricultural products have practical purposes. For example, cotton can be used to make textiles and clothing and its seeds used to produce oil or animal feed. Bamboo can be used for many different purposes including furniture-making, flooring, artistic carvings and also clothing. A number of agricultural products are being exploited as sources of fuel, for example ethanol, which is produced from sugar cane.

Savings and capital investment

A person who puts aside some of their disposable income as savings will gain personal benefits such as greater financial security and a sense of achievement and greater self-worth. There is also an option for people to invest some of their savings. People can invest in bonds, treasury bills, shares, life insurance and retirement savings plans. People invest in such instruments because they will get a financial return at some point. Some of these investments can have a positive impact on the development of the region.

Government bonds and treasury bills

By investing in a government bond or a treasury bill, an individual is in effect loaning the government or the treasury the money they invest. The government or treasury then has the money at their disposal to use in carrying out their particular functions. Bonds and bills are another way of raising **revenue**. The bond or bill will be arranged over a set period of time and at the end of this the investor can have their money returned with interest.

Treasury bills tend to be short-term **securities** which mature in one year or less, while government bonds can be invested for years.

Company shares

Individuals are also able to invest in companies that might be owned privately or by government. If these investments are in local companies, which are then able to consolidate or expand their business, this will contribute to regional development.

KEY POINTS

1 Prudent use of foreign exchange involves limiting the amount of money spent on non-essential items from countries outside the region.

2 Leading a healthy lifestyle means people are more productive, take less time off work and are less of a drain on health services.

3 Creative use of agricultural products means consuming less foreign-inspired and imported food, and using agricultural products in innovative ways.

4 People who save are able to invest directly in a country through government bonds and treasury bills.

5 People can help local businesses by investing in shares in local companies.

Types of tourism products

Concept of tourism

Tourism is the movement of people from their usual place of abode to another destination or destinations for reasons other than work. Tourists visit places for many different reasons, but their choice is often influenced by such things as the attractiveness of the natural environment or the appeal of an area's culture or heritage.

Tourism is also the name of the industry that involves businesses that cater to the needs of travellers in regard to transportation, accommodation, food, entertainment, recreational activities and souvenirs.

For practical purposes and for statistical reasons, travellers are categorised as 'visitors' or 'tourists' depending on the length of their stay in a given destination. A person who stays for less than 24 hours is classified as a visitor.

Excursionists are people who visit a place but sleep away from the destination, for example on a cruise ship or yacht.

Tourists who are not using cruise ships or yachts are referred to as land-based tourists.

Types of tourist

Tourists are classified according to their country of residence, as Table 9.1.1 shows.

The natural beauty of the Caribbean has drawn tourists here from all over the world. As people's understanding and appreciation of the natural world and of its fragility has become more sophisticated, so tourism products are constantly adapted to address new perceptions and expectations.

Type of tourist	Description
International	Travels outside the geographical region of their home country
Regional	Travels to places within the same geographical region
Domestic	Travels within their own country

Table 9.1.1 Types of tourist

Tourism products

Most tourism products are intangible, which means they cannot be held or handled and therefore cannot be taken back with the tourist to their home. Although tourists may purchase tangible products in the form of souvenirs, the main appeal of tourism is in travelling and experiencing new and interesting places. Tourism products, therefore, are mostly to do with sights, sounds and similar sensory experiences, which create pleasant emotions and feelings.

All-inclusive tourism

Resorts are areas that have been especially developed to meet the physical needs of tourists and also create those pleasant emotions and feelings. Resort areas include hotels and similar accommodation, food courts, shopping malls, coffee bars and places of entertainment.

An all-inclusive tourism product means that everything that a tourist will need during their stay is provided within the resort.

Time-share tourism

Time-share involves individuals or groups purchasing the ownership or right to stay in a particular property. A number of parties share ownership of the property and each is allocated a certain period of time in which they may use the property.

Traditional tourism products

The Caribbean has become a major world tourist destination because of the excellent beaches, the attractive marine environment and the predominantly favourable warm weather conditions. These attractions, known in short as 'sun, sea and sand', form the basis of traditional tourism products.

New tourism products

As more places in the world develop tourism products that are in competition with the Caribbean, new tourism products need to be developed here so that visitors will continue to be attracted.

Nature/ecotourism

Nature/ecotourism caters for those who want to observe animal and plant life in natural habitats. The Caribbean offers rainforests, mangrove wetlands, bird sanctuaries, nature reserves and marine environments including coral reefs.

Sports tourism

Sports tourism offers visitors the opportunity to participate in marine or land-based sporting activities. Marine-based activities include scuba diving, water skiing, swimming, sailing, snorkelling, surfing and sea-kayaking. Other tourists visit for sport fishing activities. Land-based sporting activities include golf, cricket, football, tennis, hiking and mountain biking.

Cultural/heritage tourism

Cultural/heritage tourism provides for those who want to experience the culture of the destination, including festivals, food, music, dances, art, language and dress, and its history in the form of archaeological sites, historic buildings, museums and monuments.

Special events

These include golf tournaments, international sporting fixtures, horse races, regattas and conferences.

Music festivals

A number of festivals attract international acts and tourists from around the world. Examples include jazz festivals and Reggae Sumfest.

Health tourism

Health tourism caters for those who need particular facilities to help them recuperate following an illness and also includes facilities that provide health resorts or spas to enhance wellbeing and general health. There are many spa resorts near natural springs in Dominica, Grenada, Jamaica and St Lucia.

Factors that influence the development of tourism in the host and supply countries

Factors influencing tourism are found in both the **host country**, which is the country to which the tourists are travelling, and the **supply country**, which is the country in which they normally reside. A host country has to make efforts to be appealing to potential visitors in a number of ways. Conditions in the supply country have to be suitable to enable people to make visits elsewhere.

Factors in the host country

In addition to developing new tourism products that will continue to attract visitors (see topic 9.1), a host country has to acknowledge the requirements for meeting tourists' more practical needs.

Accessibility

A major consideration for tourists is the accessibility of their destination. This means how easy or otherwise it is to travel to the host country. For international tourists travelling by air, a major consideration would be whether or not there was a direct flight from their home country and, if there was not, how simple the transfer from the nearest international airport to their final destination would be. To cater for cruise ship passengers, the host country must have a suitable seaport.

Availability, cost and quality of tourist services

A host country needs to have an organised and regulated tourist industry. This includes having a tourism organisation, such as a ministry of tourism, to develop industry policies and guidelines, and a tourist board to focus on marketing the country and the tourism products on offer.

Tourists need to feel that they will be safe from crime, violence or harassment when they are in public places

The individuals and businesses who work in the industry to provide the actual facilities, services and amenities, such as accommodation, restaurants and attractions, must ensure that a variety of these are offered at a high level of quality and at reasonable prices. Personnel working in the industry should be trained in the skills necessary to perform their particular function.

Perception of safety and security

When people travel they often feel vulnerable. They will want to know that levels of crime or violence in the host country are at acceptable levels and be reassured that they will not be exposed to any threat or risk.

Political stability

Political stability means that there is good governance within the country and a respect for law and order. There should be healthy relationships between political parties and a sense of social harmony among the general population. Without this political stability, tourists are less likely to be attracted. Political instability would also make it more difficult to attract foreign and local investment to develop the tourist industry.

Infrastructure

A host country needs to have modern sanitation arrangements. Sanitation is mainly concerned with a system for the provision of clean water for washing and a system for efficient removal of solid waste and sewage.

A modern, safe and well-maintained road network is also important for tourism. Tourists sometimes want to travel to different sites within the host country. Facilities such as hotels and restaurants also rely on the efficient delivery of such things as food supplies.

Host countries also need an adequate and reliable electrical supply system and modern internet and telecommunications systems.

Airports and sea ports

Air and sea ports need to be modern and capable of handling modern aircraft and ships, as well as accommodating large numbers of passengers. In the Caribbean, steps were recently taken to upgrade airport facilities.

Factors in the supply country

The tourists that the host country is hoping to attract must:

- have a disposable income that allows them to travel on holiday
- be made aware of the destination by tourism promoters from the host country and travel agents in the supply country
- have specific and detailed information about transportation, accommodation, attractions and amenities at the destination
- have easy access to affordable and reliable transportation to and from the destination.

ACTIVITY

Outline three recent developments in tourism facilities in your country, other than the expansion or reconditioning of airport facilities.

KEY POINTS

1 A host country must:
- be easily accessible through the provision of airports and sea ports
- have a range of reasonably priced, good-quality tourist services
- be perceived to be safe and secure
- have political stability
- have a good infrastructure.

2 People in the supply country must have:
- an adequate disposable income
- knowledge of the destination
- adequate information about travel and accommodation
- easy access.

How does tourism contribute to the Commonwealth Caribbean economy?

A craftsperson is employed indirectly in the tourism industry, while a person working in a hotel is employed directly

The economic impact of tourism

The tourism industry is a major element of the economy of most Caribbean countries. The industry earns foreign exchange and produces other **revenues** for governments. Tourism provides employment directly, for workers in the industry, and indirectly, through associated industries such as agriculture and construction.

Foreign exchange earnings

Tourism is the largest foreign exchange earner for most Caribbean countries. These foreign exchange earnings pay for a country's imports and repayments on international loans.

Employment

Tourism provides direct employment for workers in tourist facilities such as hotels, restaurants, clubs and specific tourist attractions. There are also many more indirect employment opportunities through links with other industries that support tourism, for example:

• agriculture – providing local produce for hotels and restaurants
• transportation – providing access to and from destinations and movement within a country
• construction – building tourist accommodation and associated facilities
• distribution – delivering items to hotels and restaurants
• general services – helping to maintain facilities in safe, reliable and clean conditions.

Government revenue

Tourism contributes significantly to a government's revenue through:

• landing fees for aircraft and berthing fees for cruise liners
• taxes on goods and services purchased by tourists
• taxes on wages of those employed in the tourism industry
• taxes on businesses in the tourism industry, for example hotel and restaurant taxes
• import duties on items brought into the country for the tourism industry
• head and departure taxes on visitors.

This revenue is used to pay for services provided by government, for example health, sanitation, welfare and education. It also contributes to **infrastructure** programmes such as road-building or housing development.

Government expenditure

Governments also spend a good deal of their revenue in developing the tourist industry, for example in improving or expanding airports. It is important that such expenditure does not simply benefit the tourists but residents as well. Programmes promoting community tourism, where visitors are encouraged to stay in smaller, family-run hotels away from the major resorts, would help to ensure this happens.

Developing good infrastructure systems in resort areas, for water supplies and sewage disposal for example, can generate employment and also provides the possibility of improvements to such systems in other parts of a country. Again, it is important that such improvements in the resort areas do not come at the expense of improvements elsewhere.

The agricultural sector

An **economic link** is formed when the output of one industry becomes an input for another. The link between agriculture and tourism forms when local agriculture is able to supply hotels and restaurants with produce. The link exists but is not particularly strong given the requirement of most tourists to consume items that generally need to be imported.

The tourism industry also has some potentially negative effects on the agricultural sector. The tourism sector can offer higher wages and so workers leave the agricultural sector, meaning that there can be an inadequate supply of labour. The development of tourist sites, such as hotels and golf clubs, can often take place on prime agricultural land, reducing the amount of land available for food production and having possible implications regarding food security.

Imports

Large quantities of food are imported to feed tourists, which increase a country's food import bill. It is necessary to balance the income from tourists and tourist consumption against these additional costs. The tourists' consumption habits often reinforce messages contained in foreign media and together these may influence local residents' tastes and habits over time.

Real estate values

When facilities in popular resort areas are to be developed or expanded, the land on which they will be built becomes increasingly expensive and unaffordable for local people. A similar situation arises in resort areas where real estate prices can rise due to expenditure and improvements in the area. Real estate prices are pushed beyond the reach of local residents.

Rents charged for some tourist accommodation in residential areas can affect the rents charged to local residents.

Economic leakage of foreign exchange

Some foreign exchange earnings from tourism go back out of the country. This is known as **economic leakage**.

Economic leakage happens when money is spent on importing food items for tourist consumption or importing materials to produce items to meet tourists' demands, for example souvenirs. Leakage also occurs if tourist facilities are owned and operated by foreign companies. In such a case, profits from the business go back to the country from where the owner operates.

KEY POINTS

1 Tourism is the main contributor to the economies of most Caribbean countries.

2 Tourism contributes to the economy by providing direct and indirect employment and by providing government revenues and foreign exchange earnings.

3 Tourism can take land away from other uses, such as agriculture, and does not necessarily have strong links with other economic sectors.

4 Economic leakage of foreign exchange occurs when earnings go back out of the country, for example on importing food for tourists.

Career and employment opportunities in tourism

This young woman is learning the skills necessary to prepare her for work in a professional kitchen

Tourism is a service industry, which puts it in the tertiary sector of employment. The services provided are varied and as a consequence so are the employment and career opportunities available within the industry.

Employment and facilities in tourism

The tourism industry provides transportation, accommodation, food, entertainment and recreational facilities, as shown in Table 9.4.1. Employment opportunities include managerial, administrative, professional, technical, clerical and unskilled roles, as shown in Table 9.4.2.

Facility	Employment
Hotels	Managers, accountants, reception desk personnel, porters, secretaries, bar staff, chefs, waiting staff, cleaners, maintenance personnel, grounds keepers, entertainment organisers, entertainers, sound and lighting technicians, ICT specialists
National parks	Managers and secretarial staff, wardens, guides, enforcement officers, education and 'outreach' personnel, computer operatives, audiovisual specialists, publicists, public relations experts
Airports	Managers and secretarial staff, airline maintenance personnel, air traffic controllers, baggage handlers, customs officials, security personnel, aircraft refuelling technicians, fire service personnel
Publicity agencies	Translators, copywriters, camera operators, photographers, graphic designers, website designers
Other	Engineers, computer programmers, lawyers, human resources managers, interior designers, gardeners, drivers

Table 9.4.1 Facilities and related employment in the tourist sector

Types of occupation	Examples
Managerial	Managers are needed in hotels, sales departments, human resources departments, tour operators, travel agents, etc.
Professional	Accountant, pilot, chef, conservationist
Administrative	Secretary, supervisor
Technical	IT specialist, web designer, heating engineer, electrician
Clerical	Receptionist, front desk clerk, cashier
Catering	Cook, bar tender, waiter/waitress
Sanitary	Maid, cleaner
Transport	Taxi driver, airline worker
Unskilled	Maintenance, gardener, bellboy, porter

Table 9.4.2 Occupations in the tourist sector

Conditions of employment

Conditions of employment will vary depending on the role of the person concerned and the terms of their engagement. Some people will be able to join a relevant trade union. Unions represent workers and ensure they receive fair wages, job security, fringe benefits, holiday entitlements and other benefits.

Qualifications

A number of institutions provide opportunities for gaining academic qualifications and specialised training in preparation for work in the hospitality sector. Areas covered include catering, housekeeping, hotel and resort management and guest relations.

Opportunities for training

A number of regional organisations provide training for tourism workers such as:

- the Caribbean Hotel and Tourism Association
- the Caribbean Tourism Organization's Human Resource Development unit
- the Tourism Product Development Company Ltd in Jamaica
- the University of the West Indies Centre for Hotel and Tourism Management
- the Heart Trust/NTA, Jamaica
- the Barbados Community College: Hospitality Institute
- the Trinidad and Tobago Hospitality and Tourism Institute.

Entrepreneurship

Tourism offers a number of opportunities for people to establish small businesses. For example, individuals can become owners of small hotels or guesthouses, restaurants, taxis and operations providing services, such as boat trips, water sports and guided walks.

KEY POINTS

1 Occupations in the tourist industry include managerial, clerical, administrative, technical, professional and unskilled work.

2 Workers in the tourist industry can expect the same kind of trade union representation and benefits as workers in other sectors of the economy.

3 A number of organisations offer education and training in many aspects of work within the tourist industry.

CASE STUDY

A local entrepreneur and his wife are planning to start a small hotel business in the Caribbean. They are hoping to appeal particularly to the ecotourist who wishes to experience some of the natural beauty in the area and who is keen on seeing some of the flora and fauna found in these special habitats. The couple have seen an existing hotel, set in its own grounds, which they believe would be suitable for their needs, although it will need some modernising and upgrading of facilities. When completed, they will offer comfortable accommodation, cooked meals and some planned excursions and activities.

Questions

1 Make a list of the jobs that will be created through the period in which the hotel is being prepared for new customers.

2 Make another list of the jobs that might be available when the new hotel opens.

3 Name a training institute in your country that might prepare people to work for this new business.

At the end of this topic you will be able to:

- assess the impact of the tourism industry on the physical environment of the Commonwealth Caribbean.

The natural environment of the Caribbean contains many beautiful **natural resources** including landscapes, beaches and marine life that form the basis for attracting tourists to the region. At the same time, there is a danger that elements of the tourist industry can cause disruption and damage to the very same environment. It is important to know that tourism activities can damage the environment and to think how the industry can work to minimise such damage, and how some tourist products can be developed that will actually assist in maintaining and preserving the environment.

Number of visitors

When considering the environmental impact of tourism, an important factor to take into account is the actual number of visitors who arrive each year, compared to the resident population. Table 9.5.1 shows the number of cruise passengers and stopover visitors compared to the permanent population of the host countries. This raises particular questions regarding, among other issues, accommodation, food supplies, water supply, waste generation, the impact on the natural environment and the changes to the environment made to accommodate the tourists.

These questions address the issues of capacity. How many people can a small island nation cater for and accommodate given a small physical size, small size of population, limited space and limited resources?

Country	Population (2009)	Stop-over tourist arrivals (2010)	Cruise passengers (2010)
Antigua and Barbuda	87,884	231,305	557,635
Barbados	276,302	532,180	664,747
Grenada	108,419	106,156	333,556
Jamaica	2,705,800	1,921,678	909,619
St Lucia	166,522	305,937	670,043
St Vincent and the Grenadines	103,869	72,478	110,955
Trinidad and Tobago	1,317,714	158,117 (Jan–May)	71,802 (Jan–May)

Sources: Population figures: July 2011 estimates from The World Factbook *(except Barbados: Barbados Statistical Service (BSS) Estimate at end of 2010; Jamaica: Statistical Institute of Jamaica 2010; St Lucia: Census 2010; Trinidad: Central Statistics Office 2010); Tourist figures: Caribbean Tourism Organization, June 2011 www.onecaribbean.org*

Table 9.5.1 Number of cruise passengers and stopover visitors compared to the permanent population of the Caribbean host countries

Use of natural resources

The natural resources of Caribbean countries include land, forests, beaches, sea, landscapes, wetlands, and other natural features. Each of these can be utilised as part of a tourism product. Each can also be misused, overused or abused, as the examples in Table 9.5.2 show.

Resources	Use	Examples of misuse, overuse or abuse
Forest	Nature tours (e.g. bird-watching), products for souvenirs	Rare species of flora and fauna removed by tourists Removal of trees to create nature trails, which may lead to soil erosion
Land	Nature tours (e.g. hiking), construction of resorts and hotels, golf courses	Removal of land from agricultural use can disrupt ecosystems Possibility that heavy use of chemicals in preparation and maintenance of golf courses pollutes soil and water supply Increase in solid waste production increases requirement for land-fill sites
Beaches and wetlands	Locations for hotels and resort areas, recreation and leisure, sand mining for construction of hotels	Hotel construction too close to beaches and on wetlands can increase risks of beach erosion and loss of natural flood defences Dumping of litter damages the beach environment Sand mining can lead to beach erosion Dredging to create harbours disrupts natural ecosystems Use of wetlands removes important natural habitats
Sea	Marine-based sports, desalinated water to supplement potable water supplies, dumping area for hotel sewage	Divers and swimmers breaking off coral Anchors damaging coral reef Hotels and pleasure craft dumping waste and sewage, polluting water and disrupting ecosystems Cruise ships washing out tanks at sea causing pollution
Landscapes and natural features	Nature tours	Hotel and resort construction reduces aesthetic appeal of views Road and path construction removes natural vegetation, increases run-off and likelihood of soil erosion

Table 9.5.2 The impact of tourism on natural resources

The disposal of solid waste is a serious problem around the world and landfill sites are a common solution. Tourism generates significant amounts of additional waste and solutions need to be developed to minimise the negative impact on the environment.

At the end of this topic you will
be able to:

- assess the impact of the
  tourism industry on the
  physical environment of the
  Commonwealth Caribbean.

The Caroni Lagoon National Park in Trinidad
is a haven for many wildlife species and
a major attraction for tourists. Could you
prepare an argument that supports the idea
that tourism can actually help to preserve
areas such as this?

ACTIVITY

1 Carry out some research into
  the changes in environmental
  laws in your country over the
  last 30 years, and assess the
  impact these will have had
  on the tourism industry.

2 Suggest some further
  strategies to assist the
  tourist industry to become
  more sustainable and
  environmentally friendly in
  the future.

Impact of tourism

Resort development

Table 9.5.2 (see page 165) shows how land is used to provide tourist
facilities such as hotels and resorts. The resort developers obviously
want to place their facilities in or near areas of natural beauty since this
is what attracts tourists. The development will destroy some of that
natural resource and **sustainable development** relies on achieving a
balance between construction and **conservation**.

Changes in ecology

The tourism industry involves activities that can have long-lasting
and even permanent effects on a country's ecological systems. The
most obvious impact is where land is developed. All natural areas are
habitats supporting a unique range of flora and fauna and the loss
of any of these has an impact on the local ecology. The cases causing
greatest concern in this regard are perhaps those involving wetlands.

The other extremely important and also extremely sensitive
environment is the coral reef. These can be damaged directly by
divers removing pieces for souvenirs but they are also badly affected
by even slight changes to the condition of the seawater. There are
direct consequences from the tourist industry, such as the dumping of
sewage, and indirect consequences when, for example, road and resort
construction results in tree removal, increased run-off and soil erosion.
The soil that washes into the sea as a result of this changes the sunlight
levels, which kills off the algae on which the coral depend.

Tourism and conservation

The tourism industry can respond to the environmental challenges in
two ways. Firstly, it can seek to educate current and future operators,
and their customers, regarding environmental issues. Secondly, it can
develop and promote tourism products that are less damaging or
even beneficial to the environment.

Damage limitation

Tourism organisations may help to reduce some of the damage to the
environment resulting from tourism activities by:

- lobbying government to construct sewage treatment plants so that
  hotels may dispose of their sewage in an environmentally safe way
- encouraging hoteliers to dispose of their sewage safely, for example
  by connecting to the sewage system
- lobbying government to enact and enforce legislation to limit sand
  mining from beaches, and illegal mining and dumping activities
- working with other organisations in establishing protected marine
  areas and land-based conservation areas

- ensuring that all development only follows environmental impact assessments
- employing good practice in terms of sustainable construction.

Ecotourism

Nature/ecotourism products recognise the appeal of the natural environment for some tourists. The logical extension of this is to understand that these natural environments need to be conserved if such tourists are going to continue to be attracted. Nature tourism/ecotourism encourages:

- the protection of terrestrial and marine flora and fauna
- the development and extension of marine parks, national parks and botanical gardens
- the development of forest reserves.

The importance of a healthy natural environment to tourism

A healthy natural environment is important to tourism because:

- clean beaches appeal to tourists
- undisturbed forest habitats encourage the sustainability of ecosystems which attract ecotourists
- healthy wetlands protect the marine environment, by reducing outflow of soil and debris, and coastal areas, by providing flood protection
- wetlands are important habitats for many species of flora and fauna which attract tourists
- coral reefs are a major tourist attraction.

EXAM TIP

In making an assessment of the impact of tourism on the natural environment, you will need to be aware of these different impacts and also be able to suggest strategies for future sustainable developments.

CASE STUDY

The Leeward Resort is at the heart of a controversy concerning damage caused to the natural environment during preparations for a deep-bed marina. In order to accommodate large, luxury yachts, a channel was dredged in Princess Alexandra National Park and the spoils were dumped on Mangrove Cay Shoal to create a 100-acre artificial island. Protestors say that incalculable damage has been done to coral reefs, grass flats, marine ecosystems and the general environment. Local businesses are facing losses, such as a conch farm and local scuba diving and snorkelling industries, due to the damage to the coral reef, which will not recover for many decades.

Questions

1 What strategies are in place to protect the natural environment in your country?

2 Are there any circumstances where the loss of, or damage to, natural environments as a result of resort development is justified?

3 Is it possible to achieve a balance between resort development and nature conservation? If so, how can this be done?

KEY POINTS

1 Resorts are often located near areas of natural beauty which can be easily damaged or destroyed.

2 Insensitive development can damage natural habitats and ecosystems.

3 The tourist industry can be developed responsibly, sometimes with government assistance.

4 Ecotourism can help to promote care and conservation of the natural environment.

5 A healthy natural environment in the Caribbean is important for tourism because the features of the natural world are one of the main reasons for tourists visiting the region.

The sociocultural impact of tourism 1

At the end of this topic you will be able to:

• assess the impact of tourism on the sociocultural environment in the Commonwealth Caribbean.

Oistins is a major fishing community in the parish of Christ Church, Barbados. Every Friday and Saturday night, there is a 'fish-fry' where hundreds of locals and visitors gather to enjoy fresh fish suppers and live musical entertainment.

Tourism brings together people of different nationalities and cultures. It provides the opportunity for visitors and locals to interact and to learn about each other's cultures, which can lead to an exchange or to a clash.

Visitors' perception of Caribbean societies

Visitors have a perception of Caribbean societies before they even arrive in the region. This perception is gained from reading tourist brochures and other material that promotes the area as a tourist destination. Promotional material is designed to create a favourable impression. Potential visitors also have access to material in the form of reports in the mass media and material on the internet which may not always present the region in a favourable light. Some visitors might interact with members of African-Caribbean communities in their home country. They can also have feedback from previous visitors. There are many websites that allow for people to review their vacations, and they are able to comment on all aspects, including the standard of accommodation, the degree of service, the quality of food, the sights to be seen and the places of interest. They can also comment on how far they were made to feel welcome, safe and secure.

One potential visitor might think of Caribbean societies as small, safe, friendly and uncomplicated. Another might think that they are undeveloped, unsafe or unfriendly. It is the role of those promoting tourism to foster the ideas of safety and friendliness. It is the role of citizens to ensure this is reflected in reality.

Influencing a visitor's perception

A tourist board may seek to influence a visitor's perception during their stay by:

• educating tourism workers on the need to display high standards of service and behaviour at all times
• promoting local Caribbean culture by sponsoring cultural shows to inform visitors
• providing for cultural exchange
• encouraging visits to rural areas
• encouraging high levels of security
• encouraging fair pricing of tourism services.

Opportunities for visitors to meet Caribbean people

Visitors and local residents can meet in a number of circumstances and places including:

• public beaches
• festivals and cultural shows
• sporting events

Suggest to a tourist board three strategies they could use to promote positive relationships between residents and visitors.

- entertainment centres
- hotels, restaurants and bars
- shopping malls
- community tourism holidays.

Relationships

Tourism is a service industry and one that very much relies on personal service and the relationships between those who are providing and receiving the service. There is a degree to which the relationship between tourists and other citizens, beyond those working in the tourist industry, is also important. In other words, tourists want to feel welcome.

Tension and conflict might arise between some citizens and some tourists if:

- residents perceive visitors as enjoying privileges that some residents are not allowed to enjoy in their own country, for example access to some beaches
- residents see visitors as wealthy and therefore exploit or even rob them
- residents offer poor service or are disrespectful
- visitors show a lack of understanding or respect for local culture
- visitors show a lack of respect for residents
- visitors do not engage with a local community but remain inside an all-inclusive resort
- returning nationals annoy residents by criticising their native country and comparing it negatively to their adopted country.

Two-way cultural exchange

Tourism offers people the chance to experience a cultural exchange. This can happen for tourists by attending festivals, especially perhaps local festivals that showcase 'the real culture' of their location. The opportunity to meet together also gives residents of the Caribbean the chance to find out about the cultures of the visitors' countries.

Influence of lifestyles, language and dress

Mass tourism can affect the way in which residents adapt their lifestyle, language and even their dress. For example, residents may change their language to suit tourists' needs.

KEY POINTS

1 Tourism brings together people from different cultures.

2 Tourism relies on good relationships between visitors and residents.

3 Residents can have different attitudes towards tourism, depending on the benefits they perceive and the fairness of treatment between visitors and residents.

4 Tourism can be used to revitalise local creativity in visual and performing arts and crafts.

EXAM TIP

You should be familiar with the ways in which visitors from outside the Caribbean might affect the lifestyle of Caribbean citizens.

The sociocultural impact of tourism 2

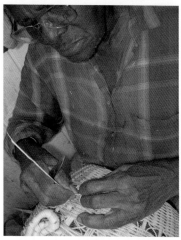

Traditional craft skills are preserved through the work of artisans throughout the region and celebrated at the annual Caribbean Arts and Crafts Festival

Attitudes to tourism

Citizens' attitudes to tourism can vary widely and they are influenced by a number of factors.

Perception of benefits of tourism

Some people are enthusiastic about tourism because it has stimulated the modernisation of their country and brought in new technologies and new infrastructure, often supported by government funding. Improved facilities are not only directly related to the tourist industry, such as airports or harbours. Upgraded roads, modern health facilities and new telecommunications systems help to encourage tourism but also benefit the country as a whole.

People working directly in tourism are likely to be fairly enthusiastic about it. However, tourism can be an 'enclave industry', which means it does not have very strong economical links with the rest of the economy. If economic benefits are not seen by the majority of the population, people may have a negative or indifferent attitude as a result.

Relationships between tourists and visitors

Tourism presents the opportunity for visitors to meet Caribbean people and for a cultural exchange to take place. A friendly and open attitude between citizens and visitors will help each group to form a good impression of the other. There is also the possibility for a two-way cultural exchange between the citizen and the visitor, with each one finding out about the other.

Since many tourists are from developed countries, some of the lifestyle, dress and **values** they present may influence local citizens, although much of this is evident in the foreign media that Caribbean citizens can access on a daily basis.

Artistic expression and national culture

Many people travel in order to experience and learn about other people's cultures. The main aspects of culture that are a feature of tourism are the creative and performing arts and local crafts.

Revitalisation of local arts and crafts

Craftspeople can use their work to express ideas, feelings, beliefs and true creativity and this may revitalise local arts and crafts. There is a temptation to water this down and to produce work that is felt will be popular with tourists.

Commercialisation of culture

Some people feel that it is important that if serious aspects of local culture are being presented to tourists, this should not be done simply for entertainment purposes. Festivals do act as tourist attractions but they should be a true representation of local culture rather than simply a tourist-friendly version.

The effects of tourism on land ownership, land use, natural beauty and the use of beaches

There can be a number of negative effects regarding land ownership and land use.

Sometimes residents are dislocated when their land, which may have been used for agricultural or residential purposes, is acquired by government for tourism developments such as airports, roads and resorts. The lack of land-use policies or the non-enforcement of these can lead to prime agricultural land being developed for tourist facilities.

Laws regarding alien land ownership make it possible for foreigners to buy land for tourism development or speculation. Foreigners are able to buy the best, beachfront properties at very high prices. This pushes up prices and makes it difficult for local people to own land.

Beachfront development stops residents from being able to enjoy these ocean views. Some hoteliers are able to deny residents access to beaches, retaining them for the exclusive use of their tourist guests.

Resort and hotel development on hillsides and elevated areas can reduce the aesthetic value of these landscapes.

Governments' tourism policies

Tourism provides the incentive and the means for governments to undertake large-scale infrastructure improvements. However, if government policies produce results that can be perceived as being mainly for the benefit of tourists rather than the local population, residents may have a negative attitude towards the industry.

Access to beaches is an area that can cause some controversy. The governments of some countries have insisted that all beaches should have unrestricted access. Other governments have allowed resort owners to own beaches and to restrict access to tourists staying in their resort. Although this allows the operator to cater for the type of client who prefers private beaches, it does mean that local residents can feel resentful about not being able to visit a part of their own country.

The argument that private beaches enhance security has been extended in some cases to restricting access for local residents to a hotel's bars and restaurant.

ACTIVITY

Consider the effect tourism has had on the sociocultural environment in your country.

- Identify some examples of where tourism has had a negative effect, for example where a hotel or resort development has spoiled a landscape or taken prime land out of agricultural use.
- Identify examples of where tourism may have had a positive effect, for example in revitalising a local craft or enabling local people to celebrate aspects of traditional culture.

KEY POINTS

1 Attitudes to tourism differ among local residents.

2 Some residents see that tourism has provided income that allows for the economic development of their country.

3 Some residents feel that the tourist industries receive too much of the financial benefit from tourism, with not enough going to the local population.

4 Tourists' attitudes to local residents have an influence on how they are perceived by local residents.

5 Tourism can help to maintain the viability of local traditional arts and crafts industries.

6 It is important to maintain the integrity of local arts and crafts when they are presented for tourist consumption.

7 Tourism can have negative effects on issues surrounding land ownership and land use.

8 Government policies should seek to balance the benefits to the tourist industry and the local populations.

Government policies and the development of tourism

The private sector and the public sector

The **private sector** comprises all the businesses and services that are owned and run by individuals or private companies. The **public sector** includes the businesses and services operated by the government. Tourism operates as a partnership because the public sector and private sector both have different roles and responsibilities, which sometimes overlap. The public sector will invest because the tourism industry produces foreign exchange earnings that can be spent by the government on economic development and social improvement for the maximum benefit of its citizens.

Public sector

The public sector is involved in marketing and promotion, infrastructure, training the workforce, environmental protection, peace and security, providing a favourable investment climate and managing attractions.

Private sector

The private sector is involved in accommodation, attractions, amenities, transportation, and marketing and promotion.

Government policies and tourism

Meeting infrastructure requirements

The tourist industry requires investment in large-scale infrastructure projects such as the construction of airports, berthing facilities, cruise ship terminals, medical facilities, water supply systems and sewage disposal systems. Other utilities, such as electricity, also need to be provided. Governments are responsible for obtaining funding, from either local or international sources.

Providing a well-trained workforce

The tourism industry requires a well-trained workforce so that tourists have the best experience during their stay. This will encourage them to return or to recommend the destination to friends and acquaintances. To help achieve this, governments establish training institutions to train new workers for employment at all levels and in all areas of the industry. Governments may also provide scholarships for students who need to obtain training that is not available locally.

Addressing environmental concerns

Tourism has serious consequences for the natural environment. Construction of tourist facilities requires land and can destroy agricultural land and natural areas. The large number of tourists also means that large amounts of solid waste and human waste are produced.

The Deep Water Harbour in Bridgetown, Barbados, is an example of large-scale infrastructure necessary for tourism in the Caribbean

Governments respond by:

- making regulations and passing legislation to reduce pollution in all its forms
- creating legal protection for coral reefs, nature reserves and other threatened environments
- providing beach patrols
- providing landfill sites and sewage treatment plants
- providing tax and other incentives to promote recycling
- enforcing existing penalties for illegal dumping
- encouraging tree preservation.

Addressing social problems

Tourists are more likely to visit a destination if they feel that it is a safe and secure place. To help create this, governments provide a well-trained police force that will protect life and property, prevent crime and violence, preserve peace and maintain order. Legislation can also be passed to protect visitors from crime and harassment.

Creating a favourable investment climate

Tourism requires investment and individuals and businesses are more likely to invest if there is a favourable investment climate. To help to create such a climate, a government needs to ensure that there is political stability, a stable economy offering reasonable returns on investments, a stable currency and financial incentives.

Providing an overseas marketing and promotional presence in key markets

Although private sector businesses are responsible for some of their own marketing and promotion, governments can also establish tourist ministries to oversee the industry as a whole and tourist offices in key markets. Funds will be made available for staff and for advertising and promotion of the destination, including promotional tours to targeted markets.

KEY POINTS

Governments support tourism by meeting infrastructure needs, providing training establishments, addressing social and environmental issues that impact on tourism, creating conditions favourable to investors and promoting and marketing the destination.

CASE STUDY

Governments can offer a range of financial incentives to investors in the tourist industry. For example they offer:

- tax holidays
- guaranteed repatriation of dividends
- relief from import duties for goods imported for the tourism industry
- low interest loans from government development banks or specially created development funds
- accelerated depreciation of plant and equipment.

Questions

1 Explain some of the benefits these incentives offer to potential investors and why this might be beneficial to a country's economy.

2 Say which of these incentives might mean that a government could lose revenue.

3 Suggest why a government might pursue a policy that appears to mean they are losing out on short-term income.

How local, regional and international agencies develop tourism

The national structure of the tourism industry

The structure of the tourism industry at national level includes:

• a ministry of tourism
• a tourist board/department/bureau
• private national organisations, such as the Barbados Hotel and Tourism Association or the Jamaica Hotel and Tourist Association.

The role of national tourism organisations

A major activity in the tourism industry is promotion. This involves marketing the destination to appropriate markets and is a primary role of a country's tourist board. The tourist board will direct its marketing towards potential tourists, travel agents, tour operators and travel writers.

A **travel agent** is a person or business that is qualified to arrange and sell tours, cruises, transportation, accommodation, meals, sightseeing and all other travel services.

A **tour operator** is responsible for arranging tour packages. The operator contracts with hotels, ground transportation companies, owners of attractions and other ancillary services to put together the ingredients for a package tour.

The Ministry of Tourism

This ministry determines national tourism policies and coordinates the work of the government's tourism agencies.

The tourist board

The tourist board has a number of functions.

• It markets and promotes the country as a preferred destination by:
  – introducing tourism products to foreign tour operators, and to regional and foreign travel agents
  – staging exhibitions, trade shows and trade fairs
  – advertising the unique features of a country's tourism product.
• It ensures accessibility to the region by:
  – securing and maintaining adequate airline services
  – creating and maintaining business with cruise companies.
• It monitors the performance of the industry by:
  – collecting statistics on visitor arrivals and expenditure
  – making comparative analyses of these statistics regionally and internationally
  – communicating its research findings to policymakers, financiers and local operators in the tourism industry.
• It seeks to create support for the industry among local communities by:
  – educating residents about the contribution of tourism to the economy

The first Valley Street Festival in Anguilla was an event organised by a partnership of the Anguilla Tourist Board and the Department of Youth and Culture. It was seen to be a vehicle for showcasing the various aspects of local cultural heritage. How might this kind of event both stimulate cultural sustainability and also help to promote the country as a tourist destination?

- informing local people of the employment opportunities available
- informing local people of their role in successful tourism.
- A tourist board is also the main link between the government and the industry.

Tourism investment or product development agency

This agency would:

- plan, develop and improve tourism products
- educate and train tourism workers
- participate in joint ventures with the private sector.

Hotel associations

Hotel associations work on behalf of hotel operators. They offer guest-related services such as staff training to members and also engage in lobbying governments to offer assistance to operators.

Hotel associations will also be engaged in promotional activities.

The role of regional tourism organisations

Caribbean Tourism Organization

The Caribbean Tourism Organization:

- monitors the industry's performance in the region
- communicates information about its findings to policymakers
- collaborates with other regional tourism organisations
- provides education and training for tourism workers
- promotes public awareness of the industry
- encourages member countries to promote the sustainable development of tourism.

Caribbean Hotel and Tourism Association

This is a federation of national hotel associations that:

- markets the region's hotels and attractions
- promotes environmental sustainability by setting environmental standards for hotels
- provides hospitality training for its members.

Hospitality training institutions

The institutions that provide training in hospitality and tourism are faculties of universities and colleges, and also facilities established by some sections within the industry itself.

The role of donor organisations

The Caribbean Development Bank (CDB) provides direct loans with long 'grace' and repayment periods for medium and large tourism projects and lines of credit to other banks for lending to borrowers of smaller amounts.

Grants and 'soft loans' come from:

- the European Union via the European Investment Bank
- the Organization of American States
- the Canadian International Development Agency.

Challenges facing the tourism industry

Cruise ship tourism is well established within the Caribbean but can be quite controversial, with many people feeling that the economic benefits do not spread to a wide enough section of the population of the countries visited

Security of funding

The commercial sector, which supplies tourism needs, significant investment in order to develop products, create new facilities, and modernise and upgrade existing facilities.

The public sector will play a large part in funding major infrastructure developments and improvements.

Marketing

Marketing extensively in established and potential markets is very important but it requires high levels of spending – some governments, tourism organisations and individual hotel operators do not have the necessary funds.

Research

A vital part of this research is establishing the tourists' needs, wants and tastes so that products, facilities and services respond to any changes.

Shortage of trained workforce and inadequate training

A successful tourism industry relies on a skilled and qualified workforce but there are shortages of suitable personnel in certain sections. This might result in some hotel owners having to recruit from overseas.

Lack of provision of hospitality training facilities can mean that students have to train away from home. A shortage of suitable trainers means that trainers must be brought in from abroad or students again have to travel to foreign institutions.

Water supply and infrastructure

An adequate supply of potable water is a major issue for the tourism industry. The large numbers of visitors who arrive each year outnumber the resident populations of most countries in the Commonwealth Caribbean.

Providing sufficient quantities of water can be challenging and expensive, and needs to be balanced with the requirements of the natural environment.

The water supply needs to be reliable and protected against problems arising from natural disasters such as hurricanes. Countries need to invest in such things as storage tanks and water purification systems.

Other elements of a country's electricity, transport and health infrastructure also need to meet the standards expected by tourists.

Global terrorism

The existence of global terrorism deters some people from travelling because they feel unsafe, while others may be put off by the delays caused by security checks.

Countries in the Caribbean rely very heavily on tourism due to its contribution to their **gross domestic product (GDP)** and so any downturn in tourism numbers will have a significant effect on existing businesses and on the possibilities for expansion.

Lack of direct air access

Some Caribbean islands lack direct air access from their major tourist-generating markets because there are no scheduled carriers servicing the route or the airports are not large enough to accommodate large, international aircraft.

Emerging destinations

Tourists are always able to consider a wide range of options for their travel. The Caribbean faces challenges from emerging destinations that:

• can offer similar experiences at competitive prices
• are nearer the traditional markets of the United States and Europe.

Tourists are looking at value for money and there are those who are conscious of the pressure to reduce long-haul flights because of the alleged impact on climate change.

The Caribbean also has emerging destinations within the region, where islands other than those with established histories of tourism are entering the market. The challenge here is to ensure that these places are able to benefit from the overall tourism market without having a negative effect on the economies of those countries already engaged in tourism.

Cruise ship policies

Port taxes and fees are charged by governments and port authorities to cruise operators to cover costs of docking and use of port facilities. Some governments also charge a head tax per passenger, which is used to maintain and improve port services and infrastructure. All these costs are passed on to the passengers. If one government's charges are higher than another's, a cruise ship operator may shift their business to a cheaper destination. To avoid this, governments need to agree on uniform taxes and fees.

KEY POINTS

1 Tourism relies on secure funding, thorough market research and effective marketing.

2 Tourism faces challenges due to:
   • a lack of trained staff
   • difficulty in providing adequate supplies of potable water
   • undeveloped infrastructure
   • global terrorism
   • limited direct air access
   • competition from emerging destinations.

3 Governments need to present a unified approach to fees and taxes regarding cruise ships.

CASE STUDY

Belize experienced a decline in cruise ship tourism during the 1990s, due in part to high taxes and limited development of infrastructure and services. The industry revived and passenger numbers increased. This was met with mixed feelings, but the government decided that cruise tourism was an important component of the tourism industry and set about developing suitable policies. A Cruise Tourism Advisory Committee was established comprising the director of product development, Belize Tourist Board and representatives from a cross-section of the cruise tourism industry and related government ministries and agencies.

Questions

1 What challenges did the Cruise Tourism Advisory Committee in Belize need to address?

2 What environmental objections might people have had to the development of cruise tourism?

3 What are the factors affecting cruise tourism in your country?

Using tourism to promote regional integration

At the end of this topic you will be able to:

- describe ways in which tourism can be used to promote regional integration.

Marketing the Caribbean as a single destination

Marketing the Caribbean as a single destination involves creating a 'brand' for the region as a whole, which has traditionally been based on the fact that it offers sun, sea and sand.

Cooperation between individuals, businesses and governments as well as between those in a particular sector within the industry, for example through the Caribbean Hotel and Tourism Association, means that the prohibitive costs are widespread marketing can be shared. The Caribbean Tourism Organization also works in this regard.

Events such as the Reggae Sumfest in Jamaica above and the St Lucia Jazz Festival draw international visitors but also appeal to fans from across the region

Recognition of the tourism products packaged by each Caribbean country

Marketing the Caribbean as a single destination has benefits for the region as a whole, but the issue still exists that not all Caribbean nations will be able to benefit directly. For example, those with airports that cannot accommodate direct international flights may attract fewer tourists.

Effectively, the different Caribbean countries are in competition with one another for a share of the overall tourist market. The challenge is to enable each one to gain access to that share and to somehow be able to compete on a level playing field.

As traditional mass-tourism products face challenges from emerging destinations and increasingly selective consumers, the need to develop new tourism products has emerged. This has produced such things as nature and ecotourism and more tourism based on a particular country's culture and heritage.

Common economic and marketing policies

The Common Single Market and Economy (CSME) calls for the free movement of people, services and capital. In respect of tourism, this will mean the free movement of:

- trained and skilled tourism professionals and of self-employed people travelling to seek work in different countries
- tourism services, which could be provided in any country by any CARICOM resident or business. Nationals from any member state would be able to purchase land, buildings or other property without discrimination
- capital, which will mean that any national from a member state will be allowed to invest in any other member state, or a company in any member states, or to establish a new company in any member state.

Creating links within the Caribbean

Economic links

These involve the free movement of goods, services, capital and skilled and trained labour.

Functional links

These links can be achieved by standardising operational processes and taxation and other forms of raising revenue.

Enterprise and tourism development

Intra-regional tourism involves developing tourist products that appeal to residents of the region who may be encouraged to visit other countries in the Caribbean. Such tourism may be developed through promoting a particular country's culture and heritage and also through events and festivals that celebrate particular aspects of Caribbean culture.

Community links

Community links occur particularly when tourists are encouraged to stay in family-type accommodation, such as bed and breakfasts. Regional associations would allow for mutual support and greater development for this form of tourism.

Environmental links

The benefits of having regional agencies with a responsibility to monitor and maintain the region's natural environment also apply to consideration of the environmental impact of tourism.

Aviation hubs

Aviation will play an important part in an integrated Caribbean tourist destination. Intra-regional flight services are important for moving goods and people around the Caribbean, but enhanced interconnections will help tourists to consider visiting more than one country during their stay. This could also remove some of the difficulties faced by those countries whose airport facilities are not of a sufficient size to accommodate large international planes. Good links between those countries with such facilities and their smaller neighbours will help the smaller nations make the most of their potential international and intra-regional tourist trade.

EXAM TIP

Think of reasons why cooperation between regional tourist destinations will assist in the growth of the industry.

KEY POINTS

1 The Caribbean region can be marketed as a single destination while recognising the particular attractions of individual countries.

2 CARICOM objectives of free movement of labour, goods, services and capital and the development of other links will assist in the regional development of tourism.

3 Improved intra-regional connections will encourage tourists to visit more than one country in the region and promote intra-regional travel by Caribbean residents.

CASE STUDY

According to its website, the Caribbean Hotel & Tourism Association believes that 'there is still insufficient awareness and understanding of the tourism industry's contribution to Caribbean countries – how it permeates the economy as well as the overall fabric of Caribbean societies'. The association works to 'sensitise public officials, the communities, and the industry itself, about its role and contribution as a foremost export sector – paving the way for a climate conducive to the sustainable development of tourism in the Caribbean'.

Question

Prepare a presentation for a meeting of public officials that seeks to increase awareness and understanding of the tourism industry's contribution to your country and the possibilities offered for sustainable development of tourism in the Caribbean.

9.13 Communications technologies and tourism

LEARNING OUTCOMES

At the end of this topic you will be able to:

- describe how communications technology impacts on the tourism industry in the Caribbean.

Information and communications technologies have had significant impacts on the tourism industry. They are used by providers to pass on information about their products and services, to collect information about their potential markets, and to detect development and trends in consumer tastes.

Due to high set-up costs and the need for highly trained specialists, the benefits of these new technologies may initially have been most accessible to larger operators. As the technologies have become more familiar and equipment more affordable, the smaller and medium-sized operators can also exploit the possibilities offered by information technology. For example, many individual hotels can set up and maintain a website which gives access to information in various forms to anyone with internet access, wherever they may be in the world.

Advertising

The tourism industry relies on providers being able to pass on high-quality and current information to their prospective customers and consumers. Tourism advertising in the Caribbean operates at various levels:

- regionally – through such organisations as the Caribbean Tourism Organization
- nationally – through such agencies as tourist boards
- locally – through towns and individual hotels, restaurant and tourist attractions.

At all these levels, advertisers can make use of new technologies, such as the internet and cell phones.

The internet allows people to research and book holidays from any location where there is internet access

Information gathering

All those involved in the tourist industry rely on having high-quality information, ranging from how consumer tastes are changing to actual numbers of visitors. The information can be used for a number of different purposes. For example, figures that indicate trends in visitor numbers and types of tourist can help to determine where best to direct investment. Analysing consumer tastes allows people to develop tourism products that will cater to these particular demands.

Visitor numbers can be collected by monitoring the arrivals of tourists at airports and seaports and is quite straightforward. Collecting information about tourists' tastes is more complicated and usually requires either direct responses to questionnaires or an analysis of types of holiday taken around the world.

The impact of the internet

The internet has made a significant difference to the way in which people research their vacations, how they make choices and how they book. An individual is able to:

- view holiday options from around the world from any location where there is internet access
- choose locations, modes of transport, operators, accommodation and other attractions
- tailor a holiday to suit his or her own very specific requirements
- book travel and accommodation.

Many more operators are able to advertise their services to a wider audience but the information presented must be accurate and constantly updated.

The search engines of the internet assist consumers as they research aspects of their holiday such as accommodation. In some cases, they are able to specify ranges of quality or price. In other cases, if they find one type of accommodation, the search engine will be able to find other examples of a similar kind.

Being able to book travel and accommodation over the internet is very convenient and therefore very appealing. Many people are happy with the security arrangements when paying with a credit or debit card over the internet and paying ahead in this way avoids the need to carry cheques or cash.

The ability to arrange and book a holiday over the internet will have had an effect on the businesses of travel agents who formerly arranged holidays.

E-ticketing

E-ticketing refers to the ability to book and pay for travel over the internet. This can avoid the need for paper tickets completely and, in the case of air travel, allow people to check-in either online or at an automatic kiosk at the airport, and so avoid lengthy queues at the airport.

Feedback

The tourism industry has to be responsive to consumer tastes, views and opinions. Customer feedback is therefore very valuable. This can be obtained by asking people to complete paper questionnaires when they are using the relevant facilities, but the internet allows for feedback to be given at any time and from any location.

ACTIVITY

Use the internet to research websites offering travel and accommodation to tourists. Look for ways in which smaller-scale operators are able to use the internet and how these are sometimes linked to countrywide and even regional sites.

KEY POINTS

1. The internet means consumers can research all aspects of a vacation from any location in the world.

2. Providers can make information available to a much wider audience.

3. Providers and tourism authorities can easily gather a wealth of information about visitor numbers, customer feedback and changing trends and tastes.

4. Booking online and the use of e-ticketing make travel less time-consuming and therefore more appealing.

C1 Communication

1 Explain some of the basic concepts of communication, the different modes of communication and how communication can break down, by answering the following questions.

  a State the four factors that are part of all successful communication.

  b Explain the main characteristics of verbal and non-verbal communication.

  c Explain the effectiveness of communications using cell phones and posters and say why each is appropriate in different circumstances. Give some examples of where both of these modes of communication are used.

  d Explain to a friend, who is experiencing difficulties with communicating with his or her parents, why a breakdown in communications may have happened and suggest some ways in which it could be restored.

2 The mass media is said to have a powerful influence today. Prepare a report that explains briefly what the term 'mass media' means and identify two modes of communication that form part of the mass media. Explain three ways in which the mass media might influence people and say how large amounts of foreign transmissions could influence sociocultural development in the Caribbean. Suggest some strategies that CARICOM governments and broadcasters could employ in order to promote the production and transmission of more locally produced programmes.

3 Write a report on how modern communications technology is being used in the development of the region. Describe three forms of electronic communication that are important in the region. Explain how each of these forms of communication is used and how each one can have a positive effect on the development of individual citizens and on organisations in the private and public sectors. Suggest one strategy to national governments that would allow the benefits of these new technologies to reach even more people and explain why you think your strategy would be successful.

C2 Consumer affairs

1 You have been asked to speak to a local community group about consumer awareness and consumer protection.

  a Prepare a list of five ways in which consumers can be exploited and five ways in which these forms of exploitation can be avoided.

  b Give a list of five consumer rights and five responsibilities.

  c Prepare a brief description of consumer groups and identify three benefits that can be obtained from these.

  d Discuss the role of different government departments in consumer protection.

2 The government of Country A is thinking about devaluing its currency.

  a Explain what the term 'devaluation' means in relation to other international currencies.

  b Outline some of the effects of devaluation on prices, employment and people's standard of living.

  c Describe some strategies that an individual consumer can take to offset some of the effects of devaluation.

  d Briefly describe a consumer cooperative and give two benefits that might be gained from forming such a group.

3 You have been asked by the government to write the text for a public information leaflet about the wise use of money in the home. Your text should give two examples of how money can be spent unnecessarily or wastefully and two examples of how it can be used wisely. You need to explain the benefits of saving and suggest two ways in which money can be made available in order to save it. You should also briefly discuss the availability of credit and the circumstances in which it is good to use it and when to avoid it.

C3 Tourism

1 You have been asked to write a newspaper article about the future development of tourism in the Caribbean.

   a Briefly describe the traditional tourism products of the region and explain why the industry needs to diversify its range of products.

   b Give three examples of new tourism products being developed in the region.

   c Explain the factors that exist in the Caribbean that attract visitors and those factors that may influence them to choose another destination.

   d Suggest two ways in which regional and national governments or agencies could assist local operators in their efforts to develop.

2 Identify the economic links between the tourism industry and the rest of the economy and suggest ways in which these could be made stronger.

3 Prepare a presentation for the tourist board to give to local hotel owners regarding the effects of tourism on the natural environment.

   a Identify three tourist-related activities that can harm the natural environment and explain the way in which this harm occurs.

   b Suggest two practices that the hotel owners can put in place that will help to ensure the health of the natural environment.

   c Briefly outline some ecotourism products that the hotel owners could promote and explain why these require a healthy natural environment and would assist in maintaining such an environment.

4 As a representative of the ministry of tourism, prepare an article explaining the significance of tourism to the country and the importance of harmonious relationships between citizens and tourists.

   a Explain briefly why there are different attitudes towards tourism and tourists among the citizens.

   b Outline some of the benefits that tourism brings to the country.

   c Suggest ways in which tourism can stimulate cultural areas such as arts and crafts.

   d Introduce two strategies that the ministry and tourist board will employ to promote positive relationships between residents and visitors.

Further practice questions and examples can be found on the accompanying CD.

Glossary

A

Alimony: payment due to one partner by the other by court order, following a divorce

Ambassadors: a diplomat, representing one sovereign or state in another country

Annulment: the legal ending of a marriage

Artisanal fishers: skilled fishermen who work individually or in small groups

Authoritarian: favouring obedience to authority over individual freedom; tyrannical

B

Balance of payments: an accounting record of all the financial transactions between one country and the rest of the world

Beneficiary: a person who is to receive an inheritance as indicated in the will of a deceased person

Bicameral: if the legislature or parliament of a country has two bodies

Bigamy: when someone marries a person when a previous marriage already exists and this is not within the law

Bilateral agreement: an agreement between two parties

Bilineal: where rights, duties and responsibilities follow both the mother's and father's lineage

Bill: a proposed law, under consideration by a legislature

Birth rate: the number of live births in a year per 1,000 people in a population

Black market: a system in which people illegally buy and sell goods, ignoring proper regulations

Brain drain: the loss of qualified and skilled personnel through emigration

Budget: a government's plan on how to raise and spend revenue

C

Cabinet: the policymaking arm of government, consisting of members of parliament appointed by the prime minister

Canvassing: to seek votes from the electorate, usually by visiting their homes or holding meetings in public

Censorship: removal of all or part of transmitted material on grounds of obscenity, sedition, etc.

Civil cases: cases brought to court by an individual, group or organisation against another but not prosecuted by the police

Civil servants: government staff responsible for implementing and administering government policies

Climate change: a long-term alteration to established weather patterns

Collateral: property put forward as security against a loan

Commercialise: to make commercial; to be able to derive a profit from something

Commodities: goods and services that can be bought and sold

Common market: the first stage towards a single market

Conservation: the safe and sustainable use of resources

Constituency: an area that contains the body of voters who elect a representative to parliament

Consumer: any individual, group or organisation that ultimately uses goods and services

Consumer durables: consumer goods that are intended to last for a number of years

Consumer goods: goods available directly to the consumer in the form in which they are intended to be used, for example bread, vegetables, shoes and televisions

Copyright: an exclusive right given to the producer of a creative work for a certain number of years

Credit: deferred payment of a debt, often used for a major purchase

Credit union: a financial cooperative, owned and controlled by its members, that provides credit facilities

Criminal cases: Cases brought to court by the police where it is believed that the law has been broken

D

Death rate: the number of deaths in a year per 1,000 people in a population

Debt burden: the debts a country has to repay

Democracy: where the government is chosen by the citizens in a general election that is free and fair

Democratic: run according to the will of all the people

Dependency ratio: the ratio of the number of dependent people in a society to the number of economically active people

Depopulation: a long-term reduction in numbers in a population

Devaluation: a decrease in value of one currency against another

Developed country: a country with a high level of economic development and standard of living

Developing country: a country moving from a state of low-level material wellbeing

Disposable income: that part of a person's income available after tax

Divorce: the process of legally ending a marriage

Dumping: a form of predatory pricing. The term is usually used when a foreign country seeks to sell subsidised goods into a local market at prices that the local producers are unable to compete with

E

Economic good: a good that commands a price

Economic leakage: when foreign exchange earnings from an industry return to individuals or companies overseas

Economic link: when the output of one industry becomes an input for another

Economies of scale: the cost advantages that can be gained by a business as it expands and unit costs of production are decreased

Electorate: all those persons eligible to vote in an election

Glossary

Emigration: people leaving a country to live elsewhere

Endogamy: to choose a partner from one's own ethnic group, tribe, religion, class, etc.

Environmental impact assessment: an assessment of the possible positive or negative impacts on the environment of a proposed project

Equality: a situation where things are equal between individuals or groups

Ethnic group: people with origins in the same part of the world who share a cultural heritage

Exchange rate: the rate at which one currency can be exchanged for another

Excursionist: a person who visits a place but sleeps away from the destination, for example on a cruise ship

Executive: having the function of executing, enacting laws, making agreements, etc.

Exogamy: to choose a partner who is not of one's own ethnic group, tribe, religion, class, etc.

Extractive industries: industries involved in taking material from the ground, for example mining and quarrying

Fertility rate: the average number of children born to each woman in a population during her lifetime

Fiscal: public revenue

Fiscal policy: government policy for managing public revenues

Floating voters: those voters not aligned to a particular party

Folkways: informal behaviours developed amongst a group of people over time

Food security: the ability of a population to feed itself

Fossil fuels: fuels such as coal and oil, created millions of years ago by the decomposition of buried organic matter

Franchise: a right to vote at a public election

Free goods: products, usually from nature that are useful and that are available in such large amounts that they have no economic value, for example air

Freedom of speech (or expression): freedom to express opinion within the law, without censorship

Generation gap: the different ideas and attitudes expressed by different generations that sometimes leads to lack of understanding or tolerance and difficulties in communication

Gerrymandering: unfairly manipulating the boundaries of a constituency in order to secure a disproportionate influence for a particular party

Global warming: the average rise in the temperature of the Earth's oceans and atmosphere

Globalisation: the process of countries coming together through communications, finance and commerce and a unification of the world's economic order

Greenhouse effect: when thermal radiation from the Earth's surface is absorbed by atmospheric gases and re-radiated, partly back towards the surface

Greenhouse gases: gases that absorb some thermal radiation from the Earth and re-radiate it back towards the surface

Gross domestic product (GDP): annual market value of all goods and services produced within a country, regardless of nationality of the producing and supplying companies

Gross national product (GNP): annual market value of all goods produced and services provided by a country's residents and enterprises, regardless of their geographical location

Host country: a country to which people are coming as tourists or visitors

Human resource: the strengths, creativity and mental abilities of a human population

Hung parliament: when no major political party has an absolute majority of seats in a parliament

Identity crisis: the point at which the conditions for being a particular or specified person are called into question

Immigration: people moving to live in a country from elsewhere

Incest: sexual intercourse between members of a family

Infant mortality rate: number of deaths of infants under one year of age for every 1,000 live births

Inflation: a sustained increase in the general price of goods and services

Infrastructure: permanent installations that support a larger whole or organisation

Inheritance: money or property that passes to a person's successors after their death

Intellectual property: the ownership of the ideas in a creator's mind that become creative or artistic works of visual or performance art

International currency: a currency in which many international transactions are carried out

International reserves: a country's stock of international currencies

Judicial: of or done by the courts of law

Justice of the peace: a lay magistrate, appointed to keep the peace and to mediate in some cases to avoid them going to court

Kinship: blood relationships within a family

Labour force: the number of people of working age within a population

Glossary

Laissez-faire: non-interference with individual actions

Legal separation: separation of a married couple by court order

Legislative: related to the enacting of laws

Libel: a false written report, published in order to damage a person's reputation

Life expectancy: the number of years a person of a given age can expect to live

Marginal seat: a constituency where a member of parliament only has a small minority and may therefore lose their seat in an election

Market: an economic structure that allows for transactions to take place

Marriage: the lawfully recognised union between a man and a woman

Mass media: forms of media used to communicate to large numbers of people

Matriarchal: where the mother or grandmother is the head or authority figure

Matrifocal: family patterns where the mother has responsibility

Matrilocal: when a couple go to live with the wife's parents

Matrilineal: where rights, duties and responsibilities follow the mother's lineage

Migration: people moving within a country or from one country to another

Monarch: sovereign or supreme ruler, with a title such as king, queen, emperor, etc.

Monetary policy: policies to control the supply of money in a country, with a view to managing inflation or economic growth

Monoculture: growing a single crop

Monogamy: where a person has only one husband or wife at one time

Mores: a form of 'norm' concerning serious matters and reflecting a society's moral values

Multilateral agreement: an agreement between a number of parties

Multinational corporation: an enterprise that manages production or delivers services in more than one country

Natural increase: when the number of births is greater than the number of deaths in a year

Natural resource: a resource from nature

Neolocal: when a couple establish their own residence

Net migration: the difference between immigration and emigration

Non-renewable resource: a resource of which there are finite supplies that will never be replaced

Norms: generally accepted unwritten rules that help to regulate behaviour within a society

Patriarchal: where the father or grandfather is the head or authority figure

Patrifocal: family patterns where the father has responsibility

Patrilineal: where rights, duties and responsibilities follow the father's lineage

Patrilocal: when a couple go to live with the husband's parents

Peer group: a group of people of a similar age, social status, experiences, interests and values

Peer pressure: the influence a peer group places on an individual to conform to the values and behaviour of the group

Per capita: literally meaning 'for each head' and used to mean 'for each person'

Petitioner: a person seeking a divorce

Plagiarism: to present another person's ideas or works as one's own

Political party: a political organisation that seeks to further political ideology, and to influence government policies by having party members elected to political

office and, ultimately, by forming a government

Pollution: materials that contaminate and degrade the environment

Polyandry: where a woman has more than one husband

Polygamy: where a person has more than one wife or husband at the same time

Polygyny: where a man has more than one wife

Population: the number of people living within a given area

Population census: an official count of a country's population

Population density: the degree of concentration of people living in a given area

Population distribution: the way in which a population is spread out

Portfolio: in parliament, the area of responsibility given to a minister

Predatory pricing: offering goods or services at a low level with a view to putting competitors out of a market or deterring new entrants into that market

Principle of collective responsibility: in government, where the whole cabinet takes responsibility for decisions made

Private sector: businesses and services operated by private individuals or companies

Producer goods: goods that are produced in order to make other goods, for example the component parts of a car

Propaganda: information transmitted in support of a particular idea, system or practice

Protectionist: an economic policy of restraining trade between nations in an attempt to reduce imports or to avoid foreign domination of a sector of the economy or the takeover of domestic companies

Psychological: of the mind

Public sector: businesses and services operated by government

Glossary

Public service: service provided by government departments for which everybody pays by means of taxation

Referendum: a chance for all eligible people to vote on a particular issue

Regionalism: a political ideology focusing on the interests of a particular region

Renewable resource: a resource that naturally replaces itself over a period of time

Resource: something that can be accessed, used and developed to satisfy wants and needs

Revenue: income, from any source

Roles: the duties associated with a person's status

Safe seat: in an election, a constituency where a sitting member of parliament has a large majority

Seat: in politics, a place in parliament

Securities: a financial instrument that has economic value, such as bonds, stocks or certificates

Sedition: agitation against the authority of a state

Self-esteem: having a favourable view of oneself; regarding oneself as valuable

Separation of powers: where legal, executive and judicial powers are given to different branches of government

Service: in economics, the non-material equivalent of a good; a task that can be performed and to which a monetary value can be assigned

Sibling: a brother or sister

Single market: a trade bloc with a free trade area and free movement of goods, services, labour and capital

Slander: a false spoken report, given with malicious intent in order to damage a person's reputation

Social institution: practices and customs that have become a socially accepted pattern of behaviour, for example, marriage

Socialisation: the process of teaching children and young people the customs and accepted behaviours of a society and nurturing attitudes that will help them to become beneficial contributors to society

Status: a social position occupied by an individual, for example father, teacher, doctor, etc.

Supplier: in economics, an individual or organisation that supplies goods or services

Supply country: the normal country of residence of tourists

Surrogate mother: a woman who gives birth to a baby on behalf of, or as a substitute for, another woman

Sustainable development: developing a country's economy, industries, infrastructure and services in a manner that means they will last over a long period of time without rapidly depleting the necessary resources

Thrift: careful and sparing use of money and other resources and materials

Tour operator: an individual or company that organises tourist package holidays

Trade liberalisation: trade policies that allow for trade across national boundaries without government interference

Trading bloc: institutions of a number of countries sharing economic and political aims, achieved through shared trading practices

Travel agent: a person or business qualified to arrange and sell tourism products

Underdeveloped country: a country not developed to its potential

Under-employment: employment that does not use skills and abilities to the full or that does not keep a person fully occupied

Unemployable: a person who is not suitable for employment

Unicameral: a parliament with only one house

Universal adult suffrage: where all competent adult persons have a right to vote

Urbanisation: the increase in the number of persons living in cities

Values: the ideas and principles that a group or society has concerning what is good or bad, right or wrong, desirable or undesirable, important or unimportant

Wealth disparity: the unequal distribution of wealth within a population

Will: a document that sets out how a person's property and wealth is to be distributed following their death

Acknowledgements

The author and the publisher would like to thank the following for permission to reproduce material:

Text

p19 United Nations Declaration on the Elimination of Violence against Women, General Assembly Resolution, December 1993 copyright © United Nations 2011

p53 Trends in Voter Turnout (1956–2003) in Barbados from www.caribbeanelections.com copyright © 2011 Knowledgewalk Institute

p123 Copyright © 2011 Caribbean Community (CARICOM)

p143 'Consumer Rights' from www.consumersinternational.org copyright © Consumers International 2011

p164 cruise passenger statistics 2009/2010 from www.onecaribbean.org copyright © Caribbean Tourism Organisation 2011

Photos

p2 Getty Images/Kin Images Inc.; p7 John Birdsall/Press Association Images; p9 Colin Babb; p13 Colin Babb; p17 Sino Pix/Rex Features; p19 Katherine James; p25 Photolibrary/Robert Harding; p26 Getty Images; p28 Shawn Banton; p30 Jamaica Environment Trust; p32 Jamaica Environment Trust; p34 2005 The Gleaner Co. Ltd; p39 Collin Reid/AP/Press Association Images; p40 Shirley Bahadur/AP/Press Association Images; p43 Office of the Parliament Republic of Trinidad and Tobago; p46 Shawn Banton; p51 Oliver Thornton; p52 Oliver Thornton; p54 AFP/Getty Images; p57 AP/Press Association Images; p58 Heidi Zech; p62 Travelshots/Alamy; p64 Shawn Banton; p67 2005 The Gleaner Co. Ltd; p69 iStockphoto; p45 Getty Images/Steve Dunwell; p72 John Cole/Science Photo Library; p74 James O'Connor; p76 iStockphoto; p79 Imagebroker/Alamy; p82 Shawn Banton; p84 2005 The Gleaner Co. Ltd; p86 Photolibrary/Eye Ubiquitous; p88 Norbert Wu/Minden Pictures/FLPA; p92 Photolibrary/Index Stock Imagery; p94 Getty Images; p96 CARICOM; p99 CARICOM; p100 Colin Babb; p102 Bernhard Edmaier/Science Photo Library; p106 Art Directors and Trip; p108 Oliver Thornton; p110 Israel Leal/AP/Press Association Images; p114 Sandy Marshall; p117 ITU; p120 Nelson Thornes; p122 Colin Babb; p124 Richard T. Nowitz/Corbis; p126 Barbados Tourist Board; p128 Fotolia; p130 Simon Belcher/Alamy; p132 Photolibrary/Joanne OBrien; p134 iStockphoto; p136 Fotolia; p139 Fiona Gartland; p140 Art Directors and Trip; p142 Getty Images/Jose Luis Pelaez Inc.; p146 Colin Babb; p148 Getty Images/Matthew Wakem; p150 Walter Bibikow/Age Fotostock/Photolibrary; p152 Colin Babb; p154 Sandy Marshall; p156 Barbados Tourist Board; p158 Photolibrary/Travel Shots; p160 Heidi Zech (top), Colin Babb (bottom); p162 Getty Images/Smith Collection; p165 Getty Images/Stephen Mallon; p166 Photolibrary/LOOK-foto; p168 Barbados Tourist Board; p170 Aragorn Dick-Read; p172 Barbados Tourist Board; p174 Anguilla Tourist Board UK; p176 iStockphoto; p178 2005 The Gleaner Co. Ltd; p180 Getty Images/Ben Bloom.